THE
MOOR'S
LAST STAND

THE MOOR'S LAST STAND

How Seven Centuries of Muslim Rule in Spain Came to an End

Elizabeth Drayson

P

PROFILE BOOKS

First published in Great Britain in 2017 by
PROFILE BOOKS LTD
3 Holford Yard
Bevin Way
London WC1X 9HD
www.profilebooks.com

1 3 5 7 9 10 8 6 4 2

Typeset in Palatino by MacGuru Ltd
Printed and bound in Great Britain by Clays, St Ives plc

A CIP catalogue record for this book is available from the British Library.

ISBN 978 1 78125 686 2
eISBN 978 1 78283 276 8

FSC
www.fsc.org
MIX
Paper from
responsible sources
FSC® C018072

For Kiernan and Fiona

Contents

Acknowledgements

First and foremost, I am deeply grateful to the Isaac Newton Trust of Trinity College, Cambridge, for awarding me a year's research leave, and to Murray Edwards College and Peterhouse, who fully supported me. In Granada, special thanks are due to Bárbara Jiménez Serrano and María del Mar Melgarejo at the archive of the Alhambra, who welcomed me and made some fascinating material available. Thanks are also due to the archivists and staff of the municipal archives, and to José María Pérez Lledó from the Ayuntamiento de Granada. I received great practical help and encouragement from Professor José María Pérez Fernández, Dra. Mercedes Castillo Ferreira, Professor Luis Bernabé Pons and Dr Teresa Tinsley, and I am extremely grateful to Dra María Luisa García Valverde, who helped me decipher some tricky medieval script. Thanks are due to Javier Balaguer and Dr Mostafa Abdulrahman, who generously shared their research on the tomb of Boabdil with me, and I also thank Professor Brad Epps, Dr Rodrigo Cacho and Professor Isabel Torres for their invaluable help, as well as the students and colleagues at Cambridge and elsewhere who have shown such interest in my project. All translations from Spanish into English are my own.

It has been a joy to work with my editor, John Davey, who has been so understanding, supportive and perceptive, and sincere thanks are also due to Penny Daniel, copy-editor Trevor Horwood and the marvellous production team at Profile Books who made this book a reality. Last but not least, heartfelt gratitude to my husband, Kiernan Ryan, who is my inspiration, and to my daughter Fiona for her good-humoured encouragement.

Illustrations

1. Statue of Muhammed I in Arjona, southern Spain. Image courtesy of Fundación El legado andalusí.
2. General view of the Alhambra. Author's photograph.
3. The Nasrid shield in the Alhambra. Photo by Jackie Ramo.
4. Court of the Lions in the Alhambra. Photo: Alamy.
5. The house of El Partal in the Alhambra, where Boabdil lived in his youth. Author's photograph.
6. Nasrid wall painting from El Partal. Photo courtesy of the Museum and Archivo del Patronato de la Alhambra y Generalife.
7. Nasrid chessboard. Photo courtesy of the Museum and Archivo del Patronato de la Alhambra y Generalife.
8. Page from the Capitulations, or terms of surrender. Photo: akg-images/Album/Oronoz.
9. Boabdil's *marlota*. Photo: akg-images/Album/Oronoz.
10. Boabdil's sword and sheath. Photo: akg-images/Album/Oronoz.
11. Boabdil with chains around his neck. Photo: akg-images/Album/Oronoz.
12. Patio of the mosque and window through which Boabdil escaped with his brother in 1482. Photo courtesy of the

Maps

Map of Arab Granada
(after Luis Seco de Paredes, 1910)

Arab buildings and
constructions still in
existence

Arab buildings and
constructions that have
disappeared

Built up areas of the city

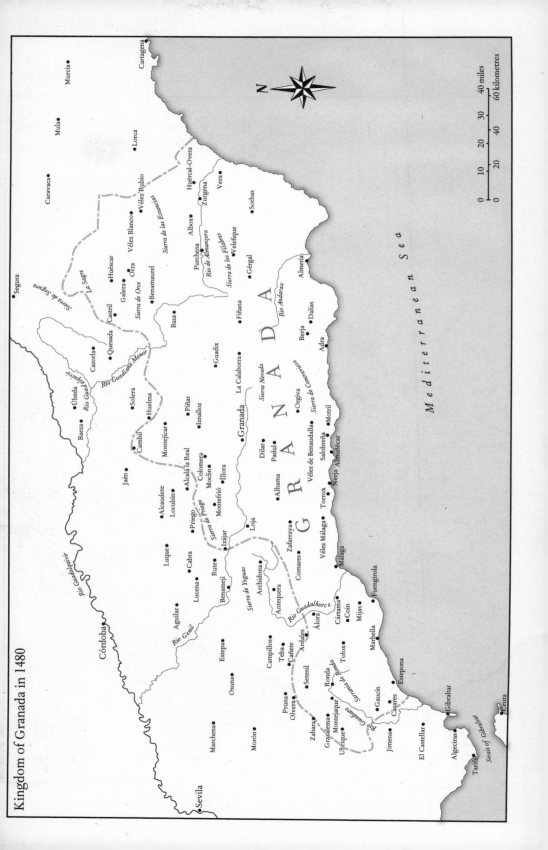

Kingdom of Granada in 1480

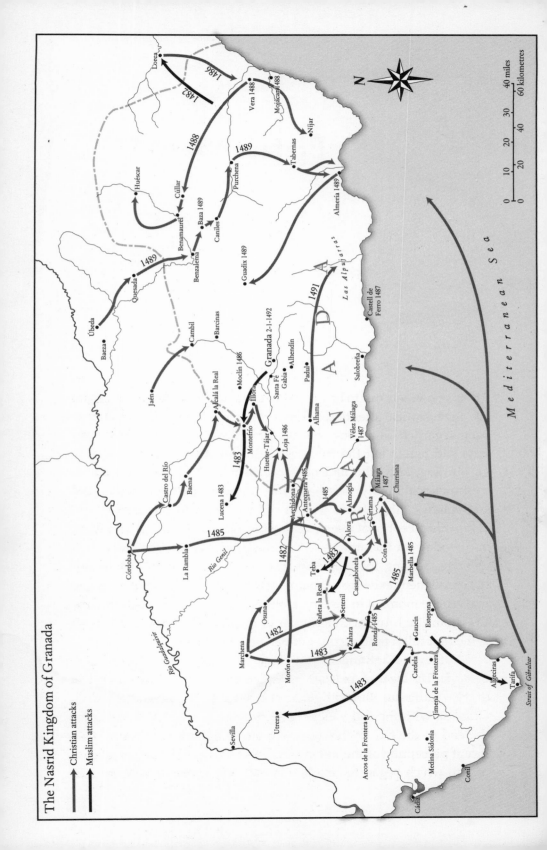

The Nasrid Kingdom of Granada

Christian attacks
Muslim attacks

Mediterranean Sea

Strait of Gibraltar

Lorca
Vera 1488
Mojácar 1488
Níjar
Cúllar
Huéscar
Tabernas
Purchena
1489
Baza 1489
Caniles
Almería 1489
Benamaurel
Benzalema
Quesada 1489
Guadix 1489
Úbeda
Baeza
Castell de Ferro 1487
Las Alpujarras
Barcinas
Cambil
Moclín 1486
Granada 2-1-1492
Santa Fé
Salobreña
Jaén
Alcalá la Real
Íllora
Montefrío
Santa Fé
Gabia Alhendín
Padul
Castro del Río
Baena
Huétor-Tájar
Loja 1486
Alhama
Vélez Málaga 1487
Córdoba
Lucena 1483
La Rambla
Río Genil
Archidona
Antequera 1485
Alora
Almogía
Málaga 1487
Churriana
Cártama
Coín
Teba
Casarabonela
Marbella 1485
Osuna
Cañeta la Real
Setenil
Marchena
Morón
Zahara
Ronda 1485
Gaucín
Estepona
Río Guadalquivir
Utrera
Sevilla
Cardela
Jimena de la Frontera
Algeciras
Tarifa
Arcos de la Frontera
Medina Sidonia
Conil
Cádiz

1482
1486
1488
1489
1491
1483
1485
1482
1483

Preface

This book sets out to bring to the fore a man who has not received the historical attention he deserves, and who has certainly never been regarded as a conventional hero. As a raw youth of twenty who had barely left the confines of the Alhambra palace except to go hunting, and who had no experience of the world outside his dysfunctional family, he rose to the throne as the twenty-third and last sultan of the Nasrid dynasty of Granada. In the ensuing ten years this exceptional man defeated his treacherous father and uncle and fended off the attacks of the indomitable Christian army with courage, bearing the inescapable loss of his Islamic kingdom and his consequent exile from Spain with dignity. He lived at a unique and crucial moment in history, at the climax of the clash between the Christian and Muslim civilisations of medieval Spain, and this book is the first full-length account of his life and times.

In Steven Nightingale's romantic homage to his adopted city, *Granada: The Light of Andalucía*, published in 2015, the author writes of 'the ludicrous Boabdil', who, he says, 'would bear down on Granada with the full weight of his fear and vulgarity and hasten the end of the city by his useless quarrelling and confusion'. This recent perception of the sultan is representative of the negative view of him which began to circulate in the early sixteenth century and which has persisted despite the more balanced and positive fictional reinventions of his life which evolved from the nineteenth century onwards. The contemporary historical biographical accounts which form the basis of this book present a different picture, one that supports the revision of various popular preconceptions of his character. The main fifteenth-century sources were written by Christian historians, with just one Arab source in existence from this time. They contain many eyewitness accounts and include the written and spoken words of the sultan himself.

The terms 'king', 'sultan' and 'emir' are all used in contemporary sources to refer to Boabdil's status as Muslim ruler, and Spanish historians favour the Christian term 'king'. These three terms are used interchangeably in this book. The term 'Moor' appears in source materials of this time, and is often employed by Christians to convey hostility, and by Muslims with a sense of pride. It refers originally to people of north African origin, but it can be imprecise. Boabdil is at times described in early Christian writing and by posterity as a Moor, yet he was a native of Spain, of Arabic descent. For us today the terms 'Moor' and 'Moorish' convey an aura of exoticism, and are associated with an architecture and culture representative of the Islamic civilisation in Spain which Boabdil evokes.

These examples show how the conflict between two major cultures in the Iberian peninsula in the Middle Ages was reflected in the vocabulary used to describe it, and permanent traces of Spain's Islamic heritage remain in the high proportion of words of Arabic origin existing in the Spanish language. Yet Islamic, Arabic-speaking Granada and the life of its last ruler have often been marginalised in history and poorly understood. The relations between the Islamic world and the West, and the tumult of recent years, suggest that the time is right to bring Boabdil's story fully into the light of day, as a history not of decline and defeat but of a courageous defence of religious and cultural identity and of a way of life. It is my hope that this book will draw wider attention to the events of his life and to their implications for the religious and cultural issues of our time.

The Nasrid Dynasty of Granada

Aking sits motionless astride his jet-black horse and waits. His black velvet robes flutter slightly in the cold breeze of an early January day and his horse paws the muddy ground impatiently. The man's bearded face betrays profound grief, though his bearing is dignified, and his sorrow is echoed in the faces of the handful of retainers watching on foot behind him. Another king and his queen are mounted face-to-face with him, their lavish clothes embroidered in red and gold, their richly caparisoned horses and vast host of attendants striking a sharp contrast with his modest, sober attire and retinue. There is utter silence. Taking one foot from the stirrup, the king bows his head slowly, then leans down to hand the bunch of magnificent keys he is holding to a page, who takes them and gives them ceremoniously to the king dressed in red. He in turn bows solemnly, and presents the keys to his queen. On seeing the joy in their faces, the vanquished king and his followers are unable to hide their pain and sadness, and the silence is broken by a sound of weeping as he turns his back on the city of Granada and leaves it for the last time. The king dressed in black is Abu Abdallah Muhammad b. Ali, or Muhammad XI, known as Boabdil, the last Moorish sultan of Granada, and head of the Nasrid dynasty. His dramatic act of handing over the keys of the city of Granada to the Christian

Monarchs, King Ferdinand and Queen Isabella, on 2 January 1492 marked a crucial moment in a centuries-old clash between two great religions and cultures. It symbolised the epoch-changing transition of the kingdom of Granada from Islamic state to Christian territory, a moment which set Spain on a course to become the greatest power in early modern Europe.

In the ten years before 1492, the kingdom of Granada was the theatre of one of the most significant wars in European history. The Nasrid sultan's territory was the last Spanish stronghold of a Muslim empire which had originally stretched to the Pyrenees and beyond, and had included northern Spanish cities such as Barcelona and Pamplona. Spanish Islamic society had been a part of the European continent for the best part of 1,000 years. It had existed there from the time of the Venerable Bede and King Alfred, through the reigns of William the Conqueror and the great medieval English kings, the creation of the universities and Gothic cathedrals and the advent of printed books, right up to Tudor times. The fall of Granada was the culmination of that ancient battle between two major and opposing civilisations, which not only settled the cultural fate of a large part of Europe but also established the basis for the discovery of the Americas. The year 1492 is generally seen as a beginning, whether of modern Spain or the discovery of the New World, but what had ended was equally significant. For nearly 800 years the Spanish peninsula had been home to a group of people who came as invaders and stayed to create a unique and sophisticated civilisation which bequeathed to Spain a lasting cultural heritage. The conquest of Granada was one of the most memorable events in Spanish history, yet the pivotal role that Boabdil played in these events has not been the focus of history, although he lives on in legend and fiction. History conspired with myth either to demonise or to romanticise the image of the last Moorish king, while the true nature of Boabdil has proved elusive. This book tells the story of his life and times and reassesses the verdict of history, which has marginalised him and favoured his conquerors. It explores his decisive role in late fifteenth-century Spain, using contemporary historical accounts as well as the views of later historians. It asks how Boabdil's reputation was created and preserved, and how he became the stuff of legend. His story speaks to us now, as we consider what the relationships might be between Spain's multireligious, multicultural medieval legacy and the conflicts that confront the modern West and the Islamic world.

The tales of invasion and conquest involving first Roderick, last king of the Spanish Visigoths, and then Boabdil, have grown in importance in the light of existing religious tensions between Islam and the West, and important oppositions, such as those between Hispanic and Arabic ethnicities, between Christian and Muslim, history and myth, are fundamental to the story of Boabdil and emphasise its perennial relevance and value inside and outside Spain. We can recognise the crucial role of Spain in the Middle Ages as the meeting point of Europe and the Orient, of Christianity and Islam, set against the negative medieval perception of Islam by Christians, and of Christianity by Muslims. The early medieval Christian image of Islam identified Muhammad as a pseudo-prophet, an impostor and heretic whose followers were men of blood and violence. It was an image that arose from the Christian view of Muslims as conquerors, and of Islam as an aberrant form of Christianity. On the other hand, Muslims had an attitude of lofty disdain towards Christians, believing them to be uncouth and barbaric.

To make sense of Boabdil's life and set it in its cultural and historical context, we need to go back in time as far as the eighth century, to understand how Islam began in Spain and how it managed to survive there against all odds when it seemed to be condemned to obliteration by the rising power of a Christian Reconquest whose roots lay in the Muslim invasion of the Iberian peninsula. Boabdil's fateful role as the king who lost the last Islamic kingdom in the peninsula has a striking if inverted parallel with the situation of Roderick, who ruled Spain for just two years from 710–711, and lost his own Christian kingdom to the Islamic invaders when his army was defeated by a Moorish raiding party on 19 July 711. Their reigns mark the beginning and the end of Islamic rule in Spain, and the abiding interest in rewriting the lives of both men owes much of its fascination to the ambivalence of their image. In a similar way to Boabdil, Roderick's life became part of fiction and myth as the king on whose watch the Iberian peninsula was conquered by Arab and Berber tribes from north Africa. It gave rise to the founding story of the Spanish people, in which Roderick's alleged love affair with the beautiful woman known as La Cava, the Whore, was blamed for the Muslim invasion, which established a powerful Arab presence in Spain for nearly eight centuries.

Boabdil's religion had been established as a faith for less than a hundred years at the time of the Moorish invasion of Spain. The earliest Christian to write about Islam was John of Damascus, who composed *A Dialogue between a Saracen and a Christian* sometime around 745. The English monk known as the Venerable Bede, also writing in the eighth century, describes the Christian idea of the legendary origin of the Muslims, who were allegedly descended from Hagar, whom the Christians believed to be Abraham's concubine, while Christians came from his lawful son Isaac. Bede's story of origins rendered all Muslims illegitimate, while Christians belonged to the legitimate albeit incestuous blood line, as Sarah was Abraham's half-sister. The issue of lineage and legitimacy to rule was a matter of vital importance to Muslims and it became central to the unfolding of Boabdil's reign. Early Christians also believed that Muslims were inherently violent, because they were the direct descendants of Cain, the murderer. When Muslims invaded the eastern Mediterranean as early as 634, just two years after the death of the Prophet Muhammad, Christian accounts described it as catastrophic, as the wreaking of the symbolic vengeance of God upon his sinful people. To them the instrument of that vengeance was the bastard line of Abraham, protected by God and yet at an infinite distance from the love of Christ. When King Roderick came to the throne of Spain in 710, Christian prejudice against and fear of Islam was already rife.

The Nasrid dynasty of sultans of which Boabdil was the last did not come into being until 500 years later, in the thirteenth century. To appreciate the historical and cultural circumstances which led from the end of Roderick's Visigothic kingdom to the origins of that dynasty and its demise, we need a sense of the broader picture of life in Spain from the eighth century until the early 1200s. The seventeenth-century Arab historian al-Maqqari describes the history of the Spanish Muslims as simultaneously the colonisation of a green and pleasant land and the end of a great civilisation. Invasion followed by conquest was to become a familiar pattern in the long battle for the land of Spain and its inhabitants, and religion became the main criterion of allegiance. In 418, in an earlier act of colonisation, the Germanic tribe of the Visigoths had invaded Spain, defeated the Vandals and established a thriving kingdom whose religion was Catholicism. The expansion of the Arab states came 300 years later, corresponding to the rise of Islam during the lifetime of the Prophet Muhammad in the seventh century. By 711 Islam was growing powerful, and Spain's proximity to Africa made it vulnerable to attack. There had already been friendly trading expeditions to Spain from north Africa for some years, and these sorties emboldened the Muslims in their desire to possess the Spanish lands they had glimpsed. Added to this, the newly crowned Visigothic king Roderick was vulnerable from the start of his reign, because of questions concerning his legitimacy to rule. He was not in direct royal line to the throne, and had been presented as a candidate by members of the nobility who were at odds with the sons of the previous king, Witiza. Roderick was perceived by some powerful factions to be a usurper. This weakened his position and exposed his authority to challenges that he attempted to counter with a bold display of fighting prowess.

While he was away flexing his military muscle against the Basques in the north of Spain, disaster struck in the south. Musa ibn Nusayr, the powerful Arab governor of Ifrikiya, as north Africa was known then, sent a militant raiding party to Spain under the command of his former slave Tariq. In panic Roderick hurried south to meet the invaders, who defeated his army in the valley of the river Guadalete near Medina Sidonia. His demise may have been hastened by the betrayal of the usurped sons of Witiza, who deserted their king in his final battle and colluded with the enemy. The battle ended Roderick's reign and the Visigothic kingdom with it. His death is shrouded in mystery. It was not recorded in any reliable accounts, and some believe he escaped to Portugal, though the general assumption is that he died in battle.

Spurred on by this unexpected success, Tariq quickly captured Toledo, and his victories encouraged Musa to follow his lead and capture Seville. The daring invasion and the easy victory of the Arabs took on an apocalyptic quality for both the conquered and the conquerors. The earliest Muslim histories describe premonitory stories heralding the invasion and the fabulous treasure that the victors acquired afterwards, including the original Table of Solomon, made of gold and silver with inlays of precious stones, which had belonged to King Solomon himself. It had been carried from Jerusalem to Spain and was discovered by the Muslims at a fortress near Toledo. For Islamic historians as well as for Christian writers, the conquest of Spain was an event of overwhelming significance, encouraging the Arabic vision of conquest and victory fostered by the policy of expansion proclaimed by the government of Damascus. The occupation of Hispania, the old Latin name for Spain, was part of a much wider Islamic conquest taking place outside the peninsula and late-Roman empire, and in Arab histories it was not seen as divine punishment for Spanish corruption, as it was in Christian history writing, which portrays it as a catastrophe equal in magnitude to the fall of Troy. For both early Islamic and Christian historians, Roderick was a man of destiny, albeit an equivocal destiny, fundamental to the fortunes and futures of both sides, creating a conspicuous parallel with the destiny of Boabdil. For Christian writers, Roderick was the vessel through which God wreaked punishment upon the corrupt through defeat and invasion, and for Islamic historians he was the instrument of conquest.

The Muslims wasted no time in vanquishing all of Spain, failing only in the northern kingdom of Asturias, and reached beyond the harsh, snowy northern Pyrenees as far as what is now southern France in pursuit of the jihad or holy war, but their defeat in 732 by Charlemagne's grandson Charles Martel at Poitiers put an end to their expansion north, and to the prospect of what would have been a very different Europe under Muslim rule. They soon settled in the southern area of Spain known as al-Andalus, modern-day Andalusia, a term said to derive from Arabic geographers' descriptions of the Vandals who had settled in Hispania as 'al-Andlish'. Between 716 and 756, al-Andalus was ruled by a rapid succession of Arab governors from two tribal groups, one from Yemen and the other from Syria. These tribal groups and the native population intermarried and the local Visigoths and Hispano-Romans were given the choice of conversion to Islam or of pursuing their own religion, provided they submitted to certain rules and paid a tax to do so.

Then, in 756, a dramatic and far-reaching event sparked nearly two centuries of brilliant cultural and social development which left the rest of Europe far behind. A member of the ruling Umayyad family in Damascus, Abd al-Rahman, fled to Spain to escape the massacre of his family by the rival Abbasid dynasty, and proclaimed himself emir or temporal Muslim ruler, with his capital at Cordoba. His enforced exile led to an era of unprecedented growth and abundance, and the emir encouraged a firm Islamic orientation in every facet of life. Schools were built, the construction of the Great Mosque was begun, literature flourished and a famous law school was established. The first Spanish emir died in 788 and was succeeded by his peaceable son, Hisham I, followed by the ferocious tyrant al-Hakam I. The learned and pious Abd al-Rahman II (822–856) brought a new outlook, refashioning Muslim society on models from the East, and attempting to rival Baghdad with the splendours of Cordoba. Yet by the end of the ninth century, his authority had grown weak, and rebellions arose. A political and institutional remedy was essential, but it came only much later, in the form of Abd al-Rahman III, who in 929 proclaimed himself caliph of Cordoba (from the Arabic *khalifa*, or successor), not just the temporal, but also the spiritual head of all Muslim believers in al-Andalus. With his reign the century of greatest magnificence and stability for the Muslims of al-Andalus began. The caliph held the vital reins of power, while al-Andalus was divided into territorial districts and many administrative posts were created. This firm basis for government and defence of the state was combined with the flourishing culture of tenth-century Cordoba, which boasted street lights, paving and over seventy well-stocked libraries at a time when London languished amid narrow, muddy, unlit streets. Sadly, the glory of the Umayyad caliphate was short lived: it declined as rapidly as it rose, mainly because of excessive centralisation of power, and finally collapsed in 1031.

Al-Andalus fragmented into twenty small states known as Taifa kingdoms, from the Arabic word for a group or party. While these small kingdoms weakened themselves with internal squabbles and conflict, two powerful enemies were gathering on their frontiers. A strong desire had begun to grow in the members of the Christian community of the peninsula to reassert themselves and regain what they felt was their native land. That desire manifested itself in the conception of a so-called Reconquest, encouraged by Pope Gregory IX's authorisation of the crusade to recuperate the territories that were perceived as lost to Islam after 711. Christian medieval writers of this time devoted a great deal of energy to reinforcing oppositions between themselves and the Muslims with whom they shared the peninsula and on to whom they projected an image of alienness. The chronicles of the kings of Castile resound with such statements as: 'On our side, Christ, God and man. On the Moors' side, the faithless and damned apostate Muhammad.' Fortified by this militant rhetoric, the Christians in the north mustered their forces, and their first signifi-cant victory came in 1085 when King Alfonso VI, ruler of the central kingdom of Castile, captured Toledo. So the Taifa kingdoms were menaced on their northern boundaries by the Christian advance, while in the south, a fearful threat from north Africa was looming.

The twelfth-century Muslims of al-Andalus were overrun by two independent groups of fanatical political and religious zealots and reformers from the north African coast, the Almoravids and the Almohads. The Almoravids arrived in 1090, preaching a strange combination of puritanical Islamic mysticism and practical warfare, and by 1106 they had occupied all the important cities of al-Anda-lus. Unexpectedly, they quickly succumbed to the wealth and glitter of court life, and to the steadily growing strength of the Christian reconquerors, and were finally ousted in 1145. Shortly after, the inhabitants took a second battering, this time from the Almohads, another group of religiously intolerant and anti-secular extremists. They reached the zenith of their power between 1160 and 1210: their most famous monument is the minaret of the Giralda in Seville. By 1172 they in turn had captured most of the cities of al-Andalus, and tried to stem the Christian Reconquest, but in 1212 they were deci-sively defeated by the Castilian Christian force at the Battle of Las Navas de Tolosa. With the momentum of victory behind them, the Castilians and Aragonese swept southwards and by 1248 al-Anda-lus had lost almost all its major cities, including Cordoba and Seville, to the Christians. Spain's history had reached a crossroads – Muslim power was waning and the progress of the Christian Reconquest seemed inexorable.

It looked very much as if Islamic life in the peninsula was about to founder. Then, in 1232, against all the odds, a new Muslim dynasty was founded in the small town of Arjona, set in the rolling hills near Jaén. On 18 April, as he left the mosque after Friday prayers, a local chief named Muhammad Ibn Yusuf Ibn Nasr Ibn al-Ahmar, boldly proclaimed himself ruler of a small area that included Baeza to the east, Guadix to the south and the city of Jaén itself. Just five years later, in 1237, the city of Granada became his capital, and the Nasrid dynasty was born, its identity taken from the new chief's resonant name of Nasr, meaning victory. His tribe or clan was known as the Banu Nasr, or Banu l-Ahmar, and this daring fighter proclaimed himself emir, taking the title of Muhammad I. Defying all expectations, Muhammad's kingdom became a brilliant success: he created a dynastic line that secured the presence of Islam in Spain for over 250 years at a time when its future seemed doomed.

What do we know of the kingdom of Granada in early times when Muhammad I ruled, and why did Boabdil's ancestor choose to make the city of Granada his capital? The kingdom coincided closely with today's Andalusian provinces of Granada, Malaga and Almeria, and geographical location was unquestionably the most significant factor in Muhammad's choice of capital. Its stunning setting amid the mountain range of the Sierra Nevada, whose snows melt and run into the two rivers passing through the city, the Darro and the Genil, gave it a strong defensive advantage. Its urban confines met the Granadan *vega*, a great fertile plain watered by the latest Arab technology, which supplied a profusion of fruit, nuts, vegetables and grain crops to inhabitants of the city, as well as acting as a defensive barrier. The Nasrid kingdom was bordered by the abundant coast along the Mediterranean sea from Gibraltar to Almeria, and by mountain ranges interspersed with fertile valleys and plains, giving it an alpine dimension. The only way to reach small towns and populations was often by narrow mountain passes frequented by mule trains. Its climate had violent contrasts, hot and arid near the sea, dry and cold in the mountain reaches, with rich, varied soils and climatic nuances which made it good agricultural land. With its natural mountain defences and its capacity to supply plentiful food, both kingdom and city, with its magnificent position dominating the borders of Muslim lands, seemed an ideal location for the emerging Islamic state.

Granada was already old, and had come into being as a city in the seventh century, probably founded by a Jewish community, since the Arabs called it 'city of the Jews'. Its ancient citadel, or *alcazaba*, was at the heart of the fortified city built on the hill on the east bank of the river Darro. It corresponded more or less to the ancient Roman settlement of Iliberri, and had hardly changed during Visigothic times. It wasn't until the early eleventh century that the Muslim Ziryad dynasty chose it as the capital of their new Taifa kingdom, reinforcing the old ramparts and taking them to the edge of steep natural slopes that made potential attacks very difficult. Towards the end of the century, Granada developed into a large urban centre, with its medina, the traditional Arab walled city with a castle or citadel, divided in two by the river Darro. Today, 1,000 years later, the vital centre of the city remains in the same place, confirming the clever urban planning of the Ziryads in adapting their needs to the topography of their environment.

Granada today still contains some of the fundamental features of the eleventh-century Muslim city. The church of San José was super-imposed on the site of a mosque built at that time, whose minaret is now used as the bell tower. The Muslim hammam, or public baths, in today's San Pedro area were built at the same time. By the beginning of the twelfth century, if not before, the main mosque of Granada stood in what is now the Calle de los Oficios in the city centre. The parish Church of the Sacrarium (Iglesia del Sagrario), attached to the cathedral, occupies the same plot of land. We know that the main mosque was very beautiful, with marble columns, and pillarheads and doors brought specially from Cordoba; it was in use in Boab-dil's lifetime and was converted into the church and cathedral site in 1501.

By the time Muhammad I set up the capital of his new Islamic state in the city in 1237, Granada both looked like and functioned as a city in Muslim north Africa rather than in Christian Spain. The status of the city led to two different categories of Muslims in the Iberian peninsula at this time: first, the many who lived as subjects of Christian kingdoms in Castile, Aragon and Navarre; and second, those who lived in the small, crowded independent Muslim kingdom of Granada, who spoke Arabic and who rightly considered themselves part of the Islamic world. From early days, those Muslims had a remarkably strong sense of their essential religious and cultural unity, and were proud of what they called Jazirat al-Andalus, the Peninsula of al-Andalus. It seemed to provide a guarantee that Muslims everywhere in Spain would be respected. From Muhammad I's time onwards, there is no record of native Christians anywhere in Muslim Andalusia. Those who do get mentioned are slaves, merchants, refugees or resident foreigners. Its tendency towards a culture that was purely Arabic in its expression gave the society of Granada an unusual quality: *convivencia*, the social circumstances in which three religious communities lived side by side and which had been such an important feature of Islamic Spain in earlier centuries, was entirely absent from Granada from this time until 1492.

If we follow the Nasrid dynasty from its beginnings up to the birth of Boabdil, a series of repeating political and dynastic patterns emerges from a history beset by intense confusion, conflict, betrayal and murder. Those patterns have a direct bearing upon the life and circumstances of the reign of the last sultan, and set the tone for the climactic moments leading up to the fall of Granada. In 1232 Muhammad I took the title of emir and leader of believers. The title meant an absolute dominion over his subjects, though he was held partly in check by the traditions of Islamic government in which some power is vested in theologians and thinkers; it was also tempered by the power of lesser leaders of the lineage. One aspect which would become a critical complication in Boabdil's reign was the absolute power of the emir to designate his successor. Although there was no written law on the subject, it was logical in Muslim political tradition for the father to be succeeded by his eldest son. As we will see, this right was dramatically disputed on occasions. The visual reinforcement of Muhammad I's power, the heraldic emblem of the Nasrids, was a shield with a band across it, said to have been granted to the emir by the Christian king of Castile Ferdinand III. Muhammad added the Muslim motto *Le galib ille Allah*, 'Only God is conqueror'. The colour of the Nasrid standard, and the sealing wax, seals and paper of documents from his chancellery were red, in recognition of his name as founder of the dynasty: al-Ahmar (the Red). It seems a fearful sign of the bloody future of his line.

The first Nasrid emir's takeover of Granada in 1237 as a testimony of Muslim power came at a vital moment. In their crusading zeal against the Muslims, the Christians from Castile had conquered Cordoba in 1236, and the Aragonese had won Valencia in 1238. Soon Muhammad I found himself in direct conflict with the Castilians, though how the conflict started is not clear, as Christian and Muslim accounts each lay the blame on the other. Muhammad agreed a peace settlement with Ferdinand III, in which the emir accepted the king as his overlord and was obliged to pay him handsomely in the form of 'tribute': a remuneration made periodically from one ruler to another, usually to show dependence. Two aspects of this agreement with the Castilians were crucial. The first was the decision of Muhammad I to become Ferdinand's vassal, because it set a pattern repeated throughout the existence of the Islamic state of Granada. The Granadan state never accepted subordination to Castile, and the status of vassalage was an on/off affair, initially for only twenty years and subsequently renewed and rejected many times by the rulers of Granada in the long history of fighting between the sides, often fuelled by the emir's support of Muslim rebels in Christian territories. Muhammad showed loyalty to his overlord by giving Ferdinand 500 men to help his siege of Seville in 1248, instead of helping his fellow Muslims, and in 1246 the emir relinquished the city of Jaén in an act of feudal submission. But he also made repeated acts of submission to Muslim rulers too, such as the caliph of Baghdad and the ruler of Tunis. No Arabic source mentions Muhammad I as a vassal of Christians, although Christian chronicles repeatedly describe Granada as a subject state. Muhammad must have needed to manoeuvre politically very adroitly in order to survive. As the historian of Islamic Spain L. P. Harvey points out, it was a time of kaleidoscopic reversals of alliances: there were no Muslim leaders in Spain who had not done deals with the Christians. Muslims fought for Christians and vice versa. To speak of treason or of apostasy on either side has little value in the context of the precarious balance between the two civilisations.

The second pivotal aspect of Muhammad I's agreement with

the Christians relates to religion. The scholars of Muslim religious law, the *ulama*, wielded a powerful influence on public opinion at all times until Boabdil's final surrender, and tended to favour fighting to the bitter end over diplomacy and compromise. Although religion seemed to play a minor role in the rise and fall of the Nasrid state, this hard-headed approach of Muslim theologians created great difficulty for its secular leaders. As a result, it was tricky for Muhammad I to make his peace treaty with a Christian monarch and not lose public support incited by the disapproval of the *ulama*. The tension between politics and religion in Muslim Granada would become a significant factor in the course of Boabdil's reign. The Granadan emirs took religious matters seriously, and were neither liberal nor tolerant, but all the Nasrids had to weigh the threat of defeat by the Christians against losing the support of religious opinion in a state whose fundamental existence depended on Islam.

Out of the blue, on 22 January 1273, Muhammad I fell from his horse and was killed while on a minor military expedition near Granada. His achievement had been astonishing. Undeterred by the greatest defeat suffered by the Muslims of Spain at that time, the loss of Cordoba to the Christians in 1236, he came out of nowhere to forge a comparatively safe refuge for Islam in the peninsula, built on perhaps unheroic but effective compromises with the enemy, and hindered by discords caused by the alienation of his supporters. His legacy was a need for perpetual vigilance in dealing with the Christians, a willingness to compromise and switch alliances as political power shifted, all and anything required to maintain Granada's survival.

The first emir's son, Muhammad II, succeeded his father in 1273 and reigned for almost thirty years until 1302. During this time a third factor came into play which would have dramatic repercussions for the reign of Boabdil: the power of lineage. Granadan aristocrats up to the late fifteenth century linked their existence to some of the thirty-six lineages established in tradition, which came directly or indirectly from the tribes of Arabia. The rest of the population was said to be descended from other appropriately glorious lineages. This gives us an idea of the practical and psychological importance of the agnatic link, in which persons were connected through descent from the same, usually male, ancestor. The famous Muslim scholar, jurist and historian Ibn Khaldun wrote about this solidarity of descent in the fourteenth century, coining the word *asabiyyah* to describe the group feeling, the cohesive force of the tribe or clan, that contributed in his view to social unity. In his book *The Rule of the Clan*, Mark S. Weiner explains how Islam itself rests on a vision of legal and political community understood through metaphors of kinship drawn deep from the Arabian past. Group honour, custom and feud provide the cultural connection for clans, the ancient tribal structures of Arab peoples which Islam was able to accommodate, while privileging religious identity over tribal loyalty. For the kin group to function as a support network its members must have an intimate knowledge of their lineage, a consciousness of their ancestry, in order to forge deep alliances. Intergroup harmony was maintained by the constant threat of the blood feud, by ancient rivalries with the potential to escalate. When Arabian tribes came together in common defence, their alliances were fleeting and shifting – something we shall see clearly in the case of Boabdil and his family.

One clan or *banu* closely associated with the early Nasrid sultans was the Banu Ashqilula, who had supported Muhammad I in his ambitions, but who after his death fell into a feud with his son, caused by the dead sultan's decision to exclude them from power in his new kingdom. The first sultan had enlisted the help of some Castilian noblemen against the clan rebellion, but the king of Castile at the time, the learned Alfonso X the Wise, craftily aimed to re-enlist the nobles on his own side instead of that of the Muslims. Muhammad II was at risk of losing some influential support from the Castilians, so he had the brainwave of talking to Alfonso himself. The *Chronicle of Alfonso X* tells us how Alfonso cunningly misled the sultan:

There came to Seville with them the king of Granada (Muhammad II) and Prince Philip and Don Nuño, and all the other nobles who had been in Granada, and the king received them well, and did them great honour, especially the king of Granada, and on this visit he knighted him. The king of Granada pledged him his friendship as firmly as could be, as had already been agreed in negotiations with Don Ferdinand and the queen, and promised to be Alfonso's vassal for all time, and to pay him from his revenues 300,000 maravedis in Castilian money. All through his stay in Seville, Alfonso did great honour to the king of Granada.

But once this agreement had been concluded, the queen and the nobleman Don Ferdinand pressed Muhammad to grant a truce to the Banu Ashqilula:

> The king of Granada was much grieved at this, for he could see what they wanted was to protect the Banu Ashqilula, whereas they had already taken his money, paid over to them on the understanding that they would abandon that cause.

Having learned to beware of the power of the clan and how dangerous it was to trust the Castilians, Muhammad II carried forward with great skill the project begun by his father to create a place that Andalusian Muslims could call their own. Then suddenly, in April 1302, the second sultan of Granada died gruesomely, amid rumours that he had been poisoned by a cake made specially for him by his son and heir.

Muhammad III is recorded as a dangerous, superstitious, unpredictable and disconcerting man with a schizophrenic personality, prone to brutish cruelty, as the historian Ibn al-Khatib tells us:

> At the outset of his reign, he had a group of his father's household troops, about whom he had formed an adverse judgement, arrested in a sudden swoop. He had them imprisoned in the dungeons of the Alhambra and he kept the key, threatening with death anybody who threw them food; there they remained for days, raising their voices in the agony of their hunger, and those who died first were eaten by those left alive: finally from sheer weakness and exhaustion all fell silent. One of the guards set to watch at the mouth of the dungeon, moved by compassion, threw down to them a small leftover crust of bread. Somebody reported on the guard and orders

were given for his throat to be cut on the brink of the pit, so his
blood would flow on to the prisoners.

Muhammad III's short reign marked the start of a period of
instability, betrayal, murder and violence which lasted for over a
hundred years. His undue haste to make peace with the Christians,
and a major political mistake in trying to control the port of Ceuta,
which alienated his north African allies, led on 14 March 1309 to his
being deposed in a palace revolution led by his brother Nasr, and to
his internal exile in Almuñecar. Over the next twenty-four years the
kingdom of Granada was ruled by three different sultans. Nasr, the
fourth sultan, ruled for just five years, in which time he successfully
defended the coastal towns of Almeria and Algeciras against Castile
and Aragon, which had made a concerted effort to crush Granada.
Their defeat halted the Christian Reconquest for many decades.
But Nasr, last of the direct line of the Banu al-Ahmar going back to
Muhammad I, was overthrown by his cousin Isma'il, who took the
throne in 1314, and Nasr ended his life in exile in Guadix, leaving
no heirs.

Isma'il, who had the same ancestor as Nasr, but through a different line, was cheated of a long reign by violent death. This time it
was one of Isma'il's cousins who took offence at some harsh words
and plotted to kill him. This left the emir's eldest son, a young boy, to
become Muhammad IV in 1325. The pattern of violence and bloodshed became more firmly entrenched when the sixth Nasrid sultan's
eight-year reign ended with his murder in 1333 as he was returning
to Granada from Gibraltar. Whether a plot from north Africa or from
Castile, Muhammad IV, like Isma'il, died through treachery.

In contrast, the reign of Yusuf I from 1333 to 1354 began a glorious age of Nasrid cultural achievement. The arts were cultivated
and many of the foremost writers of the time graced the royal court.
It was in Yusuf's reign that the Alhambra came into its full glory, and
there will be more to say about that great citadel in Boabdil's era. It
was customary when an emir or caliph became established to shelter
his royal personage in a palatine city, which also lodged his court,
key personnel and often his army. Such a citadel would have all that
was needed to function as an autonomous unit. When Muhammad

I founded his new capital, he created such a city in the Alhambra, whose urban structure was already clearly laid out by the time his son came to power. In Yusuf I's reign the monumental Gate of Justice was built at his orders, as was the Comares palace, containing rooms for royal receptions, with its enormous rectangular patio, fountain and wooden roof representing the Islamic conception of heaven, one of the supreme examples of Nasrid carpentry. In the great ruler Yusuf's time Granadan architecture reached its zenith.

But Yusuf could not relax. Wedged between Castile and north Africa, there was a need to be constantly wary, but this watchfulness could not prevent hostility. Like his predecessors, Yusuf made a truce with Castile, and then entered an agreement with both the Castilians and with the north African Marinids, placing Granada as a pawn between two strong powers. His reign witnessed the most significant reversal of the Muslim cause in Spain before 1492 in the Christian victory in the Battle of Salado in 1340: a decisive factor was weaponry, as it would be in the last battles of the Nasrids to save their city. The Castilian Christians plied the enemy with heavy cavalry charges, which, as Harvey explains, was a form of fighting to which western European aristocratic society had a strong ideological commitment. The lightly armed and manoeuvrable Muslim cavalry was no match for it. To make matters worse, the Castilian king Alfonso XI's crusading zeal inspired him to have another go at winning Algeciras in 1342–1343. Once again, the machinery of war was crucial. It was memorably the first major engagement in the Iberian peninsula where cannon were used, and one of the earliest anywhere. It was, in fact, the Muslims who introduced the new weapons, not the Christians, as the latter made out in their own chronicles. In the end the Muslims did not give in, and after the long siege of Algeciras, a ten-year truce was agreed in 1344.

Yusuf I's reign ended characteristically. As he was praying in the Great Mosque in Granada in 1354, an assassin, described as a lunatic in Arabic accounts, stabbed him to death. It was as if the Nasrids had a curse of violent death upon them. Yet Yusuf's genius as a ruler allowed his kingdom to last 150 years more, and established its reputation as one of the world's great sites of Islamic cultural achievement.

His son and successor Muhammad V, the great-great grandfather of Boabdil, was the first of the Nasrid sultans to experience the phenomenon of the interrupted reign, which would become a major feature of the final years of Nasrid rule. Only sixteen when he began to rule, five years later he had been replaced by another Nasrid prince in a palace coup that bore strong resemblances to future events. The Alhambra became a hotbed of sedition and treachery. A grandson of the emir Nasr, another Isma'il, and his mother Maryam had disappointed aspirations when Muhammad V was proclaimed the new ruler, though Isma'il was foolishly allowed to continue living in the Alhambra. His conspirators somehow scaled the mighty palace walls while Muhammad was outside and would not allow him back in, forcing him to flee to Guadix, with Isma'il II now on the throne due to his mother's money and their cunning plot. Alarmingly, Isma'il was assassinated in 1360 in a new plot in which his brother and court circle were also murdered; Muhammad VI the Red, a nephew of Yusuf I, took the throne. Meanwhile, Muhammad V, a staunch vassal of Castile in true Nasrid fashion, received the help of King Peter I of Castile against Muhammad the Red, whom Peter imprisoned and ultimately poisoned. Muhammad V won back the kingdom of Granada in 1362, negotiated a series of truces which led to the longest period of peace Granada experienced in its history, and reigned for thirty years until he was fifty-three. He made significant improvements to the Alhambra, including the creation of the Patio of the Lions, and many of the beautiful buildings we know today were the work of his architects and craftsmen. He died on 16 January 1391.

From then on, sultans came and went at a bewildering rate, and their history reads rather like something from tales of the Arabian nights. Over the next twenty-six years, into the fifteenth century, three sultans reigned briefly. Yusuf II, son of Muhammad V, and Boabdil's great-grandfather, reigned for just two years, under the domination of his father's faithful servant-minister Khalid, who went from tyrant to victim in a ghastly execution after Yusuf II suspected he was plotting to poison him. Ironically, Yusuf still died a terrible death soon after, when, according to Christian accounts, he put on a poisoned gold tunic sent him from the king of Fez.

Muhammad VII succeeded the poisoned sultan in 1391 and reigned for sixteen years until his own death in May 1408. The significant aspect of this time, apart from palace bloodshed and violence, was the growing strength of Castile. The Christian kingdom had recovered from the ravages of the Black Death in the 1300s, and was developing the formidable power which would eventually lead it to dominate Europe and the New World. The skilful diplomacy and boldness that had enabled the kingdom of Granada to stand up to Castile grew less effective as the Christians began to wield their muscle and refused to accept the kind of easy truces made in the past. This had had grave consequences by the time Boabdil took the throne.

While Muhammad VII was sultan, his elder brother had been imprisoned in the castle at Salobreña. Finally liberated when Muhammad VII died, he took the throne as Yusuf III and reigned for nine years from 1408 to 1417. He tried hard to negotiate peace with Ferdinand I of Aragon, but Ferdinand made a vital conquest by winning the border fortress and busy town of Antequera, which encouraged the victors and demoralised the Granadans, who lost a fine town and a fertile growing region. When Yusuf III died in 1417, the issue of clan warfare resurfaced to disrupt the next thirty-five years in what Harvey describes as an extreme example of multiple interlocking reigns. In the period up to 1453, Muhammad VIII reigned twice, 1417–1419 and 1427–1429, while Muhammad IX the Left-Handed reigned three times, 1419–1427, 1429–1445 and 1447–1453. Yusuf IV reigned from 1430–1432, Yusuf V in 1445, 1450 and 1462–1463, and his son Isma'il III from 1446 to 1447. What are we to make of this? Apart from the dizzying political instability of the Granadan state, stoked internally and also externally by interference of Castile, we can identify a new destructive factor – the fierce fighting between clan factions in Granada itself, principally between the Banu Sarraj, known as the Abencerrajes, and the Banu Bannigas, known as Venegas.

In 1419 there was a coup d'état led by the Abencerrajes, bringing down Muhammad VIII and putting Muhammad IX on the throne. He was not in direct line of succession, and this lack of legitimacy to rule began a profound internal discord which continued until the end of the emirate. By destroying the direct legitimacy of succession, the Abencerrajes hoped to bring in a political system based on respect for the power and privilege of their lineage group, and their feuding family is romanticised in various ballads and sixteenth-century stories, reminding us of the importance and influence of lineage in this society. When Muhammad VIII was reinstated in 1427 there was a change of ministers, and the Abencerraje government was replaced at its head by Ridwan Venegas, whose clan supported legitimacy of succession. Ridwan was the great enemy of Muhammad IX in the Granadan ruling elite and proposed a third candidate for the throne, Yusuf IV, supported by John II of Castile, whose story is told in the famous Castilian ballad 'Abenámar'. But by the time Muhammad IX died in 1453, the Abencerrajes had found a new pretender to the throne, Abu Nasr Sa'd, the grandson of Yusuf II and paternal grandfather of Boabdil.

Sa'd was fifty-five when he became sultan, supported by the Abencerrajes and also by the new Castilian king, Henry IV, who came to the throne in 1454. But there was a confused period of two years or so when there were two rulers in Granada – the son of Muhammad VIII, Muhammad X known as El Chiquito (the Younger), occupied the Alhambra, all Granada, Malaga and Almeria, but he proved so unpopular that he had to flee, falling into an ambush set by Sa'd's son, after which he was suffocated to death inside the Alhambra, along with all his heirs. At this point in 1455 Sa'd entered the Alhambra himself, and promptly rejected all Castilian demands for truce, vassalage and tribute, in spite of having their support.

There is a first-hand account, written from the point of view of the Christian enemy, which confirms Sa'd's bellicosity and daring, although the account also speaks volumes about the horrific cruelty of the Christians. In 1457, a Swabian knight, Jorge de Ehingen, travelled to Spain in the service of Duke Albert of Austria. While he was at the French court en route, news came that Henry of Castile was preparing an expedition against the Moors of Granada, and Ehingen left to take part. He recounts:

A solemn embassy from the king of Spain arrived asking the king of France to participate in the great crusade he intended to lead against the Moorish king of Granada, because the latter, with the help of the king of Tunis and other Moorish sovereigns from north Africa, had made many ruinous raids throughout Spain, and if they were not restrained, worse would happen.

He describes the beautiful suits of full armour each man was given, as well as one hundred crowns and a letter of recommendation for the king of Spain, and continues:

> We went in the direction of Granada [in Spring 1457] taking all the castles and small populations of this kingdom, because the Moors feared taking on so many troops. We needed to assault most of the fortresses and towns and put all the Moors to death, and the assistants and servants were ordered to knife to death the women and children, which they did. We continued to the city of Granada, ready to fight, as we suspected that the Moors, with so many soldiers, would come out to meet us, which they did. They didn't let us get close to the city but sought us out, to no advantage since we had better munitions than they did.

After this Jorge and the troops crossed the kingdom of Granada, 'bringing blood and fire to everything we found'. He escaped with his life, although his leg was badly injured during the assault of the town of Jimena.

It was into this climate of conflict, treachery, brutality and murder that Boabdil was born in the Alhambra, sometime between 1459 and 1462, under the rule of his grandfather. He entered a world in which his future would be inescapably influenced by factors prevalent in the history of his kingdom from the outset. Chief among them were vassalage to the Christians, whose power and weaponry were increasingly strong, the political power of the Muslim *ulama*, warring clans, betrayals, lethal violence, a tendency to multiple reigns, and intense discord at the heart of the royal family. Despite this, from its foundation in 1237 to the start of Sa'd's reign, the kingdom of Granada had evolved into a state with many of the characteristics of a modern European nation. Society was bonded not by a tribe but by a single religion, Islam; by a single, universal language, Arabic; and by a sense of the deep differences between the Granadan people and the Other beyond its frontier, a people who spoke a Romance language, Castilian, and who, like them, followed a single religion. At the time of Boabdil's birth, this had simultaneously created solidarity and instability, yet also formed the basis for the modern state system. These paradoxes at the heart of the Granadan life underlay the challenges Boabdil faced during his life, as he fought for his own future and that of the independent Muslim country he ruled.

2

Man of Destiny: Boabdil's Early Life

Abrilliant crescent moon is shining high above the Alhambra palace. The late-August night is hot, still and quiet, with no sound except the chirring of crickets and the gentle splash of water in the fountains. The bedroom doors to the balcony above the Patio of the Lions are wide open to let in air, and the moonbeams fall on the figure of a small boy standing on the threshold, his back to the dark room behind. The young Prince Boabdil is too hot to sleep. He is wide awake, and enchanted by the moonlight playing on the water of the fountain in the centre of the patio. He watches motionless, calmly absorbed by the sounds of the running, moonlit cascade. Suddenly the spell is broken and there are shouts, people running with lanterns, the clash of metal as sword hits sword. He doesn't understand what is happening, but he feels frightened. Behind him, a woman's anxious voice urges him to come away from the balcony, but he is rooted to the spot as he glimpses his father rushing past, sword in hand, followed by a band of soldiers. Many years later he would still remember the strange expression of exultant joy on his father's face that night as he glanced up and caught sight of his son.

This evocation of the night in 1464 when Boabdil's father, Abu l-Hasan Ali, took the Nasrid throne of Granada pinpoints two opposing dimensions of Boabdil's early years, the idyllic childhood in which he grew up surrounded by the beauty and protection of the great palace and fortress and, in disturbing contrast, the climate of danger and fear that pervaded the citadel and therefore his youth. When Abu l-Hasan became sultan, his eldest son Boabdil was around five years old. Although the exact date of his birth is unknown, chronicles describe him as in his early twenties at the start of his own reign in 1482, and his birth year is usually given as 1459 or 1460. From the start, the shadow of destiny lay over him, as court astrologers predicted that he would suffer great misfortune, to the extent that he became known by the nickname El Zogoibi (the Unlucky One). He was born in the Alhambra itself, and probably commenced the basic Islamic education designated for princes at the age of five, close to the time of his father's accession. Perhaps sometimes in the mosque of the Alhambra, and mostly with a private tutor, he began by learning how to write the ninety-nine names of Allah, and verses from the Koran. Then he would have studied the Koran thoroughly, and started to learn arithmetic, and later, at the citadel's madrasa, he is likely to have been taught advanced Arabic grammar, poetry, logic, algebra, science, history, law and theology. Boabdil's schooling was designed to make him an educated and widely read adult, an image hinted at in Christian chronicles and developed in his fictional representations. A future sultan also needed practical expertise, and the young prince was bound to have been taught how to ride and care for horses very early. He became a highly skilled horseman in hunting, a pursuit which was excellent training for war and a measure of his nobility. Arab coursers were renowned for being small yet powerful, agile and adaptable, and Boabdil must have ridden these fearless horses to hunt bears, boars and hares with the weapons of war, a lance, perhaps a crossbow, a knife and sword. The twin poles of his life would have been his Islamic education and his immersion in the arts of horsemanship, hunting and war.

Such a path from childhood to manhood must have been full of interest, activity and companionship as he grew up with his younger brother, Yusuf, and his sister, Aixa. Yet the unique privilege of living in the Alhambra palace, one of the wonders of the world in its elegance, grace and beauty, with its running and still water features, and its walls adorned with Islamic poetry, was marred by a darker side. As we saw in the reign of his ancestors, the palace had become increasingly a site of murder and violence, 'a monument to murder, slavery, poverty and fear', as the writer and historian Robert Irwin described it, referring to the violent 'red' or bloody deaths there of seven sultans and numerous viziers as well as the cruel imprisonment of Christian slaves in the underground pits of the fortress. The very palace the sultans had built for their recreation and protection became a place of terror and subversion, where they lived in fear of their lives.

In the first three or four years of Boabdil's life, his grandfather Sa'd had lived and reigned in the Alhambra. The year 1461 is remembered with horror in the history of Granada as the time when Sultan Sa'd ordered the assassination of the Abencerrajes, the Banu Sarraj, who had always been his supporters and promoters. Why he did this isn't certain. Whether he wanted to deflect attention from the fact that he had failed to keep the Castilians at bay, or whether they had in reality kept some tribute money for themselves which should have been paid to the Castilians, the terrible story goes that he invited them all to a banquet at the Alhambra and had nearly the entire clan slaughtered there, including his own minister Mufarrij. Only a few escaped and fled to Malaga.

Then, in a bizarre turn of fate, Sa'd was overthrown by his own son, Boabdil's father, on that August night in 1464. There is much disagreement about what happened to the sixty-five-year-old Sa'd after he had been deposed. Some say Abu l-Hasan attempted a reconciliation with his father and asked him to return, but that Sa'd refused, preferring to establish himself in Almería. The Morisco chronicler Hernando de Baeza recounts instead, and more convincingly, that he was sent to Salobreña castle under a kind of house arrest, where he is said to have died on 20 April 1465. Abu l-Hasan himself must have been over twenty-eight years old at the time, as the Egyptian writer Abd al-Basit tells us that he was born in 1436/7. If his reign might not have been decisive in bringing about the final demise of his kingdom, it was undoubtedly critical in terms of his relationship with his eldest son and in its repercussions on the latter's reign. A man who overthrows his father must be constantly looking over his shoulder at his own sons and questioning their intentions.

The two defining aspects of Abu l-Hasan's character were his warlike, cruel nature, and his weakness for sensual indulgence. He must have seemed a frightening man to his children. Following the lead of the *ulama*, he maintained a persistently militant attitude towards the Christian enemy, always favouring fighting over diplomacy. He was known to them as Muley Hacén, 'Muley' being the Castilian version of the Arabic for 'My Lord' and 'Hacén' the Christian version of his own name, Hasan. The sultan's unshakeable defiance of the Christians is clear, and he is reputed to have refused to pay a tribute to the Castilian Queen Isabella because, he claimed, the places in Granada where coins were minted were forging lance-heads to make war, not to pay the Christians.

At the start of his reign Abu l-Hasan still had to deal with the rebel Abencerraje clan, whose survivors remained in Malaga, where they formed a centre of opposition from 1470 onwards with the help of Abu l-Hasan's younger brother, Abu Abdallah Muhammad, known as El Zagal (the Valiant), uncle of Boabdil, who had set himself up as leader of the region with Malaga as its capital. The Abencerrajes proclaimed him as their king, and civil war erupted. Promising better living conditions, and the strict observance of Islamic rules and law, the sultan took charge and won over the inhabitants. The brothers were reconciled, and Abu l-Hasan once more imposed his authority with the same aim of exterminating the rogue clan that his father had pursued. Realising their number was up if they stayed put, the Abencerrajes departed to shelter with the Christian nobles who lived close to the frontier, in particular with the Medina Sidonia family. With the uprising quashed and his brother toeing the line, Abu l-Hasan's kingdom enjoyed a period of economic and military prosperity. His constant attacks on the Christians in the form of raiding parties forced the enemy to sign a series of truces, leading to a relatively long period of peace from 1465 until 1481, a situation greatly helped by destructive outbreaks of internecine violence among the Christians, which showed that the Nasrids of Granada were not unique in their internal feuding. Abu l-Hasan took good advantage of this to ally himself with the powerful Christian Count of Cabra, who would support him in future conflicts. In 1472, the sultan personally signed a general peace treaty covering the entire frontier for three years until January 1475. Henry IV of Castile undertook not to help any of the rebels from the Abencerraje clan, which suggests the latter were still an active threat.

So far, so good. Abu l-Hasan's militant politics allowed his kingdom to flourish. But events conspired against the continued peace of the Nasrid state in the form of two new and very powerful monarchs, Isabella of Castile and Ferdinand of Aragon, who had married in 1469. Isabella had come to the throne of Castile in 1474 when Henry IV died in his palace in Madrid. When the king of Aragon, John II, also died in 1479, his son Ferdinand took his place, and the two kingdoms were united. In the same year civil war in Castile ended, and peace was made between Castile and Portugal. These circumstances were decisive for the Nasrid kingdom of Granada, and for the end of Andalusian Islam, as Ferdinand and Isabella could now concentrate on war against Granada. Their aim was to abolish the Muslim state for ever.

The Arab historian al-Maqqari tells us of ominous warnings given to the Granadan Muslims of an approaching divine punishment and the ruin of their empire. He describes an ancient weathercock in the old casbah of the city which bore a verse foretelling an unspecified calamity that would ruin both the Alhambra palace and its incumbent. Hernando de Baeza also describes the appearance of a comet, broad and long like a sword, which appeared from two hours before dawn until daylight, for a period of thirty days. The king's astrologers told him that this was a portent of major war and great destruction. The year 1478 brought another omen, shortly after Abu l-Hasan had signed a new treaty with the Catholic Monarchs, as Ferdinand and Isabella were collectively known, who at that stage were still involved with war against Portugal and did not insist on the payment of tribute. Enamoured of increasing his military strength, Abu l-Hasan at that time had more cavalry, artillery and other weapons than any of his predecessors, and his soldiers were self-confident and not intimidated by Castilian military might. In April of that year he decided to organise a great parade and inspection of all his troops, a marvellous public spectacle to demonstrate his growing military prowess, and surreptitiously to prime his people to accept a tax increase. It is likely that Boabdil, then eighteen or nineteen, was present, as his father's heir. But the sultan's triumphal parade, which lasted for days on end, culminated in disaster. al-Maqqari gives us a vivid description of what happened:

> On this occasion the soldiers were clad in suits of polished steel armour, dressed in gorgeous silken robes, mounted on fleet steeds, and having their swords, spears and shields richly embossed with gold and silver. One day when the sultan was as usual seated under the pavilion and the troops were passing before him, the summit and the sides of the neighbouring hill of as-Sabíkah being crowded with spectators who had left their dwellings for the purpose of witnessing the pageant, God permitted that all of a sudden the rain should fall down in torrents, and that the river Darro should overflow its banks. Such was the fury of the devastating element, which came pouring down from the neighbouring mountains, carrying along large stones and whole trees, that it destroyed everything in its way, and that houses, shops, mills, inns, markets, bridges and garden walls were the prey of the devastating flood. The water reached as far as the square where the great mosque stands. So frightful an inundation had never before been experienced in the country, and the people naturally looked upon it as the harbinger of the dreadful calamities which awaited Muslims in just chastisement for their perversity and their sins.

This catastrophe had a terrible effect on Abu l-Hasan, who seems to have suffered some sort of breakdown. The anonymous Arabic author of the fifteenth-century chronicle known as the *Nubdhat*, the only contemporary historical source surviving in Arabic, censoriously declares that from this time on, the sultan grew confused and began to decline. He reviles him for devoting himself to pleasure and lust, and amusing himself with singing and dancing girls. At the same time, Abu l-Hasan cut back the pay of his soldiers, so that they had to sell their equipment to live, and acted cruelly towards his people, crippling them with vastly increased taxes – perhaps to pay the cost of cleaning up after the floods, although it sounds as if the hike was planned before the day of the disaster. No doubt the shock of the sudden inundation did adversely affect Abu l-Hasan, but his abandonment to hedonism was nothing new. His naturally lustful nature had intense and far-reaching consequences for both his kingdom and his family, Boabdil in particular.

Abu l-Hasan's wife Aixa was a powerful Nasrid princess, said to have been descended in a direct line from the Prophet Muhammad. She was the daughter of Muhammad IX, Boabdil's maternal grandfather, making her a distant relative of her second husband. She was also the widow of Muhammad X, who was executed by Abu l-Hasan on behalf of his father, Sa'd. In spite of this melodramatic background, their marriage was peaceful for twenty years, during which time their three children were born, all of whom, according to Hernando de Baeza, were 'notable and brave persons'. Abu l-Hasan and Aixa were two very strong personalities, and while they had personal interests in common, things went well between them. But harmony turned into hatred when another woman came into Abu l-Hasan's life. The sultan had organised an attack on the small Christian town of Aguilar on 29 September 1471, when, in Baeza's account, the raiding party captured some children watering their animals at the fountain. Among them was a young girl of about twelve, who was taken to Granada and sold into the king's household. She was given the task of chambermaid, sweeping the royal rooms. Abu l-Hasan somehow got involved with the girl, using one of his pages as a go-between, but Aixa's ladies found out that she had been taken to her husband's royal chamber, and beat her severely when she emerged, leaving her half dead. Abu l-Hasan, believing his wife to have ordered the beating, was distraught. He ordered beautiful clothes to be made for the girl, and gave her magnificent jewellery fit for a queen, and on the next festival day he ordered his subjects to make reverence to 'La Romía', which was the name used to describe a Christian woman who had become Moorish.

The young Christian captive was almost certainly Isabel de Solís, the daughter of the knight commander of the town of La Higuera de Martos, Sancho Jiménez de Solís. She converted to Islam and took the name Zoraya from the name of a star in the Pleiades constellation. Legend has created an image of her dazzling beauty which bewitched the sultan, although Hernando de Baeza, who lived at the royal court, wrote that he knew her many years later, and he didn't think much of her appearance or character. Whatever the case, something about her must have captivated Abu l-Hasan, who gave her land, houses and a privileged position at court. He is alleged to have bribed some judges into legalising a new marriage, which created furious resentment in Aixa and her sons. He gave Zoraya as her personal residence the palace known as Daralcotola, which stood where the monastery of Santa Isabel la Real is now located in the Alcazaba Cadima in the Albaicin. The sultan bought it expressly for her, and improvements were made before she moved in. Baeza continues that, from then on, the sultan made his life with her, recognised her as queen and neither spoke to nor saw Aixa ever again.

To a proud noblewoman like Boabdil's mother, such an insult must have been hard to bear, and we learn from the chronicles of Aixa's bitter jealousy. Being scorned as queen by her husband and substituted by a young girl with no social status, a renegade Christian to boot, ruined Aixa's relationship with Abu l-Hasan and caused a lasting enmity between the sultan and his wife, his family and members of his court, most of whom were loyal to her. Because of Abu l-Hasan's impetuous, cruel and angry nature, Aixa feared for her children, so she allowed matters to proceed uneventfully for a time while he indulged in his passions. What tipped the balance was the threat posed to Boabdil by the two sons her ex-husband had fathered by Zoraya, Sa'd and Nasr. From birth they were considered royal princes, and as such they grew up in the Granadan court. Abu l-Hasan gave them their own property and personal wealth, which came from the inheritance an aunt had bequeathed him, and enabled Sa'd and Nasr to escape from what would inevitably have been a precarious financial situation in later life. The position for Aixa gradually became intolerable – she lived in the rooms surrounding the Patio of the Lions with her children and loyal servants and advisers, while Zoraya lived with Abu l-Hasan in the Comares tower of the Alhambra close by. Clearly ambitious for her firstborn, she saw the danger to Boabdil's succession to the Nasrid throne, fearing that in his deluded state, his father would favour one of his and Zoraya's sons over his legitimate heir. But Aixa had a very important card up her sleeve. Her status as a Nasrid princess meant that she benefited from the link of kinship through blood relationship down the female line, which had existed among the Nasrids since the fourteenth century. By virtue of this connection, women of royal blood could transmit rights to the throne, rights which she exercised as mother of the next true Nasrid sultan. Determined that her son should inherit the throne, this power and her dominant character made her a protagonist in many political events, in particular in relation to Boabdil, and later historians have suggested that her son's personal and political conduct was very much dictated by his mother, although the contemporary sources we have available don't bear this out: they tend to portray Boabdil as his own man in those matters.

There is an echo in this tale of passion and jealousy of the love affair of King Roderick and La Cava, back in 711. In both cases a woman provokes important events leading to the loss of a kingdom. In fact, a Sephardic Jewish chronicle written by the historian Moses Capsali contains an imagined account of Abu l-Hasan's first glimpse of Zoraya which strongly hints at the Visigothic king's first sight of La Cava:

> One day the king looked out of the window and saw a young girl his servants had carried off from Christian Spain. The young girl was very beautiful and of good appearance; for this reason they called her Zoraya, which means 'lamp' in Hebrew. And the king ardently desired her beauty, and he hid her for many days, because it was a humiliation that the king should bring a concubine into his home and take other women in place of his wife.

This anecdote is similar to the stories which describe Roderick looking out of a window and seeing La Cava having fun with her ladies-in-waiting, when he is overcome by her beauty. In the same way that Christians accounted for the Muslim invasion of Spain by blaming Roderick's lust and debauchery, the Andalusians wanted to find a concrete reason for the fall of Granada, and often attributed it to the discord at the Nasrid court caused by the sultan's alliance with Zoraya. The importance of these intrigues has been exaggerated, and

certainly other factors were equally if not more crucial in the demise
of the sultanate, but that they increased the internal conflicts that
were mortally destructive to the Nasrids and intensified the climate
of conspiracy there is no doubt.

In this complex web of family relationships between Abu
l-Hasan, Aixa, Zoraya and Boabdil, Abu l-Hasan's brother Muhammad, El Zagal, played a significant part in the events leading to the
end of the kingdom. El Zagal's date of birth is vague, sometime after
1437. His wife was a daughter of Yusuf IV, in what had perhaps been
a marriage arranged by his father Sa'd to curry favour with the dissi-
dent political powers in Granada, especially with the ever-powerful
Abencerrajes. As valiant as his sobriquet, and as warlike and ambitious as his brother, he had been defeated by him in Malaga in 1470,
and reverted to being subject to Abu l-Hasan, remaining loyal to him
for the rest of his reign. There will be much more to say about El Zagal
later on, but I have introduced him at this point because of what his
connection with Zoraya shows us about her cunning and rivalry with
Aixa. While Abu l-Hasan was alive, the Christian convert stayed
close to him as his wife and queen, but when he died she turned to
El Zagal for protection. There were strong rumours that although
her two sons were with their father at his death in Salobreña, Zoraya
remained in the Alhambra as queen consort at the express wish of
El Zagal, who pressed her to marry him when his brother died. She
refused, proposing that her elder son Sa'd should take the throne. On
this occasion, the *alfaquíes*, the priests of Islam, ignored her demands
as they deemed it more useful for El Zagal to reign instead.

In 1482, amid these family crises, Boabdil married Moraima,
who was not a princess, but the daughter of Ali al-Attar, governor
of the town of Loja and a member of the royal court, and soon they
had a daughter, Aixa, presumably named after her grandmother,
and later, two sons, Ahmed and Yusuf. The future Moorish king
lived with his new family as well as his brother, sister and mother in
the close-knit community of the Alhambra, in the Patio of the Lions,
under the shadow of his father's licentious lifestyle and increasingly severe rule. As if these tensions inside the royal city were not
enough, the Granadans were faced with a severe threat from outside
the kingdom.

Despite the material and psychological setback of the great flood of 1478, Abu l-Hasan persevered with constant raiding parties into Christian territory for booty and captives, and there was an encouraging victory in December 1481 when the Nasrid troops recaptured the town of Zahara from the Christians. It didn't take long for the Christians to retaliate with a deeply damaging blow to Granadan defences. Their surprise attack on the fortified town of Alhama signalled that the hostilities had reached a new and unprecedented stage. Alhama was a border town famed for its baths, perched in a magnificent location at the edge of a great ravine amid rough, mountainous terrain which the Granadans believed made it impregnable. It was not a large place, but it was strategically situated more or less in the centre of the kingdom, between Granada, Malaga and Ronda. There were other routes to the two main cities, but if the Christians could take Alhama, it would give them a vital base from which to wreak further destruction on Granadan territory.

There is a vivid account of the Battle of Alhama by the royal secretary and chronicler Fernando del Pulgar, a Jew who had converted to Christianity. He tells us that the Christian assault was a major undertaking, planned in great secrecy. Not even the troops were told their objective until they started out on the road. The skilled campaign veteran Rodrigo Ponce de León was in charge of one of the columns, and he managed to assemble 25,000 cavalrymen and 3,000 infantry at the town of Marchena, about thirty miles (forty-five kilometres) east of Seville, and take them undetected along perilous cross-country mountain tracks to bring them to the outskirts of Alhama at dawn on 28 February 1482. It was an astonishing feat of leadership and military training. Ponce de León also had scouts known as *escuchas*, or listeners, posted to spy out which side of the town was most vulnerable. Fifteen troops led by a man called Juan de Ortega scaled ladders to climb the citadel, where they managed to kill the lone guard and his sleeping companion undetected. Alhama's main defences were unmanned because the *alcaide*, or governor of the fortress, was away at a wedding. His womenfolk were captured and the gates were opened to admit Ponce de León and his Sevillian soldiers.

Alhama was taken by surprise, but its townsfolk fought back

with a vengeance, hoping against hope for help from Granada, only a
few hours' march away. The fire from crossbows and firearms was so
intense that it kept the Christians at bay inside the castle, desperate
with fear because they also realised that Abu l-Hasan would come
to the rescue. But they were trapped, and were driven to knocking
through the castle walls from the inside, amid a hail of fire. The royal
historian Pulgar recounts how

> the Moors put all their strength and all their heart into the
> fighting, as a courageous man is bound to do when defending
> his life, his wife and his children from the threat of death or
> enslavement. So in the hope of saving some of the survivors,
> they did not flinch from battling on over the corpses of their
> children, their brothers, those near and dear to them, fallen
> before them in the struggle.

Up to 4,000 women and children were captured, and more than 1,000
were killed in the streets. Vital food supplies such as oil, honey and
flour were destroyed and a great deal of gold, silver and cattle were
taken as booty. These terrible events are recounted from a Moorish
point of view in the Spanish ballad 'Ay de mi Alhama', still sung
today.

News reached Granada of the outrageous attack, and the sultan
was pressured into leaving at once to defend his compatriots. Abu
l-Hasan and his troops duly arrived the next morning and were
greeted by the horrific sight of piles of corpses tipped over the city
walls by the Christians, where the local dogs were making a meal of
them. Abu l-Hasan killed the dogs. The Christian accounts and the
Arabic *Nubdhat* agree that the counter-attack was strong and courageous, but somehow the Christian forces held on and smuggled out
a message asking for relief. The Duke of Medina Sidonia and other
noblemen arrived with their troops and broke the siege, forcing Abu
l-Hasan to retreat. The Arabic chronicle, which ought to have been
sympathetic, insinuates that the sultan and his vizier faked an intelligence report claiming that the Christians had amassed a mighty
army which was descending on Alhama, using this as a reason to
withdraw with all speed. This seems unlikely, for Abu l-Hasan was

not a coward, and he made two more attempts to retake the town in April and in early July, without success.

Events proved Abu l-Hasan right in abandoning the siege of Alhama. News reached him that the Christian forces were marching over the mountains from Écija to attack Loja, the town governed by Boabdil's father-in-law Ali al-Attar. The small town lay in a beautiful location in a narrow valley on the western edge of the fertile Granadan *vega*, occupying an important strategic position in Moorish defences. A Christian attack so close to the city of Granada posed a grave threat to the Muslim state, and the sultan rushed to help Ali al-Attar, who fought valiantly in its defence. When the relief troops arrived, the Christians were already on the back foot, and suddenly withdrew in confusion, leaving a great deal of their siege equipment and artillery in the battlefield as they left. If Alhama had been a triumph for Ferdinand, Loja was a disaster, and the Christian monarch was obliged to return to distant Cordoba to rebuild his army. Abu l-Hasan had sent him a clear message – they were not going to surrender meekly.

Meanwhile, in the Alhambra, tensions were reaching boiling point. Boabdil found himself at the centre of a feud that gravely affected his life from then on. His natural position as the rightful heir to the Nasrid throne drove his mother's ambitions of power and status, with lineage and clan loyalty once more vital factors. The temperament of Boabdil's father, half-warrior, half-libertine, not only threatened his elder son's safety but also drew him into his mother's jealous revenge and hatred of her husband, while El Zagal, his equally warlike uncle, also aspired to the throne and destabilised the prince's situation. At twenty-two, Boabdil was caught between love for and loyalty to his mother, his siblings and his own wife and children, and fear of his father and uncle, between his fondness for learning and fine verse and a growing ambition to reign that required him to act as a military commander and autocrat. Thus the circumstances of Boabdil's lineage and early life conspired to shape his destiny. By the middle of July 1482, things had reached a tipping point, and a new drama was set to be played out on the political stage of Granada.

3

From Knight to King:
Boabdil Reigns in Granada

Sometime in early 1482, Boabdil and his brother Yusuf fled from the Alhambra. The Arabic author of the *Nubdhat* describes these events in veiled language, avoiding naming any individuals, as if he were expecting his readers to be already in the know, or perhaps to protect himself. He mentions certain 'devils with the faces of men' who tempted Aixa, suggesting her sons were in mortal danger because of the impetuous temper of their father and the ill-feeling between her and Zoraya. These schemers kept on with their insinuations until she yielded to them and removed Boabdil and Yusuf from their quarters in the Alhambra. The 'devils' were probably the Abencerrajes, who had always supported Aixa. Whoever they were, they conceived a dramatic plot to oust the reigning sultan and replace him with his son.

The Morisco chronicler Hernando de Baeza, who knew Boabdil personally and worked with him for many years, gives us a more detailed account of his daring escape with his brother:

It had been arranged for a Mudejar, a Muslim living under Christian rule, called Abrahen de Mora, who came from the town of Mora in the kingdom of Toledo but who was living in Granada at that time, to enter the queen's house, under the pretext of selling wrought copper. This gave him the opportunity to give some letters to the prince, and by means of these and other missives, they made an agreement with certain noblemen from Guadix. There were two in particular, both very brave men, Aben-adi and Abenecid, with whom Abrahen de Mora dealt. I knew Abrahen personally as a friend, and he was a good man, and very astute in matters of war. He sent some letters to Guadix addressed to those men, concealing them among some pots that he gave to a lad called Abrahen Robledo, from Guadalajara, who worked for some tinkers, and whose job it was to take pots and pans to sell throughout the kingdom. The agreement was that on a designated night, at about ten o'clock, six people should take nine horses with them, to an irrigation channel on the outskirts of the Generalife gardens, just two hundred paces from where the prince lived. The men went on foot, and were joined by Abrahen de Mora at the foot of the wall of the prince's house, where he would be waiting for them, and would recognise them by a certain sign. Once the sign had been given, the prince appeared immediately, like one who hadn't slept, and threw down a thin rope by hand, as agreed, and they tied a much thicker woollen rope to it, which he then tied to a marble pillar and climbed down on it, followed by his brother. Both were treated with due reverence and respect, and were given a sword and dagger each. They say that the prince and his brother, although still lads, encouraged the men and spoke to them with great maturity. They reached the place where others were waiting with horses, which they mounted, and everyone left at dawn for Guadix. Once they had entered the town, the same men who had brought them sent other men from Guadix to the city of Almeria with the prince's younger brother, as had been arranged. Once Yusuf had arrived in Almeria, they gave homage and obedience to him there, and proclaimed Boabdil king in Guadix.

The city of Guadix lies on the banks of the river Guadix, 1,000 feet (300 metres) above sea level in the Sierra Nevada, and from the time

of the Muslim invasion of 711, it had been a Muslim trading centre
with its own fortress and mosque. It is about thirty-eight miles
(sixty kilometres) from Granada, far enough for Boabdil to feel some
degree of safety, yet still within striking distance of the city. For
several months there was constant communication between certain
noblemen in Granada and Boabdil and his supporters, who had con-
cealed him with the intention of raising him as king in Granada. On
the very day that Abu l-Hasan was celebrating the victory at Loja
in July 1482, the news reached him that, with the help of the Abencerrajes, his son had arrived in Granada with his vizier Yusuf b.
Kumasha Aben Comixa, and occupied the Alhambra, taking advantage of his father's absence. Abu l-Hasan was forced to flee first
to the Alpujarras and then to Malaga, where he set up his capital
with his vizier Abu l-Qasim Venegas, accompanied by his brother
El Zagal. His eldest son now became head of the Nasrid dynasty:
Boabdil was proclaimed Sultan Muhammad XI on 14 or 15 July 1482,
adopting the honorary title al-Galib bi-Llah, Conqueror by the Grace
of God, the Nasrid motto which is inscribed on walls throughout the
Alhambra. The name by which he was known to the Christians, and
by which we know him now, Boabdil, comes from Abu Abdallah,
the sultan's *kunya*, the title he assumed in combat and for official
purposes, as it sounded to the Christians when spoken in the Granadan Arabic dialect. While Boabdil controlled Granada and Almeria,
his father governed Malaga and Ronda. Abu l-Hasan began to live
through the same painful experience he had inflicted upon his father
of being ousted from the throne by his own son, and so Granada
became divided, with two monarchs disputing the throne. The historian Fernando del Pulgar, the chronicler to Ferdinand and Isabella,
records how Abu l-Hasan attempted a return to Granada, getting
one of his men to scale the walls of the Alhambra and allow in some
1,500 Moors who killed many of those on guard. Pulgar goes on:

> Then the former king went out into the city of Granada and
> started fighting in the streets with those he found there. And
> the people from the city and Albaicin who were on the side of
> his son came together and fought against him and his men.
> They threw him out of the city and he took refuge in an old

fortress nearby, while the captain Aben Comixa went back to reclaim the Alhambra.

The accounts of various Christian and Arab chroniclers reveal a good deal of confusion over the dates and details of the plot to oust Abu l-Hasan. The only contemporary Arabic source, the *Nubdhat*, claims that it was his sons' escape from the Alhambra that Abu l-Hasan heard of on the day of his victory at Loja, but that would give Boabdil insufficient time – six months, according to Hernando de Baeza – to muster his supporters in Guadix and be proclaimed emir in mid-July 1482. This date seems certain, so we must assume that the princes had made it to Guadix in January of that year. There is also a divergence of opinion over the reason for Boabdil's over-throw of his father. The royal historian Luis del Mármol Carvajal, writing a long time after the events, in 1600, describes Abu l-Hasan as old and ill in 1482, and completely in thrall to Zoraya. He attri-butes Boabdil's rebellion to the bad feeling between his mother and Zoraya, which led all the foremost people in the kingdom to hate the sultan and conspire against him. On the other hand, the Chris-tian chronicler Andrés Bernáldez, writing some time before 1513, so much nearer in time to these events, tells us that the main cause of Abu l-Hasan's downfall was the envy of certain Granadan noblemen because of the great favour in which he held Abulcacim Venegas, royal constable of Granada, chosen as vizier by the sultan, and who, says Bernáldez, ruled the city and kingdom much better than Abu l-Hasan himself. Venegas was of Christian lineage from Cordoba, with a Christian father and grandfather, although he was born in Moorish lands. Clearly the illustrious Muslim clans of Granada objected to the great power of this man with Christian ancestors at the heart of the royal court. Possibly both sexual rivalry, with its implicit threat to royal succession, and the jealous rivalry of the clans conspired against Abu l-Hasan, allowing his rightful heir to take his place. Whatever the case, this grave split or *fitna* in the Nasrid family began to weaken Granada in a way that would eventually prove fatal, and one which the Castilians knew how to exploit.

Yet in spite of a retaliatory attack by Abu l-Hasan against Boabdil's troops, resulting in their flight back to Guadix, a city as enthralled by the son as it was hostile to the father, the first six months of Boabdil's reign were relatively peaceful. What kind of city did the young sultan rule over? What did it look like, who lived and worked there, and what did daily life in the Alhambra precinct consist of? The cityscape of Granada was typical of other Andalusian and north African Islamic cities, with a walled central nucleus – or medina – where the main religious, commercial and military buildings were situated, next to the main royal palace and fortress of the Alhambra. Around the medina were suburbs, some big, some small, each with its own gates, usually open all day for the purpose of collecting taxes on the merchandise coming in or going out, but closed at night to isolate and protect the city dwellers. The names of some of these suburbs came from the place of origin of their first inhabitants, such as the district of Gomeres at the present-day entrance to the Alhambra, where lived the black Berber tribesmen who came overseas to fight for the Granadans. Others came from their occupants' profession – the Albaicin, or al-Bayyazin, means the district of the falconers, for example. The layout so characteristic of Muslim cities was one of winding thoroughfares with many smaller streets branching off the main routes, twisting and undulating and often leading to dead ends. Some were, and still are, so narrow that a soldier wearing armour and holding a lance couldn't walk down them. Passages linked the upper floors of houses above the street, many of which had attics that protruded outwards, creating sharp contrasts of light and shadow that accentuated their irregularity. Granada is a city that speaks through its architecture. The separation and isolation of the districts, the narrow tortuousness of the streets, the many labyrinthine passageways, mighty walls and entry gates all point to a primordial need for defence against attack. They suggest a society closed off from the outside world, living with an ever-present threat of assault and persecution which, given the long history of Christian attempts at reconquest, seems entirely understandable.

This closed-in quality also had an effect on the houses of its inhabitants, of which there were about 50,000 at the end of the fifteenth century. The majority of Granadans in Boabdil's time lived in very restricted, enclosed spaces. Records left by the Christian conquerors show that their families often needed between two and six dwellings of the size used by the same number of Muslims. The sheltered nature of Muslim houses reflected their concept of urban domestic life as a refuge from the hubbub of the street. With their inner central patios, fountains and potted plants surrounded by living areas and bedrooms, their dwellings were places of intimacy away from prying eyes and the fierce summer heat, with few windows facing out, often just balconies with wooden shutters. Water was supplied using irrigation channels from rivers and streams, and sewage was fed into an external drain. Their furniture was poor and sparse, mainly consisting of low tables or dressers, chests, mattresses and cushions, carpets and rugs. There were copper or clay pots, rarely glass, and better-off families had oil lamps, bed clothes and table coverings.

Outside, in the town, the main buildings bespoke the importance of trade. The *alcaicería*, situated near the main mosque, was devoted to commerce, particularly buying and selling the beautiful silk which was one of Granada's most important products. It was a large area full of stalls and small shops, almost 200 in all, with ten access doors, and was owned by the sultan, Boabdil in this case, who collected tributes from the stall holders. In addition, the *alhóndiga* or *fundaq* was a kind of corn exchange where grain was stored and sold, as well as other merchandise. The building known as the Corral del Carbón in modern Granada is the only old corn exchange preserved in Spain. There was also a specialist *alhóndiga* called the Zaida, which in Boabdil's time sold oil, honey, cheese and dried fruit. The third areas devoted to trade were the *zocos*, the permanent or regular markets, of which there were many in the streets and squares of the medina and in the city suburbs, and they were inevitably the noisiest, busiest places in Granada. The city also had many mosques. The German traveller Hieronymus Münzer estimated that there were over 200 when he visited Granada in 1494, though most of them were small, private places of worship. All the large mosques were converted to churches when the city came under Christian rule, and nothing remains of them apart from two minarets, converted to the bell-towers of the churches of San José and San Juan de los Reyes. The madrasa is still in Calle Oficios near the cathedral, and continues to fulfil an educational function as part of the University of Granada, as well as being open to tourists.

A wide variety of people lived inside the city walls. Rich Muslims who were landowners, merchants or members of a distinguished family lived in big houses in the suburbs, while the majority of the population consisted of artisans, many of whom lived in specific streets or *barrios*, according to their areas of expertise. Most of the professional army lived in the city, along with artists, men of letters, lawyers and religious leaders. A large part of the Granadan lower class was made up of agricultural workers from the *vega*, who lived outside the city walls in small communities and villages. A number of native Castilians, either captive or free depending on their religious status, had an influence on politics, since many religious renegades, or *elches*, found asylum and important positions in the Nasrid army and at court. As we have seen, there were no Christians native to Granada because the Mozarabs, or Christians living under Islamic rule, had disappeared from the area before the emirate was formed. There were a few Jews, no more than 3,000, who lived in the city and on the coast, working as craftsmen and traders, as well as doctors and interpreters. The city ruled by Boabdil was a thriving cultural, religious, commercial, artisanal and agricultural centre, in a privileged position of access to the ports of Malaga and Almeria, with north Africa within easy reach. Genoese merchants called regularly at these ports and eagerly bought local silk, sugar and fruit, so the economy would have flourished if the Granadan treasury had not had to pay enormous sums in tribute to Castile.

The new sultan lived once more in the city of the Alhambra, which in his time was an entirely self-sufficient urban settlement, and the last example of a palace which was both a fortress and a city, a model devised in Mesopotamia millennia ago. The palaces formed part of the citadel, which contained arms stores, at least twenty-five houses belonging to senior officials, the gardens of the Generalife, a mosque which had a beautiful bronze lamp now in the National Archaeological Museum in Madrid, public baths and its own madrasa. There were even ceramic and glass-making workshops and a tannery. All Boabdil's administrative staff worked in the palace of the Abencerrajes, halfway along Calle Real (Royal Street), down which a drainage channel flowed supplying water to the entire precinct. This bustling city within a city was also a place of leisure and delight, with its many cooling fountains, spectacular views of the city and the *vega*, and its gardens designed with the Muslim concept of paradise in mind, an oasis of delight appealing to all five senses through their colour, scent and texture, the taste of their fruit and the sound of flowing water. The sultans drank wine despite its Koranic prohibition, and they also enjoyed milk, orange or rose water, quince and pomegranate syrup or fruit juice. Their food was refined and varied, including lamb, goat and chicken, couscous, harissa, cheese and honey, with a wealth of fresh vegetables, fruit and nuts from the *vega*, especially almonds, figs, pomegranates and raisins.

We can see from this that Boabdil's life as sultan in the Alhambra was luxurious and pleasurable from a material point of view, but his political landscape was less attractive. Although he ruled exclusively in his capacity as emir, the policy, actions and affairs of state were conducted and influenced by divergent groups and individuals, the most prominent of whom was the vizier, or *wazir*. Since the emir was above all a military leader whose mission was to defend Granadan Muslims from danger, the military government of territory was more important than civil government. To maintain his personal power Boabdil had to spend a good part of his income on maintaining the garrison and troops on a salary, and he needed to rely on his vizier to act on his behalf in civil matters, although the minister had to obey the superior jurisdiction of the emir, could not interfere in the decisions of religious authorities and did not have any right of succession. The appointment or dismissal of the vizier was the will of the emir, and many of those appointed to the post became personal friends of their masters, such as Boabdil's vizier Aben Comixa, who served him loyally to the end, in contrast to the viziers of some earlier rulers who were notoriously vicious to their enemies. The vizier had a virtually all-embracing power derived from the trust and friendship of the emir. He conveyed and fulfilled the emir's orders, organised all administration, drew up decrees and official correspondence, as well as being head of diplomacy and leader of the Granadan part of the army, although the emir held overall jurisdiction and power as military commander.

The *qadis*, or judges who reviewed civil, legal and religious matters according to Islamic law, were trained in theology at the madrasa in the city, and were entirely independent of the emir. In the late fifteenth century they had all the power of the doctors of Muslim law, the *fuqaha*, behind them. Both groups could dictate policy on the strength of their opinions, and they were both ferociously opposed to any emir who countenanced concord with or subjection to Castile, which did not augur well for Boabdil. Religion was inseparable from the administration of justice, and the existence of a civil, secular judicial body was unthinkable. So Boabdil ruled surrounded in theory by friendly collaborators in the vizier and the *qadis*, to which we should add the ever-present pressure groups and unions of interest formed by the lineages, including the Abencerrajes who had supported both Aixa and Boabdil, and also the military who were the masters of physical force. The uniqueness of existence in Granada rested on this social and political edifice.

Looking out from the belvederes of the royal apartments, an abundant city of gardens, groves of trees and private orchards surrounding its walls was laid out before Boabdil, with the inimitable *vega* beyond. This fertile plain acted as a natural defence for the city as it was a barrier between Granada and the mountains. It was also vital for providing food, and flourished at the hands of Muslims expert in horticulture and irrigation. In common with other Nasrid cities, Granada had intimate contact with its rural surroundings. This was in strong contrast with its Christian conquerors, who scorned the local countryside. City dwellers went to the country for harvest celebrations and festival days, while there was a constant flow of Granadans from the *vega* entering at the city gates to sell their vegetables and fruit.

Beyond the *vega* lay the omnipresent frontier. This area of land, known to the Castilians as the *banda morisca*, the Morisco border, was a vital factor in the material and psychological life of the Granadan state. It is one of the most fascinating features of the war between Christian Spain and Muslim Granada. The Spanish historian Miguel Ángel Ladero Quesada makes a telling point when he writes that this frontier was unusual because it divided a place that had a previous history and identity as Hispania, and separated populations mostly descended from natives of Hispania on both Christian and Muslim sides. In that sense it could not be compared to other medieval frontiers between Christianity and Islam such as Byzantium or the Crusades in areas of the Mediterranean. It was not officially a border between two countries, but in all other respects it might just as well have been, as it separated two cultural systems, two religions, two societies. No independent new culture ever emerged as there was little possibility for coexistence or mixing. The frontier was a precise one, a line or strip marked out by towers and fortresses, a line of demarcation not only geographically but also symbolically. As L. P. Harvey puts it, it was also a frontier of the mind. It was the tangible manifestation of an ancestral confrontation between two worlds which opposed each other from ideological and religious positions that were reciprocally exclusive.

The land frontier that delimited the territory of the Granadan emirate consisted of about 11,600 square miles (30,000 square kilometres) of what is now eastern Andalusia, and it had existed for nearly 250 years when Boabdil became sultan in 1482. The territory was a paradoxical place of peace and also of hostility. There, truces were fulfilled and goods exchanged, while daily hostilities and confrontation created a permanent need for both defence and attack along the border. The truces helped to suspend and defuse large-scale hostilities and ease the pressure of the intense life of frontier coexistence, where at times relations were peaceful and even neighbourly, but mostly consisted of rivalry, violence and reprisal. There were some measures in place for maintaining peaceful coexistence on a daily basis in the form of the *juez de frontera*, or frontier judge, a kind of arbitrator between Moors and Christians, and usually there was one representative from either side, both of whom resolved the petitions of the opposing group. There were also special frontier police, the *fieles de rastro*, and *exeas*, or interpreters, who were indispensable for commerce, in the exchange of captives between the two parties, and as guides for merchants. Often a Christian interpreter let his beard grow and wore Muslim clothes in order to be better accepted by the Granadans. Direct evidence of the vital role played by interpreters is brought to light in a letter written by King Ferdinand and Queen Isabella to Boabdil much later, in June 1488, regarding a number of Moors, as they describe them, who managed to infiltrate the province of Malaga, under Christian command by that time, and who committed some unspecified crimes. The monarchs command Boabdil to make public announcements stating that no Moors should visit these areas without a Christian interpreter, otherwise they would be taken captive.

Castile was perennially the counterpoint to Granada, and nowhere more so than on the frontier. The attitude of the Castilian Christians to the Muslim emirate speaks of a fundamental difference in perception between the opposing sides. Castile perceived Granada as a vassal kingdom whose emirs held illegitimate power because the creation of the Muslim state by Muhammad I was in their eyes an act of vassalage. Granada naturally took a different view, and never accepted its subservience to the Christians. The social and political aspirations of the Christian noblemen of Andalusia largely revolved around the frontier, where many died or were wounded; these showed in their chivalric ideals and in the poetic memory of that unique time recorded in the famous Spanish frontier ballads then and later. The pattern of violence and reprisal provided the opportunity for heroism on the frontier, through the kind of hostility that did not break any truce in force, such as surprise assaults and horseback raids on fortresses and other local places, with the intention of seizing booty, wearing down the enemy and capturing a frontier outpost. These sorties fed a desire for fame and for fulfilment of the ideal of fighting the infidel.

For the Granadans, *ribat*, which was the obligation to fight on the frontier, was a religious one, and their involvement in frontier warfare was essentially defensive since there was little hope of them ever being able to expand their territory significantly owing to its geographical location. Yet, however seriously both sides might have taken their obligation to fight for their God and for their people, the immediate aim was often the commandeering of a herd of cattle or a recently harvested crop. The frontier fighters developed a way of life which was transferred to the New World discovered by Columbus, where cattle raiding and hard riding formed part of the myth of how the West was won, and was also echoed in the life of the Argentinian gauchos.

The major preoccupation of Boabdil's life up to the time he became sultan was the inner discord in Granada and in his own family. But the Christian threat on and beyond the frontier that lurked constantly in the background began to come to the fore in 1482. The Granada campaign now started in earnest. In 1479 the Warrior Pope Julius II had issued a crusading bull calling for war against Granada. This chilling order from the head of the Catholic Church was reissued in 1482, reinforcing the ingrained idea that the war against the Moors was part of the culture of the fighting and ruling classes of late medieval Spain. The popularity of great novels of chivalry such as *Tirant lo blanc* (*Tirante the White*) and *Amadís de Gaula* (*Amadeus of Gaul*), whose world of valour and often super-human strength of arms reinforced traditional values, proclaimed the need to restore chivalric ideals among the knights of Spain. The Muslim preoccupation with lineage was to an extent mirrored by the Christian anxiety over *limpieza de sangre*, or purity of blood. Aris-tocratic families were desperate to assert their unsullied bloodline going back to the ancient Visigoths. In Castile in particular, being the son of someone of note, an *hijodalgo* – from which the word hidalgo comes – was an important distinction.

The Christian chroniclers of the war emphasised the idea that their campaign could be vindicated as a reconquest of territory lost a long time ago to the Moors. It was a taking back, a restoration of what was rightly theirs, the overcoming of a wicked political enclave and a holy war against the unbeliever. It was also a positive way of channelling the violence among the aristocracy of Castile which had threatened to ruin the kingdom in recent years. The accounts of those historians are inevitably biased towards the victors, and we have to take this into consideration when we attempt to build up a picture of what really happened. With the exception of the anony-mous Arabic *Nubdhat* and al-Maqqari's long history, nearly all the accounts of the Granadan war were written by Christians, though it is true to say that they often present the Muslim enemy in a respect-ful light, and even with admiration at times.

As life on the frontier continued with its raids, skirmishes and minor victories on both sides, the event took place which proved to be the catalyst for a final, focused Christian campaign against Granada. While Boabdil and his supporters were in Guadix in early 1482 plotting the next moves in their plan to set the prince on the

Granadan throne, the Christians made the surprise assault on the fortified town of Alhama described in Chapter 2, when Abu l-Hasan so boldly defended its people against the odds. The success of the Christians in this battle moved the war into a new phase and, as we have seen, Abu l-Hasan was quick to retaliate in successfully defending Loja. But this did not deter King Ferdinand for long. He regrouped his men and resorted to a strategy known as the *tala*, which consisted of burning and destroying crops. It was a ploy he had used before, except that this time it was in the *vega* of Granada, very close to the city, and in an area which provided much of its essential grain, fruit and vegetables. It was a dreadful, slow and devastating process, against which the Granadans could do nothing. If their food supplies were destroyed, there could be no hope of survival.

In his territory of the now divided kingdom of Granada, Abu l-Hasan carried on doing what he did best – raiding and attacking frontier outposts. By early 1483, the Christians had decided to try to capitalise on their success at Alhama and invade the large and beautiful coastal area east of Abu l-Hasan's territory of Malaga, known as the Ajarquía. Their strategy was not entirely clear, other than perhaps to boost their morale, and that lack of clarity of intention was matched by an equal indecisiveness regarding which way they should go. A council of war assembled in the town of Antequera and a long discussion took place. Fears were expressed about the rough mountainous terrain and steep drops which favoured the enemy, and which would be little use to the Christians if they did capture it. In the end they did decide to make a raid, but their fears proved to be well founded, since the local inhabitants led them into a disastrous trap. Pulgar tells us what happened:

> The scouts who were entrusted with guiding them along the safest route took them across a mountain track so high and steep that a man on foot would have found it difficult. According to their custom, the Moors kept fires lit all day and all night on the tops of mountains and other high points, as a way of summoning those who lived in those areas. They lay in wait for the Christians and inflicted heavy casualties by raining

rocks down on them and firing arrows from the side and rear.
As the Christians struggled to extricate themselves, night fell.
Fearing they would suffer even greater casualties if they kept
on the track, they went back down a deep river valley under a
high mountain which the Moors had already climbed. When
they saw that the Christians had taken this route they threw
rocks and stones down on them, killing many. Some who tried
to escape by climbing the cliffs fell to their deaths because in
the darkness they couldn't see any of the footholds. They could
hear the war-cries of the Moors, and terrified by the darkness
of the night and the rugged terrain, they lost heart and did not
know how to escape.

The experienced soldier Rodrigo Ponce de León managed to escape
only by taking another man's horse. Many Christians gave themselves up rather than face the mountainous ravines around them,
and quite a number were captured in the countryside by brave
Muslim women who came out from Malaga to hunt for them. More
than 1,000 prisoners were taken. Pulgar naturally blamed the scouts,
although he also criticises the excessive pride of the Christians. Abu
l-Hasan did well out of the victory, as the booty won was sent to
Malaga to be shared out, but it inevitably ended up in the hands of
his officials.

Back in Granada, the news of the Christians' demoralising
defeat reached Boabdil, and his advisers and other noblemen felt
that on the back of this, the new sultan should make some kind
of sortie into Christian territory to please his people and show his
mettle. So Boabdil and his troops left the Alhambra with a great
display of power and aplomb, and passed through the towns of
Luque, Baena and other areas before returning to Granada, where
he was welcomed back joyfully. It was a successful PR exercise, and
gave Boabdil a sense of his own strength and responsibility. The
mood was high. From the shelter of the palatine city he could survey
his domain, the still prosperous city below him. His father was out
of the way in Malaga, and in spite of the ruined crops in the *vega*,
supplies still arrived from outlying towns and villages. The enemy
was demoralised and the sultan, aged twenty-one or twenty-two

at the time, was persuaded to undertake a more daring plan for his next military outing. Little did he know that he was to meet his nemesis.

4

Captured

The Museum of the Alhambra has a Nasrid chessboard on display dating from the fifteenth century. Its beautiful inlaid wooden squares, made of walnut and birch, are well worn, a visual testimony to its everyday use in Nasrid domestic life. Chess is one of the oldest games of war, and has been played in Spain longer than anywhere else in Europe, by Spanish Muslims since their arrival in the eighth century, and by Spanish Christians and Jews since the early tenth century. It started in ancient India, and the original pieces represented the units of the Indian army – foot soldiers, cavalry, armed chariots and elephants. The infantry, or pawns, were led on the chessboard as in life by the king and his senior minister, his vizier. Some people think it was a game modelled on Alexander the Great's campaigns in Persia, in which his squadrons were aligned in ranks of sixty-four squares, the number of squares on a chessboard.

The game reached Europe through Moorish Spain, where in Islamic chess, opening moves had romantic names such as the Sword opening, or Pharaoh's Fortress. As it spread to medieval Europe, the pieces changed to reflect the feudal social environment of the times. Kings and pawns stayed the same, but the elephant piece was replaced in Christian chess by the bishop, a powerful figure in the medieval Church. In Spanish Muslim chess, the bishop is just an *alfil*, meaning a chess piece and nothing more. The horse of the Indian game became the knight, a symbol of feudal chivalry, the old armed chariot became the castle (or rook in English, which comes from the Persian word for chariot), and the vizier changed into the queen. By the late fifteenth century, when the Nasrids were playing chess on the Alhambra chessboard, a dramatic change had taken place. The queen was no longer the weaker companion of the king – she was the most powerful piece on the chessboard, with new long-range striking power. There was only one way to win the game, and that was through the irrevocable cornering and capture of the enemy king.

In some respects this updated game of chess was to be played out in real life on the frontier between Granada and Castile. The Muslim king and his vizier were pitted against the Christian king and his often militant bishops in their struggles to conquer or defend the frontier fortresses and castles marking the boundary. The powerful new presence of the chess queen was mirrored in the royal personage of Isabella of Castile, and the king the Christians needed to corner and capture was Boabdil.

After his first foray into the kingdom of Granada as sultan, Boabdil decided to take his men deep into Christian territory. The historians give different views on why he hit upon this bold plan. Fernando del Pulgar thought it was because the sultan saw that he now had greater power than his father, and realised that his people warmed to a king who took war to the Christians. Jerónimo Zurita, royal chronicler of the crown of Aragon, and close to King Ferdinand, claimed that Boabdil was envious of the good fortune his father had in his victorious campaign in the Ajarquía, when he conquered the Andalusian cavalry with so few troops of his own. Zurita says that Boabdil was very brave and spirited, perhaps carried away with the idea of military glory and prestige, and felt that he needed to do something outstanding in order to outshine Abu l-Hasan. On the other hand, the Morisco chronicler Hernando de Baeza suggests that the sultan was more hesitant and prudent, since it was the opinion of the Granadan grandees that before celebrating his first outing he should follow up with a second, which, Baeza says, was almost against Boabdil's wishes, although he eventually went along with their suggestion. It was perhaps hard for a new sultan, and a young, inexperienced man to boot, to go against his more experienced advisers, but it turned out that he should have followed his instincts on this occasion.

On Monday, 21 April, 1483, Boabdil took 1,500 cavalry and 7,000 infantry out of the kingdom of Granada into enemy territory to raid the Christian town of Lucena and destroy its wheatfields and vineyards in a countermove to King Ferdinand's devastation of the crops in the *vega* of Granada. As the sultan and his troops left the city they passed through the Gate of Elvira, where the point of Boabdil's lance hit the arch of the gate, and was broken. This sinister omen was followed by another, more alarming one, when a fox crossed the path of the army, ran through the ranks and, in spite of the showers of missiles thrown at it, escaped unhurt. Undeterred, Boabdil and his men pressed on, because the time seemed ripe for attack. The idea was that the populations on the frontiers of Cordoba, Écija and the surrounding areas would have fewer people to defend them after the defeats the Christians had already suffered in March, and that they would put up little resistance. Although it was not a great stronghold, Lucena was a large, wealthy town deep in Christian territory beyond Loja and Rute, sixty-five miles (105 kilometres) north-west of Granada itself. But there was something the Granadans had not taken into account. Having heard of Boabdil's recent exploits in the towns of Baena and Luque, and fearing a new attack, the renowned Count of Cabra, Diego Fernández de Córdoba, and his identically named nephew had placed sentries to warn the inhabitants of any approach from the Moors. There is a Christian story that the battle plan may have been betrayed by a Moorish convert to Christianity, although the theme of the religious convert who gives away vital military information is a common one in Christian accounts, so we may need to take it with a pinch of salt.

Boabdil and his large army of troops arrived at Lucena as dawn was breaking and set up their camp. According to Zurita, they began to attack the town, many of whose inhabitants were badly injured by arrows and Moorish musket fire. The Muslim soldiers then started to destroy the olive groves and vines. The agreed signal between the lookouts in Lucena and the Count of Cabra was that at the first sight of any approaching Moors, they would burn straw or wood to make smoke signals, which they did as soon as they got wind of the approaching Muslim company. When the Count of Cabra saw the signal he arrived with just a handful of his people, though the Moors had not seen his approach, and didn't know how many men he had with him. The count ordered his flag to be hoisted alongside other similar pennants, and drums and trumpets to be sounded, all within sight of Boabdil's army camp. The violent noise and sight of the Christian flags fluttering, plus the men grouped at the top of the nearby hill, tricked the Muslim contingent into thinking a great cohort of cavalry awaited them. Assuming their plan had been discovered days ago, and believing that half of Andalusia was against them and was gathering there, some of the Granadans thought Boabdil should turn back before more Christian aggressors joined the fray. Others were of the opinion that the sultan should advance by crossing a minor river called Martín González, where the Christians always had difficulties. They knew this because some of the Muslims had been there on previous raids, when the Christians had been unable to ford the stream. Their idea was that, as Boabdil had brought such a strong force, he should cross to the other side and gather his men before the Christians came, because if they turned their backs and retreated, the enemy would catch up with them and they would be shamed.

Hernando de Baeza tells us that at this point a new voice spoke up:

> He was a dealer in perfumes and spices from the town of Loja, a very ancient man of over eighty years old. He was astute and very wise in matters of war, and he said to the king: 'Sir, your Highness should not follow any of this advice, stay where you are. Since you have such power in numbers, we will have at least as many if not more soldiers than it is possible for the Christians to gather here from now till the evening, then night will cover us and your Highness can decide what is the best thing to do. What is more, we have the stream between us and them, which gives us an advantage.'

The spice dealer was, in fact, Boabdil's father-in-law, Ali al-Attar, the governor and captain of Loja. He was insistent that his advice should be followed, because, he said, whoever crossed the river, whether Moor or Christian, would be lost.

But for whatever reason, Boabdil and his men did not follow his father-in-law's advice, and went ahead to cross the stream with a great sound of drums and pipes, with the sultan on horseback in the second battalion. Here disaster struck. The Christians began a surprise rearguard attack, and the sultan attempted to fight back, but his soldiers panicked and started to flee wildly across the stream. Although Boabdil realised Christian numbers were small, he couldn't hold his men back. So many horses and riders had already splashed their way across the water that the riverbed was churned up with mud, stones and weed, and many cowardly Muslims went in all directions with no thought for their king who remained behind in grave danger. Boabdil's white horse entered the water and sank down into the mud, stuck fast and unable to move. Hernando de Baeza gives us another vivid picture of those moments:

While the king was in this state of anguish and distress, a Christian foot-soldier came to the edge of the riverbank and raised his lance to strike the king. A cavalryman named Santa Cruz, who was a Muslim living under Christian rule in Toledo, whose own horse was stuck in the stream alongside the king, shouted to the foot-soldier, 'Stop, stop, you fool, don't kill him, he's the king.' The soldier stopped in his tracks and at that moment another infantryman came up, this one from the town of Baena, along with another man riding a pack mule laden with baskets. The other soldier said to him 'That's the Moorish king!' and together they lifted him from his saddle and put him on the mule. One jumped on the animal and rode with him, and the other led it by the halter, and together they took him a good part of the way to Baena. When the captain of the new recruits and some of his men in Baena were alerted to this, four or five of them went on horseback and took the king from them, and setting him on a horse, they took him to Lucena.

The priest and historian Andrés Bernáldez describes how a Moor named Cidi Caleb, a nephew of the chief lawyer of the Albaicin of Granada, returned to the town of Loja on horseback. His lone arrival caused a great commotion and the townsfolk came out to ask him where the king and his men were. Cidi Caleb told them that they were still in Lucena, where the sky had fallen upon them and they were all lost or dead. There was great grief and weeping at this news, and Caleb then went on to Granada to tell the same tale, although it is not clear whether he thought the king was dead or captured. Certainly, many of Boabdil's troops were killed on that day, possibly as many as 1,000, along with many principal figures in Boabdil's court and family, including Ali al-Attar. Hernando de Baeza recounts a poignant anecdote in which Ali al-Attar could not bear to see Boabdil captured, so he plunged into the waters of the stream and drowned.

Although he had been recognised, Boabdil at first told his captors he was the son of Abenlaxar, a nobleman who was the constable of Granada. There was no reason that the Christians should have recognised Boabdil, as he had rarely left the city of Granada in his life, and had never been outside the kingdom until 1483, as far as we know. He could easily have passed as a member of the Granadan nobility, but his identity had been revealed to the Christians by some of their prisoners. It is interesting in Baeza's account of his capture that it is a Moorish convert who realises who he is, perhaps because he recognised or was familiar with what Boabdil was wearing. One thing that came out of this disastrous day for the sultan and his people is the clear idea it has given us of Boabdil's appearance, his clothes and weaponry at the Battle of Lucena. There is an old manuscript in the National Library in Madrid which contains a description of the young sultan written by the Abbot of Rute in the province of Cordoba, Francisco Fernández de Córdoba. The abbot tells us that Boabdil went into battle riding a white horse, richly caparisoned, and that he rode with short stirrups in the Arab style. He was armed with a strong cuirass or body armour, lined with crimson velvet secured by gilded fasteners, under a Moorish tunic of brocade and velvet. On his head was a dark red and gold helmet. He carried a Nasrid sword embellished with silver, a dagger inlaid with gold and silver and a strong shield and lance.

Boabdil's clothes and weapons were given away as booty to his captors. They ended up in the possession of the Marquises of Villa-seca, whose family eventually gifted them to the nation. Some can now be seen in the Army Museum in Toledo. The well-preserved clothing shows that Boabdil wore recently made winter garments for his first military campaign, and the arms he carried were part of the regalia of a Nasrid sultan. His white linen turban, the distinctive sign of his sovereignty, taken from him when he was prisoner, has also been preserved along with his luxurious *marlota* or tunic in costly red velvet from the East, the colour of the Nasrid dynasty, all embroidered with gold leaves, branches and pomegranates. There is also a pair of leather boots reaching to the knee, and a pair of leather indoor shoes which show no wear or dirt from use, nor the wrinkles and ridges formed by moulding themselves to the person's feet, which again suggests that they were recently worn for the first time by Boabdil. Perhaps he had the soft light brown shoes made of goatskin with him to change into after dismounting, when his long boots were wet. Kings wearing similar clothing are depicted in the paintings of several artists of the late fifteenth century, such as Pedro Berruguete and Vincenzo Foppa, and these help to date the apparel from the 1480s. The museum also possesses his belt with its leather pouch to hold the Koran. It is quite likely that all these items were specially made for him once he had taken the Nasrid throne: the *marlota* is a garment made for cold or changeable weather, as it often is in Granada in April. We can confirm from the size and length of Boabdil's boots and outer clothing that he was a person of average build, quite short in stature, probably about 5'4" or 1m 65, with small feet. There was a myth that Boabdil had fair skin and hair and blue eyes, which arose because of a portrait depicting him like that in the Alhambra. In contrast, the Abbot of Rute describes him more plausibly as 'of reasonable height, well-built, with a long face, dark skin, black hair, beard and eyes, large eyes with a melancholy expression, unless it was an expression of royal composure'.

Boabdil's magnificent sword and rapier of the Nasrid royal house were ancestral symbols of his dynasty. They were more court ceremonial arms than for fighting; the enamelled Damascene sword came from the time of the second emirate of Muhammad

V (1362–1391) and the rapier, with its palm-tree ornamentation on
the hilt, was made in the era of Yusuf I (1333–1354). But in battle
they were as good as the most up-to-date versions. Boabdil's recent
accession to the throne explains why he, rather than his father, bore
the two best swords and the extraordinary dagger from the Nasrid
emirs' armoury, inherited from his forebears and representing his
legitimacy as Nasrid sultan. Boabdil went into his first battle against
the Christians dressed in a way befitting a Nasrid sultan – his splendid arms and attire were a display of his legitimacy and power to
his own men, and no doubt gave him courage and confidence. They
linked him to his dynastic ancestors and gave him the weight and
authority of history. While his ceremonial weapons suggest that he
may have planned not to engage in direct combat, at the same time
they conveyed a show of courage, boldness, pride and a willingness
to fight if it came to it. Boabdil may have quailed inside, but he cut
an impressive figure at the head of his army.

Once the enemy had gathered the booty, they took Boabdil
before the Count of Cabra, who saw that fortune had turned his
prisoner from a powerful king into a powerless subject in a very
short space of time, felt sympathy for him and gave him some kindly
advice. If a wise man considered the rapid changes of human life,
he said, he should not be disturbed by the prosperity he had a short
time before, nor afflicted by the adversity which had assailed him so
quickly. Since the good things of the past were not constant, present
misfortune could also change in a similar way. With these words of
consolation, and with the respect due to a sovereign, the count took
his prisoner to his house in Baena. He then wrote to King Ferdinand
and Queen Isabella, who were in Cordoba, telling them of their
victory and of the capture of the Nasrid sultan. At the orders of the
Christian Monarchs, Boabdil was taken a good distance north to the
castle at Porcuna, where the tower in which he was imprisoned can
be visited today. There he was treated with great honour, and was
accompanied by many of his own servants. For the Christians, the
capture of Boabdil was a matter of political transcendence. Ferdinand
saw at once that this stroke of luck could well allow him to achieve
his aim of conquering the whole of al-Andalus. The author of the
Arabic *Nubdhat* viewed things from the perspective of the Granadan

Muslims, and he states quite clearly that the disaster at Lucena was shameful, the most shameful part being the capture of Boabdil. This may seem melodramatic but it hits the mark: his imprisonment led to the loss of their homeland.

Ferdinand wanted time to consult his royal council on how to play this ace that had fallen into his hands. While he was still in Cordoba he received messengers sent by Boabdil's mother, and by other noblemen and leaders of the kingdom of Granada, who begged him to free Boabdil and return him to his kingdom. Their logic was that if he remained captive the Christians would receive no tribute money; they said that if Ferdinand released him, they would offer him as the Christian king's vassal, and give him 12,000 gold doubloons each year as long as there was a truce, as well as 300 Christians, whom the king could choose from those who were captive in Moorish territory. As security, said the messengers, they promised to give one of the emir's legitimate sons, Ahmed, as a hostage, as well as ten sons of other governors and heads of the kingdom of Granada. They also asked Ferdinand to send troops to fight against those areas and fortified towns that had reverted to supporting Boabdil's father while his son was in prison. They made it clear that if Ferdinand refused to release the emir, all the main noblemen of the kingdom, as well as the cities, towns, castles and areas that supported Boabdil, would turn to his father if they lost hope of the emir's liberation. Abu l-Hasan also sent messengers to negotiate his son's release, but although we do not know what his terms were, we can suspect that his motives were dubious and may well have been threatening to his son's life.

When Ferdinand heard all this he ordered the Count of Cabra to bring Boabdil to Cordoba. On the day of his arrival, all the grandees, noblemen and other courtiers were ordered to go out to greet him as he approached, riding between the count and the governor of the army recruits. Boabdil came soberly but regally dressed in black, on a well-caparisoned dark brown horse, and he was greeted by drum rolls and trumpets playing along the route to the house of the Bishop of Cordoba, where Ferdinand had ordered his lodgings to be made ready. Here the grandees took their leave, while the count and the governor dismounted with the sultan and showed him to his quarters. Ferdinand then received the count, but did not want to see Boabdil until it had been decided whether to release him or not. Instead he sent Martín de Alarcón, who had held the fortress at Porcuna and was charged with guarding him, to say that the sultan should take heart, and be cheered by the hope of freedom. When he heard this Boabdil replied with dignity and diplomacy:

> Tell my lord the king of Castile that I can't be sad while I'm in the power of such noble and powerful monarchs as the king and queen his wife, especially when they are so kind, and have so much of the grace that God gives the kings he loves. Tell him also that for some days I've been thinking that I would place myself in his power, in order to receive the kingdom of Granada from his hands, as my grandfather the king received it from King John your father-in-law, father of the queen. And that the greatest misfortune I have had while in this prison is to be forced to do something that I had a mind to do willingly.

This courteous, diplomatic message suggests that Boabdil may have been considering passing Granada over nominally to Ferdinand, while remaining its ruler; or it may have been a response intended to placate and curry favour with an enemy masquerading as an ally.

The historian Fernando del Pulgar gives us a detailed and at times verbatim account of the high level discussions of the royal council, who had to weigh up the pros and cons of liberating their prisoner, as well as the terms offered by his mother and his father. Opinions were sharply divided, with some members feeling they should go along with Boabdil's request to be released, and also that he should be given some military assistance. Others thought that he should remain captive, and that war should be waged without let-up. The master of the knightly Order of Santiago, Alonso de Cárdenas, held the opinion that the sultan should not be liberated:

> If you set this imprisoned king free you will give us a signifi-cant enemy in a young, healthy man, instead of an old and ailing one [he is referring to Boabdil's father here]. The power of the Moors is nothing without the king they love. They are

now without the captain they need and will regain the king they most desire, so it follows that the enemy who is now weak and spent for lack of a good leader will be strong and united under this one. Nor should we trust the discord amongst them, because how can we know that father and son won't be reconciled and end up stronger together to rebel against you, as the kings of Granada have done against the kings who were your ancestors every time they have had an opportunity to do so?

Cárdenas also thought that Boabdil's request for troops should be refused, because if Ferdinand was going to risk the lives of his troops to win the country for him, it would be better to win it for himself. The aim was, as he pointed out, to wage and win the war of Granada, and not to stop until the desired end had been achieved.

The Marquis of Cádiz, Rodrigo Ponce de León, expressed the opposite view:

Before Boabdil's capture, the war between him and his father was an advantage to us, because they couldn't defend their kingdom so well under those circumstances. I say that he should be released, as he is the cause of the split; then they will need to fight two wars, one amongst themselves and the other against us. In that way we will be more successful, and they will be less able to defend themselves. Since two kings can't reign at the same time, whether they are father and son or not, the latter won't stop fighting until he has the obedience of the entire kingdom, and the former won't stop fighting until he is the only king, like he was before.

These divergent opinions give us a good idea of the Castilian perception of the situation in the kingdom of Granada at that time, and in particular the relationship between Boabdil and Abu l-Hasan. It gives a strong impression that Boabdil was greatly loved by his people, and certainly not a puppet of the Christians, but rather a man to be feared as a potentially dangerous enemy who could rally the loyalty of the Granadans. Because the opinions of Ferdinand's royal council were evenly balanced, the Castilian king asked his wife Isabella to make the final decision. She chose to release Boabdil under some severe and compromising conditions. The sultan would become the vassal of the ruling Catholics, obey their orders and come whenever they called him. In addition, the Granadans would hand over 400 Christian captives, not the 300 suggested by Aixa, and a sum greater than the 12,000 gold doubloons she and her advisers had offered. All the cities and towns supporting Boabdil would be obliged to give safe passage and maintenance to the captains and retinue of Ferdinand and Isabella to enable them to wage war on the places which still supported his father. Boabdil had little choice but to swear to fulfil these stipulations, after which Ferdinand granted a two-year truce to the sultan and all places obedient to him, or obedient within thirty days of his release. An interesting additional clause shows that Boabdil's only request was to allow the Moor Muhammad Abencerrax, or Abencerraje, to cross the sea from Africa to join him.

Once the sultan had capitulated, Ferdinand demonstrated his largesse. He ordered the Moorish king and his retinue of fifty knights to be given clothing in rich fabrics, brocades and silks, and other luxurious adornments, plus all the money they needed to make the journey back to their own lands. So far the Catholic king had avoided a face-to-face meeting with his Muslim counterpart, but the ritual of court demanded a fitting leave-taking of his unwilling guest. But what was the correct procedure? Should Boabdil kiss Ferdinand's hand? The sultan was willing, but Ferdinand thought not. If Boabdil were free and in his own kingdom, he would have done so, he said, but he did not want to humiliate the emir by requiring him to do so as his prisoner. He lifted the kneeling Boabdil from the ground, upon which the latter thanked him profusely and began to praise his magnanimity. But Ferdinand interrupted him and spoke to his interpreter: 'This gratification isn't necessary. I trust in his goodness, and that he will do everything a good man and king should do.' The awkward goodbye over, Boabdil and his retinue were given an armed guard to accompany them to the safety of their kingdom.

This first encounter between the two men set the tone for their future relationship. The sultan was not hostile in his manner, but shrewdly compliant. Unlike his father, he was statesmanlike and courteous in the face of his enemy. Ferdinand was born in Aragon in

1452, so was about ten years older than Boabdil. He had the upper hand not only because of his age but also because the sultan was his prisoner. To all intents and purposes he appeared generous and benevolent to his captive, but there are signs of an underlying coldness and suspicion, a calculating quality. His reluctance to meet Boabdil in person, the awkwardness of the encounter, the crippling terms of the capitulation and the insistence on the sultan's subservience to Castile and Aragon all belie the veneer of friendliness and bonhomie. While the capture of Boabdil seemed to play into Ferdinand's hands, at the same time he clearly saw the sultan as a serious threat to his ambitions who needed to be held in check.

Those ambitions had grown and taken full hold of Ferdinand since the start of 1482. If the stars had predicted Boabdil's unfortunate destiny, great things had been prophesied for Ferdinand. On 6 January of that year, a few days before the news arrived that Abu l-Hasan had captured the Christian fortress of Zahara, he and Isabella were returning to Castile from the parliament held in Valencia, and they stopped off at Teruel, where Epiphany celebrations were organised for their stay. As part of the fiestas, Ferdinand listened to a sung eulogy which contained a prediction about his future:

> *It is prophesied*
> *in ancient tomes*
> *that the one to conquer Jerusalem and Granada*
> *would be called Ferdinand.*
> *Your name is right*
> *and your chosen path shows.*
> *That you will conquer them*
> *go on your way, have no doubts*
> *God will be your guide.*

His first major step along this path, his defence of Alhama with 6,000 cavalry, 1,000 foot soldiers and full supplies, had sent a message that he intended to keep the town free of Moors. Its negative impact on the Granadans, who staged three unsuccessful attempts to recover Alhama under Abu l-Hasan's leadership, showed the power of psychological strategies, in which the king was expert. Rulers in the rest of the Iberian peninsula viewed Ferdinand's expansionist ideas with some trepidation, as did the king of France, Louis XI, who feared his potential power if he acquired more territory. This policy coincided with the decision of the Catholic Monarchs to extend the reach of the Inquisition in 1482 to other parts of their kingdom beyond Castile, starting in Cordoba and then moving into Ferdinand's native Aragon.

Ferdinand was not only skilled in psychological warfare but also a formidable planner of military strategy. After the great victory of the Granadans at Loja, which was to come in 1485 and was perceived by the Christians as a real disaster, Ferdinand realised he needed to refurbish his army. He turned it into a stable professional unit based on cavalry and infantry, with a powerful bank of artillery and specialist equipment. He knew it needed a good communication system to ensure it received the correct provisions, as well as an efficient transport and mail system to coordinate movements. It was Queen Isabella's innovation to establish a campaign hospital fully equipped with nurses, surgeons and medical supplies. Four hundred covered wagons were armed against attack and set aside as ambulances. Ferdinand's military strategy against Granada was centred on annual campaigns lasting eighty to ninety days, with the aim of taking an important strategic city each time and avoiding battles in the field. As we saw in the previous chapter, the plan involved the most deadly of Ferdinand's weapons, the slow but sure devastation of crops known as the *tala*. As the war wore on, his army did not consist of Castilian and Andalusian troops alone, but also European knights, Germans from the Order of the Holy Trinity, English soldiers captained by Count Rivers, and artillerymen from Brittany and Burgundy.

In spite of his apparent amicability with Boabdil, it is obvious that Ferdinand had every intention of using him to worsen the internal divisions in the Nasrid camp. In a letter written to his sister Juana, the queen of Naples, on 26 August 1483, just a few days after seeing the captured sultan, he told her that it had been decided to release him because his objective was 'to create such division in the kingdom in Granada that it would bring about its complete and utter ruin'.

While Boabdil had been imprisoned, events had taken place which seemed to confirm Ferdinand's opinion of the disarray of the Nasrid royal family. Taking advantage of his eldest son's enforced absence, Abu l-Hasan returned to the city of Granada and regained the throne at the end of April 1483, beginning a precarious second reign which lasted barely two more years. The dynastic conflict, far from being resolved by his son's capture, became more intense. In Almeria, Boabdil's brother Yusuf remained independent from his father and supported his sibling. While Boabdil's partisans, headed by Aben Comixa, had gone to Ferdinand in Cordoba to negotiate his release, Abu l-Hasan had also tried the same thing, but the Catholic king had accepted the first offer, clearly because he thought it would be more damaging to aggravate the internal divisions to which his eventual agreement with Boabdil would give rise.

Unable to return to Granada with his father now in his place on the throne, Boabdil went once more to the favoured town of Guadix and set up a base there from October 1483. Yet any aspirations he had to return to the capital suffered a severe setback because of the intervention of the Granadan *alfaquíes* or *ulama*, the Muslim doctors of law, on a religious matter. Although Abu l-Hasan's supporters in the city had been able to reassert themselves, there was still a lot of resistance from those citizens who were loyal to Boabdil. The reinstated emir took a bold step to quash any possible rebellion. He went to the *ulama* and asked for a ruling on the legitimacy of his son's uprising against him, and they delivered their verdict through a *fatwa*, which was the basic manifestation of the activities of Muslim jurists. In fifteenth-century Granada, a *fatwa* could be used to assess the orthodoxy of a doctrine, or the morality of someone's conduct, although in practice it often degenerated into an argument used by litigants to make their point of view prevail. The basis for the *fatwa* was the compatibility of the verdict proposed with the fundamental principles of Islam. It was the questioning of moral conduct that was relevant in this case.

The document containing the *fatwa* exists in a collection of other similar items by the famous Muslim jurist al-Wansharisi, and is dated 17 October 1483. It describes the matter clearly from the perspective of the jurists and Abu l-Hasan, stating that a group of

Andalusian elders and noblemen abandoned their obedience to Abu
l-Hasan and proclaimed his son as sultan. It accused Boabdil of con-
niving with the Christian king to engineer their escape from Muslim
territories, and of signing a peace treaty with the Christians showing
his obedience to them. Who were the Andalusian noblemen referred
to? Members of the Abencerraje clan spring to mind, who were at
odds with Boabdil's father, and probably desperate to escape punishment and death. Or perhaps they were Christian captives who
had been seized and taken as hostages. The *fatwa* asks whether Boabdil's actions can be supported by divine law, or whether they were
purely and simply acts of rebellion and disobedience to God and his
messenger. Was it lawful, it continues, for any Muslim to help and
collaborate with these other men and shelter them, and what is the
divine sentence upon those who do such a thing?

The verdict was damning. The proclamation of Boabdil as sultan
was a violation of his sworn fidelity to his father. The jurists could
not find the least support for this in Allah's laws. It was a straight-
forward sin and an abandonment of the obedience due to Allah and
the Prophet Muhammad. Boabdil was accused of creating civil war,
denigrating Islam, spreading enmity and hatred in the hearts of
Muslims and corrupting civil harmony. On the subject of Boabdil
accepting the help of the Christians, the jurists quote Surah 5:51 of
the Koran: 'Do not take Jews and Christians as friends, because they
are the friends of each other. Whoever among you takes them as
friends will turn into one of them.' Such behaviour was prohibited,
and anyone who swore allegiance to the young sultan committed an
illicit act. The document was signed by the chief jurist Ibn al-Azraq,
the *mufti* al-Mawwaq, and others. This posed an enormous problem
for Boabdil, who wisely remained in Guadix and did not attempt
to enter the capital. Fernando del Pulgar writes that many Granadans began to hate Boabdil after the verdict was announced, because
they feared that his dealings with the Christians would lead them to
the remaining Muslim lands and capital city, so they disassociated
themselves from him.

This apparent moral and religious victory of father over son
must have given Abu l-Hasan some satisfaction, but tragic events
once more desolated the Nasrid dynasty. While Boabdil's father

took advantage of his imprisonment to return to the capital city, his mother at once took her daughter and servants to Almeria to be with her other son Yusuf, who was established there as the local ruler, at which time she had heard the news of her firstborn's capture. Baeza recounts the rumours that Zoraya turned Abu l-Hasan against Yusuf in the hope that Yusuf would be executed. Her plan seems to have been that with Boabdil permanently in jail, as she saw it, and his brother dead, the path would be clear for her own son to inherit the Nasrid throne. While this plot was hatching, Abu l-Hasan was suddenly struck down by serious ill health. Throughout 1483, and well into 1484, the fighting between Christians and Muslims had not let up, with defeats on both sides. In 1484 the initiative for the attacks was always Christian, and the most important struggles were for Álora, Alozaina and Setenil, a small town in the direction of Ronda. It is said to have taken two weeks during September 1484 for the Christians to take the castle of Setenil, which put up a characteristically fierce resistance. During this battle, Abu l-Hasan was afflicted with something similar to epilepsy, which affected his sight, gave him seizures and weakened him physically, to such an extent that he could no longer take part in the fighting, although he would not relinquish the throne. The author of the *Nubdhat*, who is unflinchingly critical of Abu l-Hasan, describes his affliction as divine punishment for his evildoing.

This was the moment Abu l-Hasan's brother El Zagal, the Valiant, had been waiting for. His celebrated strength and fierceness as a warrior gave rise to his epithet, which was also used by the Christians, and was the origin of the Spanish word *zagal*, meaning 'boy' and later 'shepherd'. With his nephew out of the way and his brother incapacitated, El Zagal stepped in to continue the defence of the kingdom. As we saw in Chapter 2, he had made his first appearance ten years before in 1470 in an uprising against his brother, setting himself up in Malaga with the help and approval of the Abencerrajes who had fled there from Abu l-Hasan. Soon defeated by his brother, he had returned to being his subject and had since remained loyal. But the situation that presented itself in 1484 encouraged him to aspire to the highest power, and El Zagal was supported in this ambition by the jurists and many Muslims from the kingdom of Granada.

As usual, tragedy was waiting in the wings. In February or mid-March 1485 El Zagal seized the city of Almeria, which had supported Boabdil, and was well disposed towards Castile. Some of the details of what happened next are not clear. The fiery Abu l-Hasan fell into a rage at his brother's rebellion, and ordered a number of eminent citizens of Almeria to be put to death. Among them were the governor of the city, Benaliscar, and all the supporters of El Zagal, including Boabdil's brother Yusuf. It appears that a black slave from Guinea was sent to carry out the murder of the prince, and it is said that the slave agreed to do so in cahoots with El Zagal. Baeza has an alternative vivid account of those events, and states that the black slave tried hard to dissuade El Zagal from the deed, begging him merely to pretend that it had been done. Yusuf was said to have been very handsome, wise and well-disposed for his age, and accepted his fate with great dignity. It appears that the slave came into the presence of the prince, who asked him if his father had sent him to behead him. The slave answered yes, and Yusuf replied: 'I have never heard of any law to say that a father can do such a thing to his son. He should consider how young I am, but may his will be done. I need to wash my body to prepare for death.' He began to undo his clothes, and went up to a patio where he washed himself in a cistern. He asked for clean vestments, according to Islamic ritual, and in the words of Baeza he departed this life with great courage and without trepidation. In this way, Boabdil lost a sibling, and his mother lost her second child.

About six months later, Abu l-Hasan took aside one of his pages and told him to go to his brother and ask him to bring his son to him, as he had a great desire to see him. A message was sent back to the effect that El Zagal didn't know what he was talking about. The sultan repeated the message, adding that it was over six months since El Zagal had kept Yusuf hidden from him. Zagal went to the constable's house and asked him to go to the sultan and tell him that his son was dead, according to his written instructions. The constable didn't much want to go on this mission, but seeing nothing could be done, he complied. In an audience with Abu l-Hasan he told him that his brother was horrified that he had asked such a question, since they had received a letter signed by the sultan ordering Yusuf to be beheaded, along with a number of others, and that he had sent his black slave to carry out his orders. Abu l-Hasan replied that clearly his brother wanted him to thank him for saving his son from death, and that if they would bring Yusuf to him, he would do so. The constable could do nothing other than repeat that Yusuf was dead, and he wouldn't be able to see him until the great Day of Judgement.

The sultan began to weep and shout. 'I have never heard of greater evil, nor of an uncle beheading his nephew. Didn't he know that I said it in anger, and not so that it would actually be done?' He spoke with sorrow and passion, as a father, and began to roar and sigh, hitting his head hard against the walls in pure agony of feeling. A few days later Abu l-Hasan went blind and suffered a series of violent seizures, as if he were possessed.

Sometime in late May or early June, after a victorious raiding party near Alhama, El Zagal made a triumphant entrance into the city of Granada, where he was proclaimed sultan by the Granadans, enthused by his victories and already primed for this event by the Muslim jurists and the cunning vizier Ridwan Bannigas. Abu l-Hasan was deposed, and, blind and bedevilled, he was sent, like his father before him, to the castle at Salobreña, where he died soon after. There is a legend that he was laid to rest at the highest point of the Sierra Nevada, from where most of the lands of his kingdom could be seen. He was said to have been buried there beneath the snow that lies at the peak for most of the year, which was named El Mulhacén, after the sultan. In fact, his body was taken back to the Alhambra and interred in the pantheon of the Nasrid emirs. Baeza speaks of his death rather tartly: 'What an admirable judgement of God. His brother treated him the way he treated his own father, even to the extent that he died in the same place!'

The fateful capture of Boabdil was a crucial event for both Christians and Muslims, a decisive moment that marked the future course of the Granadan war. The chess game had taken an unforeseen turn, since Boabdil, whose own young son was given to the Christians as a hostage, was obliged to become Ferdinand's pawn when the powerful Queen Isabella decreed his nominal release. During the time of his imprisonment, three kings had challenged each other for one throne, and two men, Boabdil's brother and his father, had died in dramatic circumstances. Now two kings were left to vie for the Nasrid kingdom, while the enemy watched and waited.

5

From King to Pawn

If you walk through the Albaicin of Granada today, you might at first think you were in a town in north Africa. In the winding, narrow streets, whose layout has changed little since Boabdil's time, small shops sell exotic Moorish perfumes, spices, leather goods and fine marquetry. Restaurants and bars serve Moroccan meals and mint tea, residents greet each other in Arabic, and posters announce Arabic courses and instruction in Islam and the Koran at the mosque. There are graffiti – one says 'No to Moors', while another is a painting on a wall just down the road from the new mosque depicting a dramatic, romantic image of a medieval princess in a tower, holding a scroll bearing an inscription celebrating the Albaicin's multireligious and multicultural environment. Although there is a feeling of timelessness, and the underlying atmosphere is tranquil, the neighbourhood is lively and animated and its popular artwork divulges latent yet familiar religious and cultural tensions.

Over 500 years ago, the Albaicin was the scene of conflict, not between religions or cultures, but between uncle and nephew, which pitted Granadans against each other in the bloody battle for the throne. The imposing El Zagal, brother of Abu l-Hasan, had the same official name – Abu Abdallah Muhammad – as his nephew Boabdil. A Christian chronicler described him as a man with a serious, dignified face, whose complexion was unusually light; he was well proportioned, neither fat nor thin, and tall in stature. His reputation for military daring and prowess was borne out during the dramatic events in Almeria in March 1485, when El Zagal had taken over the city from his brother and given the order to execute the rebels, including young prince Yusuf, his other nephew. Boabdil had fled in fear of his life to Cordoba, which was part of Christian territory, while his mother was thrown into jail. He never forgot this terrible betrayal and deception by his uncle, the re-enactment of an old Nasrid paradigm of treachery and bloodshed, and never trusted him again, later refusing offers of assistance from his uncle that, if they were genuine, might have been advantageous to him.

In spite of El Zagal's powerful position in Almeria, he could not hold back the advancing Christians. In April 1485 they conquered the fortified towns of Cártama and Coín in the west of the province, then, in late May, they besieged the allegedly unassailable town of Ronda, destroying its defences with their artillery and forcing the inhabitants to surrender. Fearing the enemy would next besiege the not too distant and strategically crucial port of Malaga, El Zagal headed straight there with 300 men as reinforcements. On the way back in early June, he managed to defeat a raiding party of Christian troops near Alhama, a victory which he celebrated with the triumphal entry into Granada when he was proclaimed sultan, officially deposing his ailing brother.

El Zagal was the twelfth Nasrid sultan to bear the name Muhammad. He succeeded in having coins minted by the Alhambra to mark his accession to the throne, which suggests the degree of power he had at that time, but his future as ruler did not look promising. As sovereign, he had sought the support of his north African Muslim brothers, and sent emissaries to Fez and Tlemcen asking for help and support, but the rulers of both those cities knew that any collaboration with the Granadans would affect the very advantageous trade relations they had with Castile at the time. The astute Ferdinand had made commercial relations with north Africa conditional on the fact that they gave no help to the Granadans. All El Zagal could get from them was an agreement to welcome Andalusi emigrants to their lands, and to rescue some captives from Malaga.

As the year wore on, El Zagal won a few minor victories, one at Moclín to the north-west of Granada, where he had gone to repair the outer walls of the town in face of an imminent attack by the enemy in early September. He managed to destroy the advance guard of the Castilian army, and captured the munitions and artillery they were transporting to lay siege to the town. The Castilians promptly retaliated by using heavy artillery to capture the two fortresses at Cambil and Alhabar, key townships on the frontier for the defence of Granada. The governor, Muhammad Lentin, negotiated with the Christians to win an assurance that the inhabitants could leave in freedom and transfer their goods to Granada itself. It was a game of tit for tat, with only one ultimate winner.

Six months had passed since Boabdil had fled from his warlike uncle, and the usurped heir had paid a price. Once again the conflicts of the Nasrid family had played into Ferdinand's hands. Ferdinand now shrewdly took advantage of the presence of Boabdil in Christian territory. Once the Christian king was apprised of the change of regime in Granada, he manoeuvred to reinforce Boabdil's position as his pawn. Rather than take on a tough adversary himself, he aimed to destroy the unity and support surrounding the older man by setting Boabdil against him. Making much of his own alliance with the nephew against the uncle, Ferdinand put pressure on Boabdil to return to the Muslim lands of the Ajarquía to the east of the province of Granada, passing through Murcia to Huéscar, twenty-five miles (forty kilometres) north-east of Baza near the Granadan frontier. His plan was for Boabdil to gain the support of these areas against the new sultan by promising them that all districts loyal to him would be saved from the horrors of war, since Ferdinand had promised peace to Boabdil and all his subjects. Most of the inhabitants of these regions, who badly wanted peace and to remain in their own homes, came out in support of the young emir.

The effect of this in Granada was immediate. While the majority of the city obeyed El Zagal, propaganda was spread in support of Boabdil by what the author of the *Nubdhat* disapprovingly describes in a phrase he had used before as 'devils in the form of men', who persuaded the people of the Albaicin, consisting mainly of peasants and cattle drovers, that peace with the Christians would be an advantage to them. They agreed to support Boabdil because they lived in great fear of the Christian army and the devastation it could bring to their crops and livelihoods. In other words, they accepted Boabdil's obedience to Ferdinand and Isabella.

Here Hernando de Baeza takes up the story:

While El Zagal was in the city of Granada, and his nephew was in the towns of Velez Blanco and Velez-Malaga, Boabdil exchanged letters with certain eminent men in the Albaicin, who promised to obey him and proclaim him sultan. Once he learned that he had their support, he departed at night, with great spirit and daring, with only twelve cavalry and about the same number of infantry, and some local scouts who led him from Velez to the city of Granada, a distance of more than sixty miles. They arrived a mile and a half from the Albaicin at the place they had agreed, and were met by nearly forty men on foot. Boabdil dismounted, and spoke to them with great energy and very warmly, thanking them for putting themselves in such danger and promising them a reward. He took a sword in one hand and a shield in the other, and with half the men in front and half behind and beside him, he went forward into the Albaicin through a secret entrance in the Fax el Lauz gate, from which his supporters had emerged to greet him, and they led him to a house where many armed men were gathered. With one voice they began to speak: 'May almighty God exalt our king, Boabdil, son of Abu l-Hasan, our lord.' Then one after another they kissed his hand and feet, and departed, leaving him there, accompanied by a dozen noblemen. As they went out into the Albaicin they started proclaiming the news that their rightful king was inside the walls with them. Then they took great care to close the gates between the Albaicin and the rest of the city, barricading them with wooden beams, stones and earth so that no one from the city could pass through.

The dangerous secret mission across harsh mountainous territory had succeeded: Boabdil was back in Granada where he belonged.

But, ironically, the king promising peace brought the return of that most terrible of conflicts: civil war.

The cruelty and ferocity of the war that followed between Boabdil and El Zagal has seemed perplexing to future generations. Religion and politics clashed with fear of the Christian enemy, as opposing ideas presented themselves to the inhabitants. El Zagal offered Granadans the possibility of maintaining their religious, political and territorial independence, thereby sustaining their Islamic ideals as well as a past they were loath to relinquish. The price for this was confronting the Christians without any concessions. On the other hand, to a populace mentally and physically fatigued from seeing their lands and towns ransacked and decimated, Boabdil represented the truce, and the prospect of being able to breathe and sleep without threat of a surprise attack. It was impossible to achieve both things, so a choice had to be made which divided the Granadans. It was exactly what Ferdinand had hoped would happen.

For over two months from March to May 1486 open war raged in the capital city, in which El Zagal's supporters used siege artillery and huge catapults to hurl rocks into the Albaicin from the ramparts of the old fortress in the Alhambra. He had ordered anyone on the side of his nephew to be killed with no mercy, taking all their possessions and casting their families from their homes. Boabdil had secret intelligence that his uncle was seeking all manner of ways to kill him too, either by poison or by sending assassins disguised as negotiators or bearing gifts. He therefore refused to see any of El Zagal's ambassadors, stating that, as the legitimate heir to his father's kingdom of Granada he would strive both to take the throne from and to behead his uncle, who had allowed his brother and his followers to be pitilessly murdered in Almeria.

The enmity between them grew, and Boabdil's partisans fought back fiercely, but there were many deaths on both sides, and the young sultan, who had fewer men, was forced to take refuge in the Albaicin. In desperation, he sent to Ferdinand and Isabella for help. True to their design of favouring Boabdil, whom they thought of as their puppet, they sent a body of troops to Granada to assist him, and the street fighting worsened.

With two sultans fighting for one throne, the Muslim doctors

of law took action to break the impasse and stem the bloodshed
by suggesting to El Zagal that he should make peace with Boabdil,
and that they should join forces against the Christians. In theory
this looked like a sensible proposition, to which El Zagal agreed.
But the *ulama* and elders were greatly distressed at Boabdil's reso-
lute response. The historian Luis de Mármol Carvajal recounts his
words, to the effect that his uncle had betrayed him so many times
and used such cruelty towards him and his friends that he would
never trust his word again, nor did he want peace or truces with
any kind of condition attached. Yet the younger man must have
been powerfully persuaded to change his mind, perhaps by his own
supporters, perhaps by the *ulama*, as uncle and nephew did come
to an agreement, but at the cost of Boabdil's sovereignty. Against
all expectation, he handed over his kingdom to El Zagal, perhaps
persuaded by the forceful arguments of the *ulama*, who had told him
that the differences between the two men would cause the downfall
of their kingdom.

The province of Granada was divided unequally between them
so that El Zagal ruled over the main cities of Granada, Malaga,
Almeria and Almuñecar while Boabdil governed the rest, including the kingdom of Murcia. With great cunning, El Zagal gave the
town of Loja due west of Granada to his nephew, as he realised
that it would be the next place Ferdinand would think of striking,
and guessed that if it was ruled by Boabdil, the Catholic Monarchs
would leave it alone under the terms of their agreement with him.
The Christians didn't share his opinion. While he was with his
troops in the field, Ferdinand heard news that Boabdil had betrayed
the loyalty and the oath sworn to the king and queen as their vassal,
and had not followed his orders, forgetting all the favours show-
ered on him by the queen. From Ferdinand's perspective, he had
broken faith with them by uniting with his uncle, and had divided
the kingdom between them so as to make war on Castile. He also
heard that Boabdil had taken a large troop of selected cavalry and
infantry to the city of Loja to defend what was now part of his territory, as he feared a Christian attack.

In what happened next Boabdil emerges as a controversial
figure of complexity and ambiguity. Different accounts give quite

divergent views of him at this vexed stage of his life. The late six-teenth-century royal chronicler to the throne of Aragon, Jerónimo Zurita, who must have had access to important documents relating to Ferdinand's affairs, writes that Boabdil sent an embassy to the Aragonese king in an effort to stall an attack on Loja. After the sultan's perceived disloyalty, furious Ferdinand was on the warpath with his troops, and Boabdil understood very well that the might of the Castilian army would be upon him and his subjects. He entreated Ferdinand not to attack, because he was a vassal and under his protection, emphasising that he and the people of Loja were there to serve him. He is also alleged to have stated that it would be easier for Ferdinand to take Malaga and Velez-Malaga, both in El Zagal's territory, than Loja. If this was true, surely it was said in the desperate hope that Ferdinand would divert his attention elsewhere. Given the enmity between Boabdil and his uncle, he might have welcomed an attack on one of El Zagal's strongholds. It was also part of the agreement between the sultan and the Christian Monarchs to work together against his uncle.

Ferdinand was not to be deterred, and launched the full might of his artillery upon Loja. Zurita remarks that brave Boabdil left the town itself with his cavalry, so that the inhabitants would not be afraid of attack because of his presence inside its walls. There was a fierce battle between the Christian forces and the sultan's 1,500 horsemen and 4,000 foot soldiers, while the battering from the artillery was so ferocious that Loja was forced to surrender on 29 May 1486. All Boabdil's captains were dead or wounded, and the sultan was himself injured, so the people of Loja requested their negotiators to be allowed to speak to King Ferdinand in safety, as they wished to hand over the town. They came before him and entreated him first of all to pardon Boabdil for breaking the promise he had made to him and to the queen. They also said that, if Boabdil relinquished the title of king of Granada, Ferdinand should make him duke or marquis of the city of Guadix within six months. He should also have safe passage in Castile, if he needed to enter that territory, or similarly if he wished to go overseas. They asked for the lives of the inhabitants of Loja to be spared, and to be allowed to take all their possessions with them, and to travel safely in the kingdoms of Castile, Aragon and Valencia, if they wished to do so. On these terms, they would hand over the city and with it all the Christian captives held there. Their negotiations were clearly successful, as most of the inhabitants still alive left as free people, with all their belongings, arms and horses. Boabdil came out of the town last, and prostrated himself before Ferdinand.

Not all the Muslims of Loja were willing to leave, though, and the chronicler Pulgar tells a story that has a ring of truth to it. One Muslim weaver carried on working at his loom while the fighting raged around him, and when his wife and neighbours urged him to flee and have at least some chance of surviving, he refused:

> Where do you want us to go? Why should we try to survive? To suffer hunger? To feel cold steel, or to be persecuted? As we have no friends to take pity on our misfortune and make it right, I'd rather wait for an enemy who covets our goods and who will kill me, so that I can be spared seeing the suffering of my own people. I'd rather die here by steel than later in shackles.

The weaver would not change his mind, and remained in his house until the Christians broke in and murdered him.

Ferdinand agreed to the terms of the Lojans, but the price was to take Boabdil prisoner once again. L. P. Harvey finds the sultan's behaviour during these events puzzling, and wonders why he had made peace with El Zagal and then rushed into battle. Was Boabdil merely putting on a show of fighting, when all the time his real objective was to surrender Loja to Ferdinand? This suggestion of treason is made on the basis of an alleged letter written by Ferdinand setting out the terms of the deal agreed with Boabdil, in which the latter was to be assisted in taking over territory, including Guadix and Baza, in return for services rendered. Harvey asks whether Boabdil could have been playing the dangerous game of hoping to get himself safely captured, but concludes that he was more likely swept along by a genuine current of patriotic enthusiasm. If the supposed letter were genuine, the term 'for services rendered' is ambiguous, and does not necessarily refer to Loja. It also seems highly unlikely that Boabdil

1. Statue of Muhammad I in his home town of Arjona in southern Spain, where the Nasrid dynasty was founded in 1232.

2. The fortress of the Alhambra viewed from the gypsy quarter of Granada under ominous skies.

3. The Nasrid shield carved on the wall of the Alhambra, inscribed with their dynastic motto 'Only God is conqueror'.

4. The Patio of the Lions in the Alhambra, the main courtyard of the palace, famous for its twelve white marble lions. It is said to be an architectural image of paradise.

5. The residence of El Partal in the Alhambra, where Boabdil lived in his youth with his mother and siblings. 6. The only remaining examples of Nasrid painting can be seen on its internal walls. Dating from the first half of the fourteenth century, they were originally brightly coloured, and depict court and ceremonial scenes, as well as the Nasrid soldiers returning to their camp with booty shown here. The paintings appear to contradict the traditional Koranic prohibition against human representation, although what the Koran actually prohibits is idolatry.

7. Nasrid chessboard, dating from the fifteenth century and made of walnut and birch wood, metal and bone. Chess was brought to Spain by the Muslim Arabs and was played by all social classes. King Alfonso X wrote an illuminated treatise on the game in the thirteenth century.

8. The page from the Capitulations or terms of surrender of
Granada showing the signatures of the sultan Boabdil, King
Ferdinand and Queen Isabella, dated 25 November 1491.

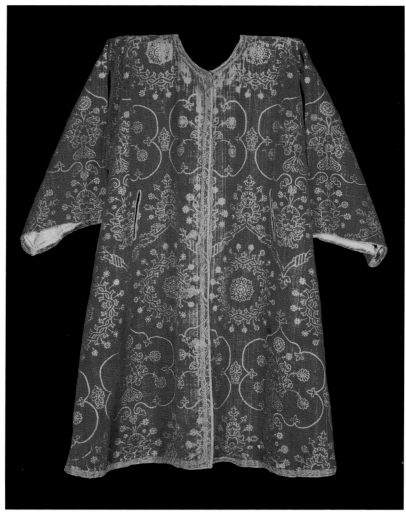

9. Boabdil's *marlota* and boots, taken as booty when he was
captured at the battle of Lucena in 1483, and gifted to the Spanish
nation by the family of the Marquises of Villaseca.

10. Boabdil's sword
and sheath, ancestral
symbols of the Nasrid
dynasty, with palm tree
ornamentation on the hilt.
These were also part of
the Christian booty taken
at the battle of Lucena.

11. Boabdil with chains around his neck, suggesting his capture by Diego Fernández de Córdoba at Lucena. An image of the enchained sultan appeared on the family shield of Fernández de Córdoba and, until recently, on several municipal shields in Andalusia.

12. The patio of the mosque and window through which Boabdil made a daring escape with his brother Yusuf in 1482, in a dramatic plot to oust the reigning sultan, his father, and take his place.

13. The Dar al-Horra palace in Granada, the last residence of Boabdil's mother Aixa before she followed her son into exile. After the fall of Granada, it became part of a monastery established on the site by Queen Isabella.

14. The *alcaicería* or old silk market in Granada, devoted to commerce and silk trading in Boabdil's time. It was owned by the sultan and contained almost two hundred shops and stalls.

15. On his return to Granada in 1487, Boabdil was proclaimed
sultan in a Nasrid royal palace in this street, the Calle de la Tiña.
The palace later became the house of the Marquis of Cenete.

16. *(inset)* Fifteenth-century anonymous portrait of Boabdil as Rey Chico de
Granada, in the collection of the Marquises of Ayamonte, Madrid. His posture,
kind expression and dark, melancholy eyes convey dignity, royal composure
and respectfulness, combined with a lack of affectation shown in his dress.

17. The monumental Gate of Justice in the Alhambra, built in 1348. The Nasrid symbols of the hand of Fatima and the key above the entrance arch contrast strongly with the Christian statue of the Virgin and Child, placed in a niche above the Arabic founding inscription at the order of the Catholic Monarchs.

18. Exterior view of the expertly restored Dar al-Horra palace in Granada, the dwelling of the sultana Aixa just prior to 1492. Here medieval Hispano-Arabic architecture meets modern graffiti.

19. *The surrender of Granada* by Francisco Pradilla y Ortiz, painted in 1882 to glorify a defining moment in Spanish history. This image of apparent Christian supremacy reveals a surprising sympathy in the depiction of Boabdil.

20. *The Moor's Last Sigh* by Francisco Pradilla y Ortiz, dated 1892, leaves no doubt of the artist's sympathy for Boabdil, who stops on his journey into exile to look back on the city he has lost.

21. Portrait of Queen Isabella I of Castile by John of Flanders, circa 1500–1504. She is wearing a white cap and veil, and her blouse is embroidered in Morisco style. Her double chin and the bags under her eyes are an uncompromisingly realistic touch.

22. Portrait of King Ferdinand II of Aragon, attributed to the Master of the legend of the Magdalen. His sober dress and demeanour belie his lust for power and ambition.

23. Muhammed I bearing the red Nasrid shield, depicted in the thirteenth-century *Cantigas de Santa María* of Alfonso X the Wise. In this contemporary portrayal Muslims are distinguished from Christians by their turbans, but are shown standing alongside Christian soldiers too, in a clear portrayal of the fluidity of religious and political allegiances at this time.

24. The *musalla* or shrine in Fez where Boabdil is believed to be buried, once a chapel dedicated to a local saint, but now a debased shelter for drunks and beggars, strewn with refuse.

25. The mountain peak of El Mulhacén, the highest point of the Sierra Nevada and the legendary burial site of Boabdil's father Abu l'Hasan. In reality he was taken back to Granada and interred in the pantheon of the Nasrid emirs.

26. Sculpture of Boabdil by Anna Hyatt Huntington in the courtyard of the Hispanic Society of America in New York, a work intended to capture the complexity of the sultan, who is wearing exotic robes and riding boots as he rides away from Granada.

27. The bronze monument to Boabdil in Granada, situated in the place where he handed the keys of the city to Ferdinand and Isabella, nowadays a small, gravelled park off the beaten tourist track, surrounded by modern blocks of flats. It was installed in 1997 to commemorate the last Nasrid emir.

had connived with Ferdinand in advance to give him Loja and again allow himself to become a prisoner. Ferdinand's rage at his disloyalty, Boabdil's frantic efforts to deflect him, subjecting himself and his people to a terrible artillery attack and being wounded, all point to something different. It does look, nevertheless, as if Boabdil was trying to play a double game – that he realised the tactical advantages of showing his compliance with Ferdinand and Isabella, but in his heart had no intention whatsoever of giving up his kingdom at this stage of the war.

In early summer 1486 a second agreement was made between Boabdil and Ferdinand in which the sultan was conceded the eastern part of the province as the feudal estate representing his vassaldom to Castile, provided he managed to take control of that region within six months. He would have to fight his uncle, whom Castile considered an illegitimate ruler; on their part, they would also fight him on all fronts. Once more playing pawn to Ferdinand as king, he was released from capture and set out for 'Velez' (either Velez Blanco, west of Lorca, or Velez-Malaga, east of Malaga). This deflection of the young emir away from his native city allowed Ferdinand to focus his thoughts on the bigger prizes of Malaga and Granada itself. To make things easier for Boabdil, on 5 June the Catholic Monarchs granted a three-year truce and peace to the city of Granada and all towns and villages who came out in favour of Boabdil.

This welcome news was proclaimed by messengers all along the frontier. Hernando de Baeza talks of his personal experience of these events in an anecdote in which we hear the words of the sultan himself. He tells us that he was sent a letter by order of Boabdil which explained recent events in part, and stated that he needed someone who could go on his behalf to the Catholic court. The sultan would be glad, the letter continued, if that person could be Hernando de Baeza himself. He describes his reactions to this personal honour:

> I didn't decide to do this at once, because it was dangerous to enter the Albaicin. The king [Boabdil] had known of me since his visit to Alcaudete on his release from prison, where he made an appeal to the grandees of Andalusia. I was living there at the time, and a great friend of mine, one of the sultan's

personal guards called Alhaje, acted as intermediary through whom he communicated in a very friendly way with me. A few days later the city proclaimed him as their king, and he wrote to me again.

So finally I went to the Albaicin, where I communicated at length with his royal person, and with his mother and wife, daughter, servants and ladies in waiting. All I have written about his imprisonment I heard in his own words, when he was speaking to me alone. He talked to me in Castilian, although he spoke it with a heavy local accent which was quite difficult to understand. One day I asked him why he didn't speak in Castilian more often, as he knew it so well, and he answered in a way I thought worthy of mentioning, saying 'Yes, I do speak it, but as I'm not completely fluent, I'm afraid of making a mistake, and a mistake in the speech of kings is very undesirable.' I felt these were the words of a great person, and as God is my witness that in the three or four years that I knew him, he was indeed great, and I really believe that if he had been a Christian, he would have been one of the best that ever was.

In spite of the inevitable religious proviso Baeza gives us, his high opinion of Boabdil as a person and as a ruler is telling, particularly in view of the chronicler's own delicate, ambiguous position as a convert to Christianity with Moorish sympathies.

The residents of the eastern areas of the kingdom, which Boabdil now ruled, soon recognised him as their leader and submitted to him in the hope of the peace and security his truce with the Christians had promised them. Encouraged by their loyalty, the sultan took the bold step of heading back to Granada. On 15 October 1486 he again entered the Albaicin secretly, where he was awaited by his supporters as before. The rest of the Granadans remained loyal to El Zagal, so once more the city was torn by street fighting between the two sides, with two men holding the title of king. At this stage, Boabdil had the military support of Castile in terms of soldiers, artillery and supplies, but in January 1487 El Zagal took the decision to enter the Albaicin by force and massacre the rebels. He roused the people of Baza and Guadix to enter through the Fax el Lauz gate, which enabled his men to take several other gates in the Albaicin, but Boabdil's partisans defended the area fiercely and succeeded in fending off the attack.

In April of 1487, Ferdinand carried out his first objective for the year, which was to besiege the town of Velez-Malaga, still loyal to El Zagal. He took his troops from Cordoba on 8 April and reached Velez-Malaga astonishingly quickly on 16 April, setting his engineers to work at once building siege-works and scaffolding. This move was decisive for Boabdil as it played into his hands, causing religious leaders to apply pressure on El Zagal to act. He was torn over what to do. Pulgar states that he offered to surrender his title to Boabdil and fight under his banner to save Velez, but his nephew did not trust him an inch, and refused the offer. Within ten days of learning of the Christian king's assault, El Zagal was obliged to divide his forces. On 26 April he left Granada with all the troops he could muster to defend Velez-Malaga. Having asked his nephew to suspend hostilities until the problem further afield had been resolved, his army took perilous mountain tracks across to Velez-Malaga, lighting great bonfires as they went and El Zagal himself appearing on a mountain top close to the city. These beacons were the signal to the local people to rally and fight. An eerie scene presented itself as the Muslims took on the Christians on the mountain slopes brightly lit by the great pyres. With the Muslims above and the Christians below, it was hard to engage in actual combat. When dawn came, El Zagal and his men had vanished – most likely because he had heard bad news from Granada. The people of Velez-Malaga had lost their would-be saviour, and were forced to give up their fierce resistance. They capitulated to Ferdinand on 2 May, although the Catholic king would have preferred to fight El Zagal, who had until then remained unwavering in his confrontation with the Christians and who still inspired his men to fight.

Boabdil was not so gullible as to wait for his uncle's return to Granada. As soon as El Zagal had departed, he roused his men and took over the city, whose inhabitants proclaimed him as sultan for the second and last time on 29 April 1487. Baeza recalls that one of the Granadans, a man over sixty with boils on his neck, who sold bathing products to the women at the baths, climbed up to one of the gate-towers and began to proclaim Boabdil as sultan. He was joined by voices from other towers, and when the sultan heard the clamour, he went down on horseback to the Elvira gate, sending out town criers announcing a general pardon to all the people of the city. In what later became the house of the Marquis of Cenete, though originally a Nasrid royal palace in the Albaicin, all the religious leaders and elders met a triumphant Boabdil, acknowledging their allegiance and kissing his feet. El Zagal retreated briskly to the Alpujarras and later established a base in Guadix, but there would be no more internal challenges to Boabdil's reign, which was just as well in view of the ever-growing Christian threat to the Islamic state of Granada.

After this victory, Ferdinand was eager to pursue his main objective of the year, which was to capture the great strategic port of Malaga. Its conquest could become a symbol of Castilian might, he surmised, lifting his subjects' spirits and deflating the Granadans' confidence in their defence. The fight for Malaga is sometimes seen as the single most important battle of the war. If Malaga was in Christian hands, then no supplies or reinforcements could reach Spanish Muslims from overseas. It turned out to be the bloodiest and most difficult part of the entire Christian campaign, and Ferdinand and Isabella narrowly escaped with their lives. To start with, they tried to negotiate a surrender without any fight, but the commander of the city, Hamete Zeli, had a garrison reinforced by fierce Berber soldiers, and he refused point-blank to enter into any kind of settlement. The Castilians were undecided over the best strategy to use – some thought a long blockade with the aim of starving the Malagans into submission would be best, while others thought a close siege and military assault would be more effective. Ferdinand felt an effective blockade would be hard to achieve, as supplies could be smuggled into Malaga by sea, so he prepared for a military attack. The king had at this point the biggest army of the entire war, but intense downpours and the rough terrain made the march difficult, especially the transport of the artillery. The lack of roads required a huge number of foot soldiers to flatten the route before the heavy artillery could move forward.

The great defences of Malaga included a series of walls and

towers of virtually impregnable thickness and size, and the twin castles of the Alcazaba and Gibralfaro which dominated the city. It presented an entirely different proposition for the Christians from their previous conquests. Also the inhabitants fought relentlessly in hand-to-hand combat on the hill leading up to the castle. The Arabic *Nubdhat* relates that 12,700 Christians were killed in a single day. While this may well have been an exaggeration, there is no doubt that the Muslims put up a heroic resistance. The battles and siege went on for three and a half months, until extreme hunger began to prevail.

During this time, Boabdil found himself once again in an extremely awkward position. As soon as he had regained the throne of Granada, he had made his chief vizier a senior governor, and had four of his main adversaries beheaded, as he reported in a letter to Ferdinand and Isabella, sending a clear message that he meant business. Writing from the fortress of the Alcazaba, Boabdil describes how Granada took his side and how he entered the city: 'Granada rose up to help us, and the flags of our party were raised, and we entered the city, established our army and deliberated on the situation . . . Your highnesses should know that we had the four main governors put to death, who were our greatest enemies.'

Boabdil had established his power in the city and had the support of the people, but the inhabitants of Malaga saw things differently. After El Zagal had vanished, they reverted to supporting Boabdil in exchange for the free movement of their merchants throughout the kingdom and also in Castile. It came as a great surprise to them to suspect that Boabdil's pact with Castile implied the potential handover of their city and the evacuation of its inhabitants. They felt betrayed and abandoned, as the sultan had sent them no assistance. In his defence, it may be said that Boabdil was performing the tricky balancing act of being appropriately subservient to Castile while maintaining his own supremacy as ruler of his beleaguered people. He was aiming to play along with the Catholic Monarchs while still harbouring the hope of saving his kingdom. And we can't forget that Ferdinand still had Boabdil's son in his power, as well as the sons of several of the sultan's closest associates.

In an incident recorded in Christian (but not Arabic) sources,

El Zagal heard of the siege of Malaga and sent a relief column. Boabdil allegedly had the column intercepted and defeated, with a few survivors fleeing to Guadix. If this account is true, then the sultan was fulfilling his agreement with the Christians, for which they seemed to have been very grateful, as they sent him gifts of horses and gilded trappings, silks and expensive perfumes. After his recent breaking of the accord with Ferdinand and its violent consequences, it was important for him to show that this time he was keeping his word. There was also the added incentive of gaining some small revenge on his treacherous uncle. Nor did he dare endanger his son or his people by showing the enemy his true inclinations.

Meanwhile, back in Malaga, the Castilian army had speedily constructed a fortress facing the Muslim ramparts. Made of timber and earthworks, it was garrisoned by 2,500 cavalry and 14,000 infantrymen, under the command of Rodrigo Ponce de León. All round the city walls they built a great ring of palisades facing inward, and a mighty exchange of cannon fire and bombardment raged on, with the Muslims aiming directly at the king's tent, which had to be removed to safety. The unflagging defence of the Malagans and the extreme exertions of the Christians had taken its toll. There was plague near the city, and the soldiers feared it would reach their camp. They also suffered from food shortages, and discontent began to spread, to the extent that some went over to the Muslim side and acted as informers.

Isabella tried to persuade Ferdinand to give up, as she feared that the army would suffer irreparable losses. The Malagans' attempt to hold out had been courageous, and Castilian morale was low. So Ferdinand asked the queen to leave Cordoba and come to campaign headquarters to raise the spirits of the troops. At no time did the Muslims panic, for they still held the harbour, and had managed to keep the enemy out. Their own morale was high, and although there is no Arabic account of life during the siege, the Spanish chroniclers are full of praise for their opponents. Pulgar comments that it was worthy of note how bold they were in battle, how obedient to their commanders, how hard working as they repaired fortifications and how astute in the ruses of war.

A strange set of circumstances put Ferdinand and Isabella in mortal danger. A holy man from Tunisia living in Guadix called Ibrahim al-Jarbi formed a plot to assassinate the king and queen. He managed to rally about 400 followers and they travelled by night, cross-country, to attack one of the temporary Christian forts. Many of the band were killed, but al-Jarbi's risky plan was to be captured. In this he was successful and he was taken to Rodrigo Ponce de León, who persuaded him to 'disclose' the information he had offered to reveal. Al-Jarbi insisted he would speak only to the king and queen, and so he was taken, wearing a burnous, with a dagger in his belt, to the royal tent. Luckily for the Christians, Ferdinand was asleep after eating a large dinner, so the Moor, who knew no Castilian, was taken to another tent to wait, in the company of some of the court retinue, including Álvaro de Portugal, son of the Duke of Braganza, and his wife Felipa. Finding himself in luxurious quarters in the company of a man and woman in fine clothes, he assumed he had reached the monarchs, drew his dagger and lunged at Álvaro, wounding him almost fatally. He then attempted to attack Felipa but was restrained by an official who rushed in and seized him. Al-Jarbi was killed and cut into pieces, and his body parts hurled over the wall using a siege catapult. The Muslims who picked up the pieces devoutly sewed them together with silk thread, washed and perfumed the body and gave it a decent funeral. In revenge, they found a Christian prisoner, killed him and stuck his corpse on an ass, which they sent out to the Christian camp.

By now, the siege was taking effect. Hunger was extreme, and the Malagans were reduced to eating donkeys, dogs and cats to stay alive, and even the leaves of the trees. They ended up surrendering and requesting safe conduct. But Ferdinand decided that it was too late for terms, and their only choices were death or captivity. Finally, the Christians relented slightly and gave safe conduct to a few men who had sued for peace. The stench of death was terrible, and the city had to be cleaned up before Ferdinand and Isabella could enter in August 1487. All those left defending its walls were imprisoned, and women and children were captured and distributed as slaves among his courtiers and captains, as well as having all their possessions seized. The *Nubdhat* expresses the anguish these people experienced: 'It fills your heart with sadness, astounds the soul, makes you weep tears of blood in the face of such a calamity.' Their grief was shared by the Granadans, who, as Pulgar intimates, did not dare show their secret feelings and desires, for fear of prejudicing the security they had been promised by the Christians. Malaga was now no longer a great Muslim seaport, but an addition to the ever-growing kingdom of Castile.

If 1487 had been a year of unavoidable diplomatic allegiance to the Christians for Boabdil, 1488 led to a shift in his perspective. The Christian army attacked and seized a number of fortresses in the Ajarquía, in spite of the entire area being included in Boabdil's realm in the agreement the Catholic Monarchs had made with him, and in spite of the truces undertaken between them. The terms were that those who wished to leave could do so, and those who wanted to stay became Mudejars, or Muslims living under Christian rule. This disloyalty on the part of Ferdinand and the breaking of the treaty served as a warning to Boabdil that the Christians were not going to honour their part of the deal. The future of the Nasrid kingdom was looking grim, and the city of Granada was becoming more isolated. In a desperate attempt to turn the tables, Boabdil did what his forebears had done, which was to look to his fellow Muslims in north Africa for help. The result was the same as it had been in the past – the lack of power of the Berber Wattasid dynasty in Fez prevented them from crossing the sea to Granada, so their sultan sent Boabdil's plea for help to the Mameluks in Egypt, where it was taken by the envoy and jurist Ibn al-Azraq. At the same time envoys were sent to the Ottoman empire with a similar request for help. We know that news of the weakness of Andalusian Islam and of the dire straits of the kingdom of Granada definitely reached the East via Andalusian pilgrims or merchants stopping off at Alexandria. The Cairo resident Ibn Iyas struck a touching personal note when he wrote that he was deeply moved by reports of lost towns, appallingly bloody battles and fights without mercy.

In November 1487 the sultan of Egypt, Qa'it Bey, received the embassy asking him for a relief army, but the great distance of Granada from his territories deterred him from sending the military help so badly needed. Instead, he put pressure on the Christian clergy of Jerusalem to intervene diplomatically on behalf of the

Nasrid Muslims, and approach Ferdinand and Isabella on the matter. Although this intervention did happen, two years later, during the siege of the town of Baza, it had absolutely no effect. Boabdil was alone and in a precarious position. In spite of the Granadans' strong desire for the peace guaranteed through their sultan's agreement with the Catholic Monarchs, they scorned him for his apparent friendship with the Christians. He couldn't win. It was equally galling that El Zagal still dominated Guadix, Baza, the Alpujarras and Almeria, had the sympathy and support of those populations in his fight against the Christians, and was able to use the income from those places to fund his army. Boabdil could scarcely cover the costs of government in the capital, and had to use violence to repress social discontent. Food was in short supply, and after 1487, only one village, Alfacar, four miles east of Granada city, still provided fruit and vegetables. So the only incursions made by the Muslims against the Christians in 1488 were carried out by El Zagal, who had a few minor successes, such as the recapture of Nerja, Torrox and Alhendín. Meanwhile, Almuñecar abandoned its support of Boabdil in favour of his uncle. By 1489, only Granada, Guadix, Baza and Almeria remained of the Islamic state.

The Nasrid sultan was not the only one to feel the strain. The exertions of 1487 had not left Ferdinand with a good feeling, despite his victory. The annals of the crown of Aragon tell us that Castile was exhausted by the war, and the royal finances could bear no more debt after the colossal expense of the military offensives. It was increasingly hard to fund the troops and maintain the army. Yet Ferdinand had regrouped by 1489: his objective for that year was the town of Baza, his aim being to put an end to the power of El Zagal, a vital step in gaining access to the ultimate prize of Granada. The siege of Baza was another turning point. There was again no question of surrender, so in June, the Christian army pitched its camp in the cultivated land around the city and prepared to strike: this proved a mistake as the ground was extremely soft, and they had to relocate it. Five months later, nothing much had changed, and the strain of maintaining the army and the blockade was beginning to tell on the Christians. The residents of Baza were praying that if they could hold out for the winter, the attack would be called off. Pulgar reveals the astonishing persistence of the besiegers, who constructed over 1,000 huts of mud and brick to protect the troops, some of whom were killed when the makeshift buildings collapsed on them. Thousands of pack animals brought food supplies to the troops, ruining the road surfaces and making them impassable. The army wanted to leave, fearful that they couldn't survive for lack of food.

Ferdinand tried the same ruse to boost morale that he had used at Malaga, which was to bring the queen and her ladies to the camp. It appeared to have an instant effect. The commander of the town, Sidi Yahya, wrote to Gutierre de Cárdenas, commander of León, asking to start negotiations, and by the end of November there was an agreement. It is clear that this did not embrace the Muslim folk who had been fighting to the death to defend their homeland, but was entirely in the interests of the Muslim ruling class. Sidi Yahya is an example of a Granadan aristocrat who became a Christian nobleman, Don Pedro de Venegas, with great alacrity, in order to preserve his wealth and land. He became Ferdinand's vassal as well as a Christian, although it was kept secret until Guadix surrendered. The *Nubdhat* describes how the negotiations were carried out behind the backs of the common people, who were evacuated and the town occupied, while the wealthy inhabitants moved out to the suburbs, in safety and with their possessions.

With his future secure, Sidi Yahya went to Guadix to speak to El Zagal in early December. Whatever he said must have had a remarkable effect, because the former sultan and king of Guadix surrendered Almeria to the Christians on 22 December and Guadix eight days later. In return he was granted an estate including a number of places in the Alpujarras, which was to be a semi-independent territory barred to Christians. He also had half the rents of the salt mines of La Malaha and 20,000 gold castellanos, a very large sum of money. It is interesting that Abu l-Hasan's widow Zoraya and her two sons were with El Zagal at the time of the surrender agreements, and he treated them generously in giving them part of the benefits stipulated. There exists a document, which is part of the agreement he reached with Ferdinand and Isabella, which links Zoraya's property and that of her sons and relatives to his own, all to be given the same consideration. But El Zagal could only bear his new situation for a few months. There was internal pressure from the Christian contingent, and from Boabdil's supporters, who conducted a smear campaign against him blaming him for all the problems of the Nasrid kingdom. It was El Zagal's turn to feel humiliation and disempowerment.

Some believe he gave up the villages and districts he ruled to Castile as an act of revenge on his nephew, since by his action Granada was cut off from the rest of the world. Perhaps he realised matters had gone too far to permit any hope of resisting the Christian advance, but it seems likely that he was also spiked by the bitter family feud. Before long he sold his estates for another 30,000 castellanos and, to the relief of Ferdinand and Isabella, crossed the sea to Oran in Algeria with his most loyal followers. Zoraya did not go with him, but stayed behind in Christian territory, and documents preserved in the Simancas archive show that in 1494 she was still a Muslim living in Cordoba, where she stayed until the end of the fifteenth century. This clever, calculating woman had apparently hoped to prevent her sons from converting to Christianity, and their former nanny, Reduan Matran, stated in a testimony she swore to be true that Zoraya had made over the title of her property in the Alcazaba Cadima, as well as her jewels and perfumes, to the secretary Hernando de Zafra in exchange for his unsuccessful intervention on her behalf with the Catholic Monarchs, whom she asked to allow her sons to go into exile in north Africa.

After 1492, Ferdinand and Isabella took a personal interest in Zoraya, perhaps because she had been a Catholic, and they took her sons to live at court and later Seville, baptising them with the names Fernando and Juan and giving them gifts and an annual allowance of half a million maravedis. This move was probably to prevent the princes being used by the Granadans as new leaders against the Christians, so they were kept a good distance from the city and had no political dealings. Her sons begged their mother to revert to her former religion, and she did so at the command of the king and queen, changing her name back to Isabel. In later documents she is referred to as Isabel of Granada, or even as Queen Isabel. The last record of Zoraya dates from 1510, when she was living in Seville. Her clear ambition to place her eldest son on the Nasrid throne together with her ability to win the protection of several powerful rulers fully justified the sultana Aixa's fears for her own family and her hatred and mistrust of her rival.

What happened to El Zagal in the end is something of a mystery. There is a story that he was imprisoned by the king of Fez, who had heard some of the rumours emanating from Boabdil's party and believed he was guilty of creating dissent among the Granadans. It is said that he had El Zagal brutally blinded and that, abandoned and helpless, the former Nasrid ruler managed to reach Velez de la Gomera, where he lived on charity until he died. He was alleged to have carried a plaque stating *This is the ill-fated king of the Andalusians*, something perhaps more appropriate for Boabdil than for his uncle. It is more likely that he lived and died in Tlemcen.

As a measure of the importance of the fall of Baza to the Castilians, Ferdinand sent news of his conquest to the princes of Naples, Bohemia, Burgundy and England, and to every city in the crown of Aragon, all of whom celebrated the news with great joy. But in Granada the mood was one of deep gloom, as Boabdil and his people were pushed to breaking point. The yearly campaigns of attack by the Catholic Monarchs left them isolated in a city desperately fighting for the survival of its unique identity. The Granadans were still riven by dissension between those who wanted to fight to the death, bolstered by the religious leaders who were unyielding in their views regarding the duties of a true Muslim, and those who favoured negotiation, including Boabdil and his advisers. Pulgar states that some Granadans accused the city leaders of negligence, telling them in secret that they had seen their enemies killing their friends, while others told them that Allah was angry with them because of their internal conflicts, which had caused them to lose land and freedom. Some inhabitants ganged up against Boabdil, who was in the Alhambra, and tried to kill him, but he found out who the ringleaders were and ordered them to be beheaded. This calmed the rebellion and the city returned to relative tranquillity. In spite of the money sent from Castile to Boabdil to swell the Granadan coffers, there was a notably hostile tinge to relations between the sultan and the Christians, and it is by no means certain that he and his council had any true intention of relinquishing the city to them. The most terrible days still lay ahead for the Nasrid capital.

6

Checkmate: The Path of Surrender

High up against the steep walls dropping straight down to the river Darro, to the north of the palatine city of the Alhambra, the palaces occupied by Boabdil as reigning sultan were well protected by the nearly vertical embankments. Next to these was the *mexuar*, or administrative area for the Nasrid kingdom, which was entered from the public square and is described for us by Ibn al-Jatib, the vizier of sultan Muhammad V, in 1362. The *mexuar* had two patios, one where the council of viziers met, and another which housed the royal chancellery, where the royal secretariat's writing office was located. This office occupied a place of great importance in Granada's political and cultural life, as the court secretaries were a group of luminaries who wrote not only documents of propaganda and legitimisation but also literary works in prose and verse. All correspondence, official letters, legal and diplomatic documents and private communications were written on the legendary red paper of the Nasrid chancellery. Although white was the most usual colour for paper, as it is today, medieval Muslim craftsmen knew how to make paper of different colours. Red represented the Nasrid dynasty, and documents issued in this shade were appropriate for the lord of the Alhambra, the red fort.

On 16 December 1489 Boabdil wrote a letter on the crimson

paper, signed in his own hand and sealed with his seal, addressed to the viziers, sheiks and dignitaries of the settlement of Ugíjar and the farmholdings of the Alpujarran village of Picena, asking for their support. What happened at Baza, he wrote, was the will of Allah, and its loss filled Muslims with pain and diminished western Islam. But now, he stated, Muslims must consider the consequences of how they behave, and reflect with all their good judgement on their situation and future. They must cease their changes of heart and hasten towards what is good with strong resolve and diligence. Boabdil told them that he had agreed an amnesty with the Christians for two years extending to all his people, and urging them to recognise his authority. He encouraged them to exalt their holy cause and confess their absolute unity in private and in public. The sultan's tone is persuasive and moralising, but also inspiring and affectionate, as he instructs them to accept what he calls 'goodness and peace'. Just over a month after this letter had been sent, something happened to change his opinion about the amnesty. Early in January 1490, Boabdil sent his trusted vizier, al-Mulih, to the court of Ferdinand and Isabella to enter into talks with them. The subject of those talks is not specified, and it may have related to the recently agreed truce, although some believe it related to the potential handover of Granada. Al-Mulih returned with a letter from the royal couple, and accompanied by two young officers, who seem to have been charged with the task of negotiating for the city itself. One of the men was Gonzalo de Córdoba, aged thirty-seven, who had been inside Granada before when he had provided support for Boabdil against El Zagal, and had also been at the Battle of Loja, where he had apparently persuaded the sultan to surrender the town. Gonzalo had patched up relations between Ferdinand and Boabdil and renewed the secret pact in which the latter was to be rewarded for fighting against his uncle with the gift of a dukedom or a high-ranking title. The other man was Martín de Alarcón, who had been in charge of the arrangements for Boabdil's imprisonment at Porcuna when he was first captured by the Castilians in 1483, from which time forward Boabdil had been the pawn of Castilian policy. Both men were well known to the sultan, although they were both associated with very negative experiences for Boabdil, which should have made him suspicious.

In his letter of reply to Ferdinand and Isabella, dated 22 January 1490, Boabdil suggested that it would be best to send his representative back to court to speak in person to the monarchs. According to Hernando de Baeza, the sultan realised that the Castilian negotiators were shifting the terms of their agreement and sent a nobleman from his household to the Castilian court at Cordoba to clarify matters. Boabdil was horrified at their response, which we can deduce was along the lines that the Muslims must surrender their arms and the city at once. This, of course, broke the pact of peace and contravened the truce signed with the Christians. Boabdil, now a man of thirty who knew his own mind, was no longer the inexperienced young sultan of 1482. He had been betrayed, imprisoned and maligned, and his son was still held hostage by the Castilians. The new demand must have seemed one betrayal too many. His immediate reaction was to provoke war, but his closest advisers warned against this, and suggested he should send his messengers back a second time. He heeded their advice and sent Aben Comixa, the senior constable of Granada, accompanied by a very good friend of Hernando de Baeza, a merchant called Abrahim Alcaiçí. They returned very unhappy, and confirmed that the Christians had no intention of keeping their word over what had already been agreed twice with the sultan. The news got out and the city was in an uproar. The stage was set once again for war.

The perception of Boabdil as the covert friend and ally of King Ferdinand of Aragon and Castile has done much to foster the idea that the Muslim leader was a traitor to his people, but it is not borne out by the textual evidence. At no time in their long association did either man pay anything but lip service to the idea of an affectionate, chummy relationship between the two. In their lengthy official correspondence, Boabdil's letters begin and end with effusive expressions of subservient respect, admiration and solicitude which might lead us to think that he was overly compliant with the wishes of the Catholic Monarchs, until we realise that this flowery rhetoric was a standard part of formal letter-writing style in Arab tradition. The communications sent by the Christians were only slightly less demonstrative and familiar, again in keeping with the habitual language of official letters in the more sober Castilian language.

More revealing of Ferdinand's true motivation is his letter to the Mameluk leader Qa'it Bey, with whom he had made a temporary alliance against the Ottoman Turks from 1488 to 1491. The Spanish sovereigns described the war against Granada as if it had marginal religious motivation. They wrote of Granada as a vassal kingdom, part of the Castilian crown, which had failed to fulfil its obligations to them, and made out that the war was a punishment of the rebels, nothing more. Those who were willing to surrender were guaranteed the preservation of their faith and freedom in their religious practices. This quite blatantly contradicts the way the war was spoken of inside Castile and by the Christian chancellery, who presented it as a crusade against the enemies of the faith. Queen Isabella's obsession with winning the war was apparently rooted in her deep Christian beliefs and piety. With crusading zeal, she longed to destroy the last remnants of Muslim power, and resented the presence of a potentially hostile kingdom of different race and religion. But her aim was political unity, fuelled by a desire to build a sense of nation and enlist the support of her people. It was obviously helpful for the alliance with the Mameluks not to show hostility towards Islam, and so the Castilians craftily harked back to the original vassaldom of the Nasrids to the Christians approved by Muhammad I in 1236. As no formal peace treaty had been signed between Boabdil and Ferdinand, only truces, this ancient agreement was still legally valid from the Christian perspective. This version of the situation as it was presented to Qa'it Bey implies that one major reason for war was the acquisition of money and power, masquerading as a religious motive. Another strategic purpose was to take the southeast of Spain from a power closely linked to the feared menace of the Turks, who might recover their strength and join with Granada in the future. So Christian Spain was sending a clear message to the Mameluks that they would do well to keep Ferdinand and Isabella as allies and not enemies.

These political and military manoeuvres reveal the cunning and duplicity of Ferdinand. The notorious Florentine diplomat and writer Machiavelli, who was a great admirer of the Catholic king, stated in his work *The Prince* that great campaigns and striking demonstrations of personal abilities brought great prestige to a prince.

He had Ferdinand in mind. As a young man, the Aragonese prince had been clever and likeable, and, like Boabdil, was an excellent horseman and hunter. The historian Fernando del Pulgar spoke of him as having 'such grace that everyone who talked to him wanted to serve him'. But his shrewdness was obvious even then – his motto was 'Like the anvil, I keep silent because of the times'. All his life he had frequented the halls of power. Aged just nine, he had been his father's deputy in Catalonia, and became its lieutenant at sixteen. He was the ideal successor to his father on the throne of Aragon, which he took over in 1477, brought up in that kingdom, but also having Castilian blood as second cousin of his wife Isabella, which made it easier to unite the two kingdoms by their marriage. In spite of this, he was a womaniser and had at least three illegitimate daughters, all relegated to convents. Historians tell us that Ferdinand was easy-going but also ruthless, devious and more cynical than his wife. The modern historian Hugh Thomas states in his book *Rivers of Gold* that his instincts were those of a calculating machine rather than a man of passion. And there were the prophecies by the clergy that he would be the king who would win back the Holy Land for Christendom. The dramatic impact of the fall of Constantinople in 1453 had renewed the crusading zeal of western Europe, reflected in the popularity of the chivalric novels of the late fifteenth-century such as *Tirante the White* and *Amadeus of Gaul*, whose mixture of chivalry and violence chimed with contemporary warfare. There was a sense, as we have seen, that Ferdinand was the man for the moment, and his successes at the siege of Malaga and the taking of the seemingly impregnable Ronda had been personal triumphs. His eye was firmly on the big prize of Granada, whose conquest would make him and Isabella rulers of virtually the whole of Spain.

Boabdil was up against a man who was obsessively ambitious, immensely powerful and an expert military strategist. He knew how to take advantage of the newest trends in warfare developed in the mid-fifteenth century, which included new weapon capabilities, tactics and administrative advances. During the course of this century almost every European army had adopted the gunpowder weapons so successful in siege operations during the Granadan war. Siege artillery had been used in Spain before the fifteenth century:

Sultan Isma'il I was reported to have captured the town of Huéscar in 1324 and Baza in 1325 using gunpowder artillery, and we know that the Spanish Muslims used cannon against the Castilian army of Alfonso XI at the siege of Algeciras in 1342. One big mistake by the Nasrids was failing to advance the use of gunpowder artillery in their military strategies. Instead, they left this to the Christians. Ferdinand modelled his siege artillery on the French weapons which had been used in the 1450s, and appointed a French Master of Artillery. The triumphs he had in the war up till 1490 would not have happened without gunpowder technology.

At the same time, Ferdinand's naval blockade on al-Andalus gave him control of the straits of Gibraltar, the narrow stretch of water between Spain and Africa which either allowed or prevented invasion. Regular Spanish patrols made it impossible for the north African Muslims to make contact with Granada. The third prong of the Christian king's military strategy was the *tala*, or devastation of crops, throughout the kingdom of Granada, but most cruelly in the *vega* surrounding the city itself. To besiege a population and destroy their food supplies at the same time is a deadly combination which Ferdinand used remorselessly. The first *tala* of the year, on 21 May 1490, destroyed the crops of the *vega*, whose castles at La Malaha and Alhendín had just been taken by his army.

Despite the threatening situation, Boabdil was in no mood to relinquish his kingdom. Granada was still formidable because of its position and defences, shielded to the east by the great mountain range of the Sierra Nevada and encircled by massive towers and walls of great strength and solidity facing the *vega*. The sultan had a change of heart and abandoned the dangerous diplomatic game he had been playing for years. Courageously, he launched an attack on the town of Padul, recently acquired by Ferdinand from El Zagal, as soon as the Castilians had withdrawn from the *tala* in June 1490. The assault was successful and, against the odds, he managed to recapture the town and surrounding area, as well as the castle of Alhendín. No doubt elated by these victories, he went to war against the coastal town of Adra, which was won back with the help of north African volunteers, but a further attack on the coastal town of Salobreña failed in September, as the Muslim army had to hurry back to Granada, where the Christian army was reported to be heading. Boabdil was trying to rebuild his kingdom with modest victories, and probably hoping to open up links from Granada to the outside world now that vital food supplies from the *vega* were practically non-existent. A chain of seaside bases might provide a tenuous life-line to allow food and other supplies to reach them from north Africa, and a link across the mountain tops to the outside world might also enable a limited amount of provisions and men to get through to Granada. During the rest of 1490, a kind of stalemate was reached. The Castilians didn't launch a full-scale offensive, but raided and skirmished, with minor successes, and destroyed the crops of the *vega* for a second time in September. Boabdil refused to surrender, although it was now that his uncle decided to leave his endangered estate and cross over to Oran.

By 1491 the writing was on the wall. Granada lived in fear and hardship, while frantic, secret negotiations went on behind the scenes. In April, once the better weather came, Ferdinand led his army once more towards Granada and intended to stay there until the city sur-rendered. On 26 April, the army camped near the fountain of a small town called Ojos de Huéscar, known as Atqa to the Muslims, just six miles west of Granada. Here they were joined once more by Queen Isabella and her ladies in waiting: the queen supervised the military preparations and inspected the encampment dressed in full armour. There is a story that she wished to get a closer view of the Muslim city, so the king and queen went to Zubia, a nearby village, and sat at a window which gave an unbroken view of the beautiful Alhambra. The feeling of being spied on by an enemy moving ever closer was too much for the Granadans to endure, and they burst out of the city gates, dragging several pieces of artillery with them, and assaulted the lines of Spanish soldiers stationed between the village and the city to protect the king and queen. The Castilians pursued them back to the city gates and a large number of Granadans were killed before they could regain safety.

The Christian army remained within striking distance of Granada throughout June and July, when Ferdinand made a remark-able decision. Seeing they might well still be in the same position as winter approached, he ordered an entire new town to be constructed on the site of the encampment. Extraordinary as this decision seems, Ferdinand was a man who had been undaunted by re-engineering mountain pathways to accommodate his troops and artillery: his plan was put into immediate action, and his soldiers became artisans. Neighbouring villages were razed to the ground to provide materials for the new buildings, which were erected in just eighty days. Where there had been temporary tents there was now permanent stone and mortar in the form of dwelling houses, plus stables for 1,000 horses. The town had the shape of a rectangular gridiron with two spacious avenues intersecting at right angles in the centre in the form of a cross, 400 paces long by 300 wide, with imposing portals at each of the four points. Inscriptions on blocks of marble recorded the relative share of labour of men from various cities in the work.

While the town was under construction Isabella had been lodged in a magnificent silk tent owned by the Marquis of Cádiz. One night a gust of wind blew over one of the lamps, which set fire to the loose hangings inside, and the blaze spread to nearby tents. It happened in the early hours when the sentinels had fallen asleep, but the Queen and her children managed to escape unharmed, although many jewels, precious silks and brocades were lost, and she had to borrow clothes from her friends. When the buildings were finished and painted in gleaming white, a mayor was appointed, a man called Francisco de Bobadilla, a war hero and commander of the military Order of Calatrava, one of the semi-religious brotherhoods whose members had played a key role in the fighting against the Muslims. The army wanted the town to be named after the queen, but she declined the honour and named it Santa Fe, Holy Faith, as a token of trust in their Christian divinity. If you visit Santa Fe today, it looks much the same as it did in 1491. The church of Santa María de la Encarnación, built later, in the sixteenth century, bears the words *¡Ave María!* and a lance sculpted in memory of a Christian nobleman, Hernán Pérez del Pulgar, who had gone to Granada at dead of night in the winter of 1490 via a secret tunnel, to pin a parchment bearing those words upon the entrance to the mosque with his dagger. It was an act straight out of the pages of chivalric romance, and suggests that many Christian knights fought for fame and glory as much as anything else. Most of the monarchs' advisers, secretaries and treasurers also went to Santa Fe, which was set up as a court as well as a military headquarters. In October 1491 Isabella actually summoned Columbus there, where he stayed all autumn, an unintentional witness to the events unfolding in nearby Granada.

In the autumn of 1491 the brazen presence of Santa Fe, with its estimated army of 80,000 men, was a huge psychological blow to the Granadans, as it proclaimed the unflagging determination of the enemy to overpower them. The *Nubdhat* gives us the Arab perspective on what was happening at this time. The author describes constant fighting between Christian troops and the Granadans, with the enemy gaining all the smallholdings in the area except for Alfacar. He describes bitter fighting for this town and its surrounding area, which was defended with great tenacity by the Muslims who feared that if it also was lost to the Christians, the siege of the city of Granada would then be formalised. There was great loss of life here and in other similar localised fighting. What comes over is the courage and ferocity of the Muslim defence – not content with armed combat, they made nocturnal incursions into the enemy camp, taking advantage of the darkness, or they attacked them on the road, stealing all they could find, including horses, mules, asses, cows and sheep. As a result of this, there was a great deal of meat available in the capital, although it was sold at a high price to the few who could afford it. The *Nubdhat* states that, during these months of fighting, the Muslim nobility all perished save for a handful of men. Around this time many Granadan Muslims departed for the region of the Alpujarras, driven by fear and hunger. The route to and from the Alpujarras across the Sierra Nevada enabled good supplies of corn, wheat, oil, raisins and other foods to reach the capital, yet the situation inside was becoming more critical, with food and manpower scarce. As winter approached, snow fell in the mountains, cutting off the route and with it the food supplies, so many Granadans were reduced to begging. At the same time, the Christians controlled the *vega* and prevented the Muslims from ploughing and sowing. Their situation was desperate.

All the time that Ferdinand and Isabella were at Santa Fe, they were pressing Boabdil to hand over the city and leave for the

Alpujarras himself, which they had promised on oath that they would grant him for himself and his descendants. The terrible reality of what Boabdil had been forced to agree to eight years before, after his capture at Lucena, resulting in a pact in which his son would be held hostage by the Catholic Monarchs until such time as he handed over Granada to them, was looming large. Perhaps he had thought that it would never happen, that he could put it off indefinitely. That was certainly what he had been attempting to do as the Christians lay in wait on his doorstep, as we can see in a letter to him from Ferdinand in response to the sultan's latest amendments to the truce, which clearly amounted to delaying tactics. Ferdinand says that he has received Boabdil's letter and one from his representatives Aben Comixa and al-Mulih, 'which undoubtedly displeases me because such new demands as you make seem too much to ask and are very unlikely to be granted, and if it was not because I wanted to honour and favour you, I would not have replied to you'. He continues by insisting that Boabdil forget such thoughts, because it is very harmful to be so far from any conclusion, and 'such delay cannot be of any advantage. I am certainly not pleased, and it is not my responsibility, but rather the blame is yours and those of your city . . . I would never have believed,' he goes on, 'that things would have got to the state they are now in. It has all been uprising and anger and discord, and none of it in my service.'

A parallel correspondence went on between Boabdil's trusted aide al-Mulih and the influential secretary to Ferdinand and Isabella, Hernando de Zafra. The formulaic language that creates a veneer of mutual respect and care between the two opposing monarchs is echoed in the letters of their representatives, but it can't cover up the underlying tension between the two parties. The royal secretary tells al-Mulih that his bosses the Catholic Monarchs know he is good and honest, and has the right intentions, while urging him to steer negotiations towards the quickest outcome 'because otherwise the misfortunes and harm arising for you from any delay will increase'. This letter relates to Ferdinand's own missive about the sultan's stalling tactics, and Zafra is trying to get round al-Mulih, although his seemingly friendly tone contains a veiled threat. Al-Mulih is not fooled for one minute, and gives as good as he gets.

Addressing Zafra as 'Special lord and true friend', he reminds him that when Aben Comixa was in Seville with him, the Christian king and queen were inclined to show great largesse to Boabdil, without any capitulation or obligation to capitulate. The series of letters between the two men are complex and involved. They reveal the intrigues, betrayals and secrecy of this time, when both sides were suspected of treachery, when messengers were liable to present false information, and when conspiracy was rife. Clearly, the correspondence between these two royal officials was deemed to be secret, despite which al-Mulih suggests to Zafra that when he needs to write something really confidential he should 'put it in a small pocket inside a letter, in case it is necessary to read the letter out before the governor, or in case the sultan wants to know what it says. In this way,' he says, 'their secrets will be safe.' This may have been a ruse to create a sense of confidence and conspiracy between the two, but there is a story that Boabdil distrusted al-Mulih, and almost had him killed. Even the most trusted advisers were liable to be untrustworthy. It is also unquestionable that Zafra used bribery. In a document dated 24 November 1491, just before the capitulations were signed, he recounts an extensive list of fine fabrics given as gifts amounting to over half a million maravedis, to reward minor betrayals by Muslims of their own people. Shockingly, Boabdil's own siblings and negotiators appear among them.

There is good reason to believe that Boabdil's mother, who now lived in the Dar al-Horra palace specially built for her in the Albaicin, had some influence on the decisions made in these dark days of the Nasrid kingdom. Hernando de Baeza suggests that Aixa, the queen mother, who had great spirit, fought with all her might against any agreement with the Catholic Monarchs. Whenever a communication from them arrived for Boabdil, she vehemently advised her son to hold firm and die as a king, like his ancestors. As a result, Boabdil began to keep quiet about his dealings with the Christians in case his mother found out. One day the sultan discovered a plot by Ferdinand to draw out the Granadans by starting a skirmish outside the city, which would allow them to enter through the open gates while the guards were being distracted. Luckily, a Muslim spy found out and told Boabdil, who told his knights in turn. They agreed to muster as many men as they could and go out to fight the Christians, rather than let such a great city be taken in such a way.

Boabdil got up early the next morning and anointed his body, which was the custom among the Muslims when their lives were in danger. He called for his arms and put them on in the presence of his mother and sister, then kissed his mother's hand and asked for her blessing. He hugged his sister and kissed her on the back of her neck, hugged his wife and kissed her on the face, and also his daughter. This was the ordinary routine each time he went to battle, but on that day he asked his mother and the other women to forgive him for any trouble he had caused them. His mother was scandalised and alarmed and asked him why he had spoken like that. Boabdil replied that it was right for him to do so, upon which his mother grabbed him and begged him to tell her where he was going and what he was going to do. She began to cry, and the other women followed suit, and they wept so loudly it was as if he were already dead. Aixa was still holding on to her son, and wouldn't let go until he told her what he had agreed with the Christians. When he told her she cried: 'Who are you commending your sad mother, wife, children, sisters, relatives, servants, and the entire city and the other towns under your command to? What account will you give Allah of giving the order for us to die by the sword and lance, leaving the others captive? Think about what you are doing, because great tribulation brings wise advice.'

Boabdil replied: 'My lady, it is much better to die once, than to live, and die many times.' 'That's true,' his mother said, 'if only you die and everyone else is saved, and the city is liberated. But such a grave miscalculation is a very bad decision.' The sultan asked her to let him go, as his knights were waiting for him, but she wouldn't release her hold on him until he had sworn on the Koran he carried with him not to put himself in danger and for his men not to leave the city gates. Boabdil went out into the field and ordered the people to be kept inside the city so that what was planned in the Christian camp could not take place. For this reason, says Baeza, many people thought that the queen mother had advised her son to make an arrangement with the Christians to allow his family and all Granadan citizens to cross over to north Africa.

By November conditions had deteriorated in the city owing to food shortages which affected the rich and poor alike, and it was clear to the citizens that the enemy intended to wear Granada down through hunger and not by force of arms. Baeza describes the heart-rending sight of Moorish women with their babies in their arms begging in the streets for food. The suffering became so great that desperate people gathered in gangs, shouting that the sultan must get the help of the Christians, and if he wouldn't, then they would. All this reached Boabdil's ears, and he felt it deeply. The *Nubdhat* tells us that a meeting of all the eminent men of the city was called, both public and private individuals, religious leaders, treasury officials, governors and artisans, as well as what remained of valiant Grana-dan knights, and many common people – in other words, all those who passed for wise and intelligent citizens. They gathered together and insisted on an audience with the emir, to whom they made clear the dire situation of the inhabitants, describing their extreme hunger and the severe lack of food and other essentials. The city is large, they told him, so if the food that was usually imported was barely enough for their needs, what would happen now that nothing was being imported because the supply routes to the Alpujarras were blocked? They also told him of the great number of brave knights who had perished, the lack of general maintenance, the impossibil-ity of ploughing and sowing crops, and the number of children who had died in recent fighting. 'None of our Muslim brothers who live on the Moroccan coast come to our aid,' they added, 'in spite of the pleas we have sent to them. Meanwhile our enemies have built a whole town to attack us better – their strength is growing and ours is weakening, they get help from their country, while we have no help at all.'

They pointed out to Boabdil that winter was upon them, and the enemy forces were temporarily dispersed and weakened owing to the bad weather, so that hostilities had been suspended for a while. They put it to him that if they entered into dealings with the enemy now, he would accept their proposals and agree to their demands, but if they waited till the spring, when the Granadans would be even weaker and more impoverished, their requests wouldn't be heard. Boabdil listened carefully, and replied: 'Do what you think is best, and try to come to a unanimous agreement in line with your interests.' This was a measured response, unlikely to provoke the wrath of the *ulama* or the patriots, and shrewdly appeared to give the decision-making power to his people. The last thing the Nasrid ruling class wanted was to be trapped in a destructive conflict caused by the very patriotic spirit they had encouraged among their people. In the end this group of noteworthy men, in consultation with the Granadan inhabitants, agreed to send a request to Ferdinand to open discussions about the fate of their city. What they didn't know, although some of them suspected it, was that negotiations had been taking place in secret for some time between both parties with a view to surrendering Granada to the Christians. These secret plans meant that Boabdil was able to avoid a much more tragic, bloody and inevitable outcome to the conflict, however much the partisans of resistance militated against them.

The correspondence between Hernando de Zafra and al-Mulih reflects the tense situation between the two opposing sides. Both men underline the importance of secrecy in the negotiations, and it is evident that the Muslims were using every delaying tactic they could think of to defer the final date of any surrender. Zafra wrote to al-Mulih:

> Dear brother and great friend, on the basis of what you write about one of your emissaries, I suspect that he may not have the best interests of my king or yours at heart, and is seeking all kind of delays to take things along another path. This will not have a good end, as he is not looking at things as they are, nor remembering that the son of his king is still captive, nor that the latter is in hourly peril of his life.

The ever-present threat of harming Boabdil's son if the Catholic Monarchs didn't get their own way resurfaces here; Zafra's comments show the veiled menace and continual suspicion cast over all dealings between Boabdil and Ferdinand, and their representatives, even when they claim to respect each other.

One Sunday in November Boabdil sent a letter to Ferdinand and Isabella in which he answered their request for a firm date for the surrender of the city. His initial suggestion of a date in May 1492 had been greeted with rage by the Christian Monarchs, and with corresponding apparent amazement on the part of the sultan at their reaction. So in this letter Boabdil backpedalled and proffered the end of March instead, when he would hand over 'the two alhambras', meaning the palaces as well as the fortress. He knew only too well that at this stage there was no way back, and surrender was inevitable, but he did all in his power to secure the best possible deal for his family and his people. Boabdil's chancellery prepared a long document on behalf of the sultan setting out his proposals for the surrender of Granada. These replaced any provisional documents drafted previously. The terms, he asserted, were such that when Ferdinand and Isabella agreed to them, he would undertake the handover. First and foremost, on the day that they received the Alhambra, they must release Boabdil's son, still prisoner in Moclín, and hand him over to his father, along with all the other hostages and their servants, without delay. The release of the prince Ahmed was almost certainly always Boabdil's central preoccupation and had been so from the time his son became a hostage.

There followed a long series of practical conditions and religious stipulations. In essence, all Granadan Muslims should be allowed to keep their religion, mosques and leaders, and the muezzin's call to prayer should continue, for all time. No Christian should be allowed to enter a mosque, nor be ordered to stay in a Muslim house, but at an inn, as they did under Muslim rule. Muslim figures of authority should be honoured, and any lawsuits between Muslims were to be judged by *qadis* and Muslim law alone. There was to be no forced religious conversion of Muslim children, and no married Muslim woman could convert until the statutory legal time had passed; nor could any *elches*, or Christians who had converted to Islam, be persecuted or forced to reconvert. Nor should any Muslim be forced to bear a distinguishing mark of any kind. Boabdil also stipulated that Jews living in Granada should have the same rights as Muslims under the terms of the surrender.

The practical conditions demanded that all Muslims should be allowed to keep their possessions for all time, including arms and horses; only a Muslim lawyer could pass judgement on their inheritances, and no punishments could be inherited. All Muslim merchants must be able to trade freely as in 'tiempo de moros', the time of the Moors, both in Granada and elsewhere in Spain, and Muslims were to live free of taxes for five years. Those Muslims who wished to leave for north Africa were to have freedom of movement overseas, as well as in Spain, taking all their possessions, with a five-year window in which to depart, and within which to return if they wished. Their property was to be sold by procurator after their departure, if necessary. All Muslim captives were to be released upon surrender of Granada, along with the hostages, and all Christian captives would be released at the same time. No Christian would have the right to speak cruelly of the past.

Boabdil's desire to preserve the religious life and customs of his people, both present and future, and to negotiate a situation which would allow them the greatest possible freedom and tolerance is plain to see. He was sensitive to their feelings and took pains to try to avoid any sense of the inferiority of Muslims under Christian domination, as his stipulation about unkind words shows. The practice of Islam, and its material manifestations of the mosque, minarets and muezzins, were paramount, as was the *aljama* or Moorish quarter of the city, from where Muslim lawyers, judges and community leaders operated. Boabdil's inclusion of the minority group of the Granadan Jews in the terms of surrender, where he states that they 'should benefit like us from these terms', is particularly poignant when just months later, in the spring and summer of 1492, all Jews, not just those from Granada, would be expelled from their native Spain by Ferdinand and Isabella.

The sultan's personal stipulations related to money, land and people. He requested 30,000 castellanos for himself, plus 10,000 castellanos each for his aides, the governors Aben Comixa and al-Mulih. Castellanos were the gold coins minted by the Castilians, especially Ferdinand and Isabella, each worth 485 maravedis, the silver or gold coins used in everyday transactions, until they were struck in copper for distribution in the New World after 1492. The sums Boabdil asked for were substantial. He also asked for all the fortresses within his jurisdiction and that of his two governors. All Muslim captives from the kingdom were to be returned within three months of surrender, starting with one hundred on the day of handover itself. The Christians, who were suspicious of an uprising, had demanded hostages over the period of transition, and Boabdil offered fifty people to act as hostages, to be handed over by Aben Comixa on the agreed day of the surrender for a period of three days while the enemy received the Alhambra and made the necessary arrangements there. He reiterates the obligation of the Catholic Monarchs to hand over his son and the other hostages, as well as the total of 50,000 castellanos, on the fated day. The details of these stipulations were set out in a long document to the Christian rulers by al-Mulih, who was even able to add a touch of humour in asking for some mules, one of which, he wrote, should be tall and broad in order to accommodate Aben Comixa, who must have been a man of generous proportions.

Ferdinand and Isabella's response to these petitions was to use Boabdil's text, but to reformulate it, subtly adjusting the terms to suit their purposes. The artfulness of drawing up the terms of surrender lay in satisfying Boabdil's requirements while leaving the path open for the conversion of the Muslim population, and the reconversion of *elches* back into the Catholic faith. The devil was in the detail. Boabdil's version expressly mentions the voice of the muezzin, who climbs the minaret of the mosque five times a day to call the faithful to prayer, maintaining a tradition attributed to the Prophet Muhammad. The words of the call proclaim 'There is no God but Allah and Muhammad is his messenger', a statement of a blasphemous nature to the Christian church. The clause finally approved by the Catholic Monarchs was subtly adjusted and refers to retaining mosques and the call to prayer, without mentioning the voice of the priest. His voice would no longer be permitted to be heard over the city of Granada.

In line with the sultan's petition, Christians who had converted to Islam would be legally protected against any insults from Christians, but the phrase 'they should not be asked to revert to Christianity' was deleted. Ferdinand and Isabella also carefully modified the clause requesting all disputes between Muslims to be judged by a Muslim *qadis* as it was under Islamic government, which was changed so that such cases should be resolved in the presence of a Christian and a Muslim judge. They also added a new clause, which didn't correspond to any of those put forward by Boabdil – that no

Muslim man or woman should be forced to become a Christian. Its inclusion was not anything new, as it was following the royal laws of Castile, set out in the legal treatise *Las Siete Partidas* (*The Seven Divisions of the Law*) by King Alfonso X in the thirteenth century. It was included in order to allay the fears of the conquered, but it was a precarious protection, which implicitly didn't extend to their descendants. The alterations made overall by the Christians paved the way for future conversion without coercion, or at least that was the plan. The inhabitants of the kingdom of Granada would become Mudejars, no longer Muslim subjects of a Muslim emir but Muslim subjects of a Christian king, similar to other Mudejar communities in Castile, Navarre and Valencia, where equivalent terms had been negotiated in the past. They had the right to remain in Granada with all their possessions, under the same tax regime, and with complete freedom of religion, law and customs. Those who wanted to emigrate to north Africa would have free passage for three years, and could take all their belongings with them, or the money from their fair and legal sale.

The negotiation of the last details of the terms of surrender, or capitulations as they were known, were finalised by Hernando de Zafra and al-Mulih on behalf of their respective sovereigns, and were signed by Ferdinand and Isabella on 25 November 1491. Boabdil had his way and the date for the surrender was set for early May 1492. It seemed that the Castilians wanted the capitulations to be accepted at all costs, and were prepared to be flexible in terms of adjustments and emendations. They wanted the war to end. Just how trustworthy their promises were is revealed in an exchange between the Christian negotiator Gonzalo de Córdoba, the Great Captain, whose knowledge of Arabic enabled him to communicate freely with the Muslims, and Boabdil's governor and vizier al-Mulih. Boabdil wanted firm guarantees that Ferdinand would fulfil the terms he had signed, and asked his vizier to make this point. Al-Mulih asked what certainty Boabdil would have that the king and queen would definitely grant him the Alpujarras, and would treat him as a relative as they had promised. The Great Captain replied tartly that their obligation and grants of land would last for as long as Boabdil remained in the service of their highnesses.

It is hard to see Boabdil's actions in this long-drawn-out process of relinquishing his kingdom as high treason, as historians such as L. P. Harvey have done. The collusion Harvey accuses the sultan of sharing with Ferdinand, as if they were close friends in cahoots, is far from the mark. The lengthy exchanges of letters between the two rulers, and between their respective envoys, are laced with suspicion and mistrust in spite of the sometimes ingratiating rhetoric of the Muslim side. These delicate negotiations, so painful to the Nasrids, had to be undertaken in secrecy. Boabdil did not want any further destruction of his weakened and impoverished people, or the devastation of his capital city as the outcome of a violent popular uprising against the Christians, who would have been merciless. He knew the score, that the end was in sight for Islamic rule in Spain, and used all the diplomatic means in his power to secure the best possible terms for himself and for the Granadans. He may well have harboured a hope that once he established himself in the Alpujarras, he might in years to come lead a counter-attack.

After 25 November 1491 the gates of the city were thus waiting to be opened, but there was an obstacle of public relations and news management. This was not because of treason at the head of the Granadan state, but because the sultan feared the consequences, practical and psychological, when the populace discovered their imminent fate. The comparatively long timescale for implementing the terms of surrender had to be shortened to avoid giving dissidents time to stir up public opinion, and to present the Granadans with an accomplished fact. It was finally agreed to hand over the fortress of the Alhambra on the Epiphany, 6 January, and as an assurance of this, on the first Sunday of the new year, Boabdil and his advisers sent 400 Granadans, young and old, as hostages to be held by the Christians until that time. This act made their impending fate self-evident to the other inhabitants, who were stirred into rebellion by individuals who went round exhorting them to praise the Prophet and telling them that they would conquer the Christians. Bernáldez wrote that over 20,000 Muslims rose up and rioted, forcing Boabdil to remain in the Alhambra. At length he went out into the Albaicin and confronted the rebels. The sultan tried to calm them as best he could, saying that it was no time to confront the enemy because of the dire straits they were in, and because it would risk the lives of all the hostages. Boabdil returned to the Alhambra in some agitation, as he feared what his people might do in such a desperate mood.

There are several accounts of those last, dark days of the Islamic state of Granada, and of the fateful day of surrender, mostly written by Christian historiographers, who had a vested interest in presenting events in terms of the powerful myth of the Christian Reconquest. We also have briefer accounts in the Arabic *Nubdhat* and from Hernando de Baeza, both of which sympathise with the conquered, yet the most compelling document of the time is one found by chance by the Spanish scholar María del Carmen Pescador del Hoyo in 1955 in the National History archive in Valladolid. It is a letter written by a man named Cifuentes to Alonso de Valdivieso, the Bishop of León, sent from the Christian camp in the *vega*. We do not know precisely who Cifuentes was, but we do know that he was in the Christian retinue in some capacity, as the dispatch is an eyewitness account of what happened immediately after Boabdil returned to the Alhambra after confronting his inconsolable people. Unlike other public accounts, this is a private letter, which did not need to be adjusted as an official version, but told things as they really were. It reveals that there were, in fact, two handovers of Granada, one official and one secret.

At nightfall on 1 January 1492 Boabdil wrote an urgent secret message to Ferdinand. Dismayed at the volatile behaviour of his subjects, and their disastrous reaction upon realising that their city would be surrendered, he knew that he needed to act immediately. He asked the Christian king to send a representative so that the handover of the Alhambra could take place that very night, in secret, since he believed that the mere sight of Christians entering their city by daylight would greatly endanger the whole process and the lives of all concerned. The Catholic Monarchs at once ordered Gutierre de Cárdenas, the commander of León who had proclaimed Isabella queen eighteen years before in Segovia, to take a Christian contingent from the royal encampment to the Alhambra at dead of night, guided by al-Mulih and Aben Comixa along a road well off the beaten track so as not to arouse any suspicion. Cifuentes discloses that the party, of which he was one, arrived at daybreak on Monday 2 January 1492, which he describes in the following detail:

We arrived at the Alhambra as dawn was breaking, and we gained access through the Alixares gate. Here al-Mulih went in to the Alhambra to let King Boabdil know that the lord commander had arrived, and the sultan asked him and all those with him to enter. He was waiting for them in the richly appointed throne room of the tower of Comares, where the commander and other captains and knights of the Christian court dismounted and went to kiss his hands. There Boabdil handed over the keys of the Alhambra to Gutierre de Cárdenas and asked for a letter signed in Cárdenas's name stating that he had received the Alhambra on behalf of their Highnesses, and that it had been Boabdil's will to hand it over.

The sultan then departed from the Alhambra and went down into the city, presumably into the Albaicin, for how long we don't know. What was Boabdil feeling during those moments? We have no written record to tell us, neither Christian nor Arabic, so we can only conjecture. Perhaps he felt great fear, relief, shame, sadness, or all of these at the same time. He knew what was at stake – nothing less than a kingdom which had existed for a quarter of a millennium, the final bastion of the Islamic faith in Spain, and of the Arab culture which had enriched the Hispanic peninsula since the eighth century. The weight of history lay upon his shoulders, as he bore the impending demise of his religion, culture and way of life in Spain.

Cárdenas lost no time in posting Christian guards at all the towers and gates of the palatine city. As soon as the fortress was secure, a Catholic priest said Mass in one of the magnificent royal chambers, and Cifuentes describes how those present were overcome with weeping, the priest included, as they gave thanks for such an extraordinary treasure coming into Christian hands. The commander then sent a message to the royal camp asking the monarchs to send over the Count of Tendilla, Íñigo López de Mendoza y Quiñones, who had been designated as governor of the Alhambra. He asked him to hurry to take over from him, along with the necessary guards and captains, and to bring the royal standard of Santiago too. So Ferdinand and Isabella along with many Christian knights cast off the mourning clothes they were wearing following the death the previous July of their son-in-law Prince Afonso of Portugal, and made the showiest preparations possible. Cifuentes takes up the story:

> They drew near to the city with their main battalions in a position where they could be seen by the inhabitants. Their Highnesses and all their noble knights, who were richly attired in *marlotas* and tunics made of silk and brocade, approached the Alhambra with the Counts of Tendilla and Cifuentes and other captains of the guard. There they climbed up and raised their flags from a high tower which could be seen clearly from the entire city and surrounding countryside.

It is striking that the Christian royalty and knighthood were all wearing Moorish dress, brocade and silk tunics with a waist sash, known as *marlotas*. This purported to be a mark of respect, a visual statement to placate, reassure and suggest commonality, which pretended to say, 'Yes, we are like you, you are not being taken over by an alien people, we are the same, and nothing is going to change.' To a Granadan watching in fear from the city, after a long period of siege, it didn't seem like that, but was rather an act of insolent appropriation, of absorption of what is Moorish by the enemy. It was an entirely ambiguous act, reflecting on the one hand the centuries-old reluctant Christian admiration for Moorish culture, for what was forbidden to them and which militated against the entire ethos of the Reconquest, and on the other a latent desire to usurp and eliminate that culture and religion. In a similar way to the Great Mosque of Cordoba, which is now a Christian cathedral clothed in an Islamic outer building, the Catholic Monarchs and their retinue presented an outer image of Moorishness which at that dramatic moment actually accentuated the impact of their victory over the Granadans. It was a very astute psychological move on the part of the conquerors, the effect of which was underlined just moments later, when the Count of Tendilla and other captains of the guard hoisted the flag of Santiago from one of the towers of the Alhambra, where it could be seen clearly from the city and the countryside alike. The Moorish tower was transformed into a Christian symbol of power.

The official surrender of Granada has captured the imagination of writers and artists up to the present day, initially as a moment of supreme conquest and later because of the extreme poignancy of that moment of transition and loss. The opening scene of this book comes vividly alive as a multitude of details from various contemporary accounts of the end of Boabdil's rule in Granada flesh out the final moments of his time in the city and help us establish what really happened. There is no doubt that the public Christian entry into Granada had a strongly ceremonial, propagandistic quality. With the Alhambra already under Christian military control, Ferdinand, Isabella and their children approached the city accompanied by the Cardinal of Spain, Pedro González de Mendoza, and a brilliant retinue of courtiers and noblemen, including Gutierre de Cárdenas and the Count of Tendilla. Christopher Columbus, who had been staying at Santa Fe the entire autumn of 1491 awaiting the decision of the monarchs regarding the finance of his proposed sea voyage, was also present as an observer. There is some discrepancy in accounts as to whether Ferdinand advanced to meet Boabdil accompanied by Isabella, or whether she and her children waited on the nearby hill of Armilla. They all agree that Ferdinand stopped about a mile from the city, near the banks of the river Genil, near what is now the chapel of San Sebastián in the Paseo del Violón, formerly a Muslim mosque, built by the Almohad prince Ishaq b. Yusuf in the1220s and converted by Ferdinand and Isabella into a Christian building.

Boabdil rode on a horse or perhaps even a mule, as Hernando de Baeza suggests, from the Gate of Seven Floors at the Alhambra, down the steep slopes towards this meeting place outside the city walls, with magnificent views of the city he was about to leave all around him. He asked for this gate never to be opened again, and although its tower is currently being renovated, his request has been honoured. Cifuentes's eyewitness account states that he was accompanied by eighty to one hundred horsemen, richly caparisoned. Some Christian reports played up the pageantry, claiming that Boabdil carried the keys of the city in one hand, and on reaching the place where Ferdinand was waiting, he began to dismount but the Christian king stopped him. Boabdil went to kiss the monarch's hand, and again Ferdinand prevented him, in a gesture of respect for the man he had conquered. But Baeza records that both Boabdil and the queen mother Aixa stood firm on refusing absolutely to ask for or kiss the hands of the Christian Monarchs, creating some discussion about this between Isabella and Cardinal González de Mendoza. It was agreed that Boabdil would take one foot from the stirrup and make a gesture of respect by carrying his headgear in his hand, and that Ferdinand would then indicate that he need do no more. Few words were exchanged. The Morisco chronicler, who greatly admired the defeated sultan, adds that Boabdil was just over thirty years old on this occasion, a man of great courage and a person of refined understanding, one who behaved as he truly was. On that fated day, his face and bearing were very sad, but he showed manly valour. This great sadness and consternation was reflected in the faces of the Granadans who were with him, unable to hide their pain at the sight of the Christians' elation. Cifuentes remarks that they had good reason for their suffering, as Granada was the most beautiful and distinguished place in the world, in its greatness, power and luxury, beside which even Seville seemed a house of straw compared with the Alhambra.

Boabdil handed the keys of his city to Ferdinand, saying in Arabic: 'God loves you greatly. Sir, these are the keys of this paradise. I and those inside it are yours.' The king then handed the keys to Isabella, and she handed them to her son, Prince Juan, who gave them to the Count of Tendilla. The seventeenth-century writer and poet Rodríguez de Ardila, who wrote a history of the noble family of Tendilla, writes that when Boabdil was told that the Count of Tendilla had been named governor of the Alhambra, he asked him to be summoned, and taking a gold ring set with a turquoise from his finger he handed it to the count, saying that Granada had been governed with this ring since the time that the Moors first won it, and he wished that he should wear it to govern as well. Boabdil wished him better luck than he had encountered in doing so. Ardila recounts that he saw the ring in the house of the Tendillas, engraved with Boabdil's name in Arabic, and that it was preserved by the family until 1656, when the last Count of Tendilla died and the ring was lost. Zurita, a Castilian chronicler, adds that Boabdil gave Ferdinand two beautiful horses, with Moorish trappings, and a priceless sword, in acknowledgement of his Christian conqueror. Boabdil's son, who had been held hostage for nine years, was handed over by Fernando Alager and Martín de Alarcón, and he was taken to his mother. The recent Granadan hostages were also given their liberty. So it was that Boabdil paid his city and kingdom for his son. At this point, Cardinal Mendoza spoke to Boabdil, consoling him, with Hernando de Baeza acting as interpreter at this most bitter moment in the life of the sultan.

What happened to Boabdil once he had made the final surrender of the last Muslim city of western Europe? Opinions are divided on the details, as some accounts describe his return to the city to collect his family, others state that he went to the royal camp at Santa Fe, where he stayed in the cardinal's apartments, and yet others claim that he left directly for the Alpujarra. What seems most likely is that he was taken to a tent provisionally set up on the banks of the river Genil to provide a resting place after the taxing events of the day. Boabdil was probably retained for a short time while the armaments of the Alhambra were handed over and the fortress was reinforced, after which he was given leave to depart. Whether or not he returned to the city briefly or passed by Santa Fe, after he took his leave of the Christian contingent he set out towards his country estate in Andarax in the Alpujarra, the lands he had been given by the Catholic Monarchs. The historian Mármol Carvajal reports the eyewitness accounts of old Moriscos, who said that Boabdil went straight to the Alpujarra without returning to the city, from where his family and courtiers had already departed with all their belongings. The royal chronicler Fernando del Pulgar gives details of what he describes as two acts of sadness on that day. It was the custom when a Moorish king crossed a river on horseback for his companions to protect and shield his legs and stirrups, but on that day, Boabdil would not allow it. Nor would he allow a pair of Moorish slippers left behind and traditionally worn by the leader of the clan to be brought to him after the ceremony of surrender. The iconic story of the Moor's Last Sigh was perhaps a Morisco tradition, and may be truth or invention. Legend has it that when the Moors reached Padul, which is the furthest place from which Granada can be seen, Boabdil began to sigh heavily, invoking the Muslim god of war, and began to weep. His harsh mother is said to have upbraided him with the words: 'You do well, my son, to cry like a woman for what you couldn't defend like a man.'

7

Exile

In 1931 a collection of essays written in the form of alternative histories entitled *If it Had Happened Otherwise* was published. Winston Churchill was one of the essayists, along with the barrister and popular historical writer Philip Guedalla, who contributed a witty and perceptive item with the title 'If the Moors in Spain had won . . .'. In the scenario imagined by Guedalla, Ferdinand and Isabella abandon their attempt to conquer Granada and escape across the Sierra Nevada to the seaport of Motril, where they embark for Valencia. A peace treaty is signed with Boabdil at Baeza in 1493, and Granada becomes a great European centre of enlightenment and culture, enriched by the finest intellects in Spain, who founded the great University of Granada under the liberal and tolerant Boabdil III. Remarking on the irreparable loss to Europe, had a less cautious strategy exposed Granada to the ravages of a crude and uncultivated conqueror, Guedalla envisages the city at its apogee in the seventeenth and eighteenth centuries, when its enlightened policies are respected throughout Europe. As the Moorish kingdom's reputation grows down the centuries, *The Times* newspaper of 1915 reports the historic spectacle of the British king, dressed in Moorish costume as a mark of respect, awaiting the arrival of his oldest ally, the sultan of Granada, wearing full colonel's uniform of his own regiment, the

Dragoon Guards, who has leapt to arms to help in the Great War effort.

In this imaginative exploration of what might have been, Islamic Granada survives as a separate political entity, weakening Spain but fostering a liberal humanist brand of Islam. Granada becomes an important military and political power and a cultural beacon. Distant though it is from the historical reality, Guedalla's version of events vividly highlights what was lost on 2 January 1492. Christopher Columbus remembered seeing the Christian flags hoisted high on the towers of the Alhambra on that day at the moment when the city became the site of transfer of cultural, religious and political power from one unique medieval society to another. It was a regime change which anticipated innumerable similar capitulations by non-Christian people to Spaniards in the Americas which Columbus was about to discover. Far from falling into a decline and dying in grief at his failed attempt at conquest, as in Guedalla's fantasy, the triumphant King Ferdinand expressed his elation in the letters he wrote to the various ruling bodies of Andalusia announcing the surrender of the city. On the day itself, he wrote to the councillors and all the people of Murcia:

> I write to inform you that it has pleased Our Lord, after enormous effort, expense and fatigue in our kingdoms, and the spilling of blood of our native subjects, to bring the war that I have engaged in with the Moors of the kingdom and city of Granada to a happy conclusion. That city, held and occupied for over 780 years, today, 2 of January of this year 1492, has come under our power and dominion, and the Alhambra and city and all its forces, together with all the other castles, fortresses and townships that remained in this kingdom for me to win, were handed over to me. As a result I determined to write to you knowing the pleasure it would give you, and so that you may thank Our Lord for such a glorious victory, and for his exaltation of our holy Catholic faith, and for the honour and increase of our kingdoms and feudal estates, and for the general honour, tranquillity and rest of all our native subjects who have served us so piously and loyally in this conquest.

Ferdinand's language reveals a ruthless, ambitious man. His first thought is not the terrible cost of human life during the conflict but the effort and expense which have been a drain on his kingdoms. He makes no reference to Boabdil, nor to any Moorish individual, emphasising the words 'I' and the royal 'Our', without mention of his queen Isabella. He also refers to Granada as held and occupied, as if the Muslims were never its rightful inhabitants. It is not surprising that Ferdinand felt this was his enterprise. The conquest fulfilled the prophecies which had circulated at the Aragonese court regarding the year 1492. It was seen as an *annus mirabilis*, a year of apocalypse. The fall of Constantinople in 1453 had been interpreted as the first sign of the imminent end of the world because it started an era of great tribulation which, according to Saint John, humanity was destined to suffer before the definitive arrival of the Messiah. Calculations made using the Kabbala, the Book of David and other holy writing predicted that this period of trials would end in 1492, and the Eastern Church fixed that year as the end of the seventh millennium of Creation, when the completion of time would occur. They were so sure about this that they didn't print any liturgical calendars for 1493. Ferdinand knew these prophecies, which needed the participation of the ultimate human hero to restore earthly order. The Aragonese used the ideas to increase Ferdinand's royal power and to suggest that he was, in fact, the chosen one. Boabdil's surrender of Granada seemed to bear this out.

While Boabdil and his entourage departed in desolation from their native city, much of Europe joined Ferdinand in celebrating what they saw as a great victory. Te Deums were chanted in Saint Paul's cathedral in London, and in Rome the Pope and his cardinals attended a special High Mass. Venice and Naples joined in the festivities, and Europe congratulated itself on the Christian conquest, which was viewed as an act of revenge against Islam for the defeat suffered forty years earlier when the Ottomans took Constantinople. In stark contrast, a bourgeois man from Cairo, Ibn Iyas, the last oriental witness, both emotional and historical, of the death throes of the Nasrid kingdom in Andalusia, records in his diary for the year 1492 the news of the fall of Granada as 'one of the most terrible catastrophes to befall Islam'.

The ill-fated last sultan of Granada shared the feelings of despair and shame of his fellow Muslims. Boabdil arrived at the country estate in Andarax conceded to him by the Christians, complete with his family, courtiers, goods and followers. Perhaps he was glad of the peace, quiet and comparative safety of what was a true mountain refuge. Although it was a densely populated area, access was extremely difficult across mountain paths, so it was almost completely cut off from any means of external assistance, or even attack. He had plenty of time to think, but also some time to relax – we know that he went hunting regularly in the country round Dalías and Berja, using hawks and greyhounds. But any peace he enjoyed was short lived. Although Ferdinand and Isabella had given the estate in Andarax to Boabdil and his family, it wasn't long before the Catholic Monarchs became discontented with this arrangement and clearly wished him to abandon the Iberian peninsula. This had almost certainly been their plan all along, to edge him out bit by bit, first sending him into internal exile a respectable distance from the city of Granada, and then overseas. They feared that his continued presence in the former Islamic kingdom might incite an uprising or another struggle in their newly acquired realm: getting Boabdil to go overseas would maintain peace in the kingdom and achieve the most rapid political and religious assimilation possible.

Eight months after the surrender, in August 1492, the royal secretary Hernando de Zafra observes that Boabdil sent a message via one of his envoys to the king of Fez asking for permission to go and live in his Moroccan capital. Boabdil's message was most probably the very long poem he ordered his brilliant court poet Abdullah Muhammad to compose on his behalf, entitled 'Garden which Pleasingly Perfumes the Spirits'. It was written partly in verse and partly in rhymed prose, and in it Boabdil laments in heartfelt tones the fate which has overtaken him despite all his efforts to fight against it. He attributes his terrible misfortune to the treachery of which he was the victim, including that of his uncle El Zagal. Although Boabdil speaks of punishment for his own errors and sins, he also rejects accusations against him on the basis that what happened was all predestined, expressing his desire for vengeance, and imploring the Moroccan king to protect him and his family. Zafra records the return of Boabdil's envoy with letters from the king of Fez to say he would receive the Granadan sultan with great pleasure. Zafra supposes that Boabdil and his close advisers were delighted.

Hernando de Zafra was a key person in the conquest and reorganisation of the kingdom of Granada and, as we know, had been in charge of the negotiations for surrender. He wrote quite unashamedly that once he had been left alone in Granada, he used all his cunning and astuteness to contrive the departure of Boabdil overseas. In a letter of September 1492 he stated that the sultan, his mother, wife and sisters were all selling their remaining inherited lands as fast as possible, so the decision must have been made at this point by Boabdil to go into exile in north Africa. The Nasrid family did not want to sell their property lightly, and were keen to make sure that they had taken full advantage of the privileges that had been agreed with the Christians. The royal secretary remarks that the sultan's property was being snapped up without its purchasers taking any account of the preferential right to this property reserved for Ferdinand and Isabella in the terms of surrender. The Moorish lands inherited by Aixa and Moraima, areas known as Beas and Huétor Santillán, were soon sold, but the Catholic Monarchs intervened and confiscated the property while they considered the best course of action.

From Zafra's letters we can see that there was an attempt to bribe Boabdil's intimate circle, al-Mulih, Aben Comixa and others, with gifts and favours, as had happened during the negotiations for the surrender of Granada. Its purpose was to oblige them to persuade the sultan of the advantages of an immediate departure overseas which would, they were told, be more beneficial to him than staying where he was, since Ferdinand and Isabella were prepared to honour him with new benefits. Pressure was applied to achieve the wishes of the Christians with the speed and diligence they wanted, while Boabdil was even offered help in any armed initiatives he might undertake in Africa, particularly any in which he might gain the sovereignty of some state or portion of territory. It is possible that the armed initiative referred to so mysteriously was aimed at the kingdom of Fez itself. The correspondence between Ferdinand and Isabella and Zafra reveals that secret negotiations had been taking place with

some of the princes and sheiks of the Moroccan coast, who had allegedly promised to form part of the Christian empire. In a letter dated
9 December 1492, Zafra referred to the Fez affair, about which he
planned to speak to Boabdil's servant El Caisí and to al-Mulih. He
expressed doubt over whether Boabdil would be interested in the
matter. It seems two messengers had already been sent to him on
the subject, but they had been rebuffed with scorn. Al-Mulih conveyed his master's response, which was that he had given his own
kingdom to live in peace, and was not prepared to go to a foreign
kingdom and have his integrity called into question, even less so
under an Arab regime. Ferdinand and Isabella's demands were a
step too far, and it is not surprising that Boabdil rejected outright
these further manifestations of their ruthless hunger for power.

By the end of 1492, it had been accepted on both sides that
Boabdil and his entourage would go overseas, provided all the necessary agreements and mutual promises had been ratified. According
to Zafra's letter of 8 December, when he must have thought that their
arrival was imminent, the departure was timed to coincide with
Ferdinand and Isabella's return to Granada. But matters took a dramatically different turn. On 7 December of that year, Ferdinand was
gravely wounded by an attack by a madman in Barcelona. His recov-
ery and pressing political negotiations affecting the crown of Aragon
made it impossible for him to return to Granada. When Boabdil
heard this news, he sent a delegation of the gentlemen of his household to visit the convalescent king, and wrote a very solicitous letter
to him in which he proposed to travel to Barcelona in February of
1493 to conclude the arrangements for his departure. Evidently, the
last thing the Catholic Monarchs wanted was to receive a visit from
the man whose kingdom they had conquered; to show favour to the
Moorish sultan in public would have looked suspect after what they
had promoted as their crusade against the infidel. Ferdinand and
Isabella resolutely opposed his coming, asking Zafra to get him to
desist, and giving the reason that it would delay his departure even
more to come to Barcelona, when the matter was best concluded in
Granada itself. They requested Zafra to deal with whatever Boabdil
demanded, and to let them know his requirements.

But Boabdil was not going to be fobbed off, and although he

didn't travel in person, he sent on his behalf Aben Comixa, who had an audience with the Christian Monarchs on 17 March 1493. His mandate was to ask them for permission for Boabdil to depart for north Africa, and to propose the purchase of his lands to them, without including rights of inheritance. The price he asked was 21,000 gold castellanos. Ferdinand and Isabella pretended that they truly wished he would remain in their kingdoms, and feigned a promise to respect his desire to go overseas and grant him the amount requested, which was to be released a week before his departure. At this point there seems to have been some cloud over Boabdil's relationship with his long-term retainer Aben Comixa. It was al-Mulih who took over the administration of the departure, and there is an unsubstantiated rumour that Comixa attempted to murder the sultan. Some old Moors averred that, when Boabdil knew the sale of lands was complete, he was so grief stricken that he would have killed Comixa if he hadn't been removed from his presence. Whatever the case, he was certainly out of favour as his name no longer appears on official documents of this time. In Granada on 15 April 1493 al-Mulih ratified the document outlining the terms of the departure, although he claimed the right to reject it if necessary. He stated that he wished to be compliant, and would grant agreement provided Ferdinand and Isabella added certain clauses specifying the particular ships and their owners that were to be used for the sea journey, which were to be well armed for protection. He also requested on Boabdil's behalf a respected and authoritative representative of the Christian Crown to accompany them for greater safety, as well as insisting that Boabdil should receive the money from the sale of his lands a month before departure, not a week.

The Catholic Monarchs finally agreed to these terms and swore to uphold them on 15 June 1493. On 8 July Boabdil did the equivalent in the town of Andarax, ratifying the document in his own hand. He must have been slow, perhaps reluctant, to send the signed and ratified document, which represented his final farewell to his native land, because Zafra told the Christians in July that he was awaiting its arrival and each day seemed like a hundred years. Still the delays continued. It proved very difficult for Zafra to evaluate the correct rents on the land sold, and to set the actual prices for their sale. The secretary tried to use a type of assessment similar to the one Boabdil had used in trade with the Genoans, but al-Mulih and Aben Comixa, now back on the scene, refused to accept it, and complained to the local archbishop. He agreed with them, and the terms of the assessment were revised, but then the actual values couldn't be agreed, as Comixa insisted on using 1492 values and Zafra 1493 rates. He was given a terrible time over this by Ferdinand and Isabella, who didn't answer his queries and requests for help for two months, so that no one knew how to proceed.

In the midst of this wrangling, tragedy struck Boabdil once more. On 28 August his beloved wife Moraima died in Andarax. She had been ill for some time, though the chronicles don't say with what. Some stories say she died of a broken heart after the years of anxiety over her son held hostage, and because of the impending exile from her homeland. This must have been a catastrophic blow for Boabdil, in the wake of what he had already endured. He left his wife buried on Spanish soil in the ancestral cemetery in Mondújar in the Valle de Lecrín, which was linked to his country estate. When he had handed over the Alhambra, the remains of his ancestors and family had been transferred there, a deed made clear by the discovery in 1925 of seventy tombs in the Nasrid mausoleum of the Rauda cemetery just outside the Moorish palace, all of which were empty except one.

Zafra announced the death of Moraima to Ferdinand and Isabella, judging heartlessly that this would be favourable to the conclusion of the matter of Boabdil's departure, since her illness had hampered the preparations. Finally, a royal decree arrived on 29 August empowering him, the local archbishop and the Count of Tendilla to arrange everything relating to the sultan's voyage. There was yet another delay while all the necessary monies owing to Boabdil were brought together, with Zafra noting in his tart manner that, in spite of his friendly relations with the Moors, they continually haggled with him, objecting to the quality of the silver coins in the payoff, and asking for them to be melted down. By 2 October 1492 he had finally overcome all the financial problems, and the fleet of ships was ready and waiting in the port of Adra. It is a coincidence of destiny that Boabdil's port of departure to Africa was the same place where the great founder of Arab Muslim civilisation in Spain, Abd al-Rahman I, disembarked when he fled from Damascus seven centuries earlier. The secretary went at once to Adra with the idea of letting his royal employers know the day and hour when Boabdil left the Granadan coast for ever, accompanied by his whole family apart from his sister, who remained in Spain and married a Christian. From a fragment of a letter dated 3 November 1493, we can deduce that this took place in mid-October, though Zafra himself didn't go on the ship. He expressed great joy at Boabdil's departure, equalled by that of Ferdinand and Isabella, whose only regret was that the sultan's son, whom they had kept prisoner for so long in Moclín and Porcuna, had left with his father, as Isabella had hopes of converting him to Christianity. There is no record of how Boabdil and his retainers, including his two sons, felt at their departure. Maybe relief as well as despair and overwhelming grief.

The Italian historian of Spain, Peter Martyr of Angleria, writing in the decades after 1492, noted the irony of Boabdil going into exile in north Africa to become the subject of weak kings when, until recently, he was 'great and fearful to all Spaniards'. This insight into the way Boabdil was perceived outside Spain flatly contradicts later perceptions of the emir as weak and ineffectual. What we know about Boabdil's life in north Africa has all the makings of a good detective story. There are conflicting opinions of what happened. One is that he disembarked in Cazaza just eleven miles (eighteen kilometres) from Melilla, which is still an autonomous Spanish town, and from there travelled to Fez, where he remained. The Arab historian al-Maqqari added that Boabdil had planned to go from Fez to Marrakech, but did not manage it, and during his journey suffered great discomfort, with outbreaks of plague all around him. Once he was established in Fez he had a royal palace built in the area of the city known as al-Andalus, where Andalusi families of Berber descent had traditionally lived. Al-Maqqari says he personally saw his house and went inside. He recorded that Boabdil died in 1532 or 1533, when he would have been about seventy-two years old, and was buried in front of the Almozala, outside the port of Xarea. According to the Arab historian, the sultan left two sons alive, Ahmed and Yusuf, and he claimed that his descendants were still living in Fez in 1627, although some said they were beggars living on alms.

An alternative theory was advanced in the late nineteenth century by the Arabist M. C. Brosselard, who claimed that Boabdil went first to Oran in western Algeria, which is the most direct route from the port of Adra, then on to Tlemcen, where he died in May 1494 at the age of about thirty-four. Brosselard's interest was piqued by the account of George Horn, a Dutch historian, who wrote in 1666 that Abu Abdullah, known as El Zogoibi, was exiled in Africa, in the realm of the king of Tlemcen. How he came upon this information isn't known, but it conflicts with the other views that Boabdil ended up in Fez. It seems strange that al-Maqqari would not have known this, as he came from Tlemcen himself, but Brosselard suggests the Arab historian was using hearsay, in spite of his claim to have visited Boabdil's palace in Fez. Brosselard thinks that the confusion between Fez and Tlemcen comes from a confusion of people and names, basing his view on his discovery near the ruined mosque of the Bani Ziyán in Tlemcen of what he believed was the Granadan sultan's tombstone, complete with epitaph. He writes that during the demolition of some old Arab houses near the Sidi Ibrahim mosque to make way for a new road, workmen were surprised to find that the threshold of one of the houses was formed of an onyx plaque covered with a long inscription. No one knew the origin of the inscription or what it meant, only that it had been there since time immemorial. It was referred to the military authorities of Tlemcen, who kept it for some years before it was given to the newly created town museum. No one had been able to decipher the inscription until Brosselard's attempt. It turned out to be an epitaph consisting of thirty-two closely written lines in Andalusian script, on an onyx marble slab three feet long by eighteen inches wide and just over two inches thick (ninety-one by forty-four by six centimetres). It states that it covers the tomb of a king who died in exile, a stranger to Tlemcen, who fought for the faith. It continues: *This tomb is that of the just, magnanimous, generous king, defender of religion, emir of the Muslims, our lord Abu-Abdullah, victorious by the grace of Allah, son of our lord the emir of Muslims, Abu l-Hasan,* and goes on to describe his war against the Christians, and his arrival in Tlemcen, where he was given a warm welcome. This revelation appears to be conclusive evidence of Boabdil's final resting place. Brosselard attributes the Fez alternative to confusion arising from the fact that El Zagal, also exiled to north Africa, arrived at Fez according to certain historians, and was alleged to have ended up begging in that city with a notice tied round his neck stating 'I am the unfortunate king of Andalusia'. El Zagal shared the same *kunya*, Abu Abdullah, with his nephew Boabdil, and both were sultans of Granada. Not surprisingly, he claimed, historians thought it was Boabdil who had gone to Fez, when it was in fact his uncle. Although the current Tlemcen town website proudly states: 'Carved epitaphs from the royal tomb of Boabdil, the last Moorish King of Granada, who died in Tlemcen in 1494 are among the treasures to be seen at the Tlemcen Museum,' Brosselard's attribution of the sepulchre and epitaph to Boabdil was discounted by some later historians on the basis that some records, notably certain letters written by Hernando de Zafra, assert that El Zagal was exiled to Tlemcen and lived there. This seems strange, considering that the epitaph refers to Abu Abdullah as the son of Abu l-Hasan and not his brother.

One account of Boabdil's death that can definitely be dismissed is that of the Spanish historian Luis del Mármol Carvajal, who wrote that Boabdil had asked the king of Fez for asylum, and after many long years in that city, he was killed in battle at the river Ouad-al-Asouad, at the head of a troop of Marinid cavalry, fighting against the troops of the Shah of Morocco. Mármol points out acidly that the king of Granada died defending a foreign kingdom when he had not wanted to risk his life in the defence of his own. The claim is eccentric, to say the least, since the battle concerned took place in 1536, when Boabdil would have been at least seventy-six years old. The story was taken up in a handful of later texts, and it unfortunately contributed to the negative image of Boabdil that has festered in the minds of certain writers and historians.

The search for Boabdil's final resting place has recently intensified, though the outcome is no less mysterious. In 2014 a team of experts including forensic anthropologists and georadar specialists, led and sponsored by Mr Mostafa Abdulrahman of Abu Dhabi and accompanied by the Spanish film-maker Javier Balaguer, went to

Fez with the aim of exhuming Boabdil's remains. They followed the references given by al-Maqqari, which suggested to them that the Granadan sultan lies buried beneath the humble mausoleum which was once a chapel dedicated to a local saint named Sidi Bel Kasen and called Bad al-Sharia, near what is now known as Bab al-Mahruq or the Gate of the Burnt One. Today the mausoleum, a square domed structure with four horseshoe-arched apertures, one on each side, is defiled by urine and faeces, broken glass bottles and rubbish of all kinds, for it has become a shelter for drunks and beggars. There is no certainty that this is Boabdil's tomb, but the results of the georadar revealed that human remains belonging to at least two skeletons are buried in that spot, marked by two tombstones. This is a good indication of the burial place of a royal personage, since sultans were habitually buried next to some important religious figure, in this case the saint Sidi Bel Kasen after whom the chapel was named. What is needed next is to extract a small sample of the remains to test its DNA and compare it with the DNA of identified people who claim to be the descendants of Boabdil. Although the Municipality of Fez was willing to support the project, and presented it as an example of cross-frontier cooperation between Spain and Morocco, it ran up against a brick wall due to problems initially with the religious community and then over whether the ministerial Department of Islamic Affairs should be in charge, or the Department of Culture. The Moroccans do not have the money or desire to finance the research themselves, in spite of firm support from the Andalusi Memories Association, which has denigrated the sorry state of the mausoleum in the press. Dr Kenza Ghali, adviser to Fez town council, asserted that there had been no proposal so far to transfer Boabdil's mortal remains back to Spain, since it was a huge decision related to the history and heritage of the sovereign country of Morocco. She described the sultan as 'a great man whose character has been blackened by certain historians'. So the impasse continues, but if Mr Abdulrahman and his team can succeed in gaining permission to carry out DNA testing, it could tell us conclusively that Boabdil was not in fact buried there, if there is no DNA match. If there is a match, the ambiguity would still remain, as there would be no foolproof way of distinguishing between Boabdil's DNA and that of his uncle, who would be the other candidate for burial as a royal personage.

Boabdil remains as enigmatic in death as in life, a spectral figure exiled and homeless, his last resting place unconfirmed. The case for a tomb in Fez rests firstly on the knowledge that Boabdil approached the king of Fez asking for protection in exile, and we know that he received a positive response, which suggests it was the sultan's first choice as a place of residence. However, it is possible that Ferdinand and Isabella's plan to use Boabdil to incite conflict in Morocco was derailed when they learned of the warm welcome awaiting him from the king of Fez. They may have tried to put him off a final destination of Fez, or he may have gone there but not remained. If his uncle, El Zagal, were already there, that would have been an added deterrent. In second place, the historical evidence that Boabdil went to Fez originates in the work of a historian who was writing over one hundred years later and had incorporated some Christian historians' work into his own. If Boabdil's earthly remains are in Fez, rarely has a king had a more unworthy resting place.

Nevertheless, the arguments for Boabdil's sepulchre lying in Tlemcen are persuasive. To reach Fez from Melilla, one suggested point of disembarkation, is a journey of over 200 miles (325 kilometres) across harsh deserts and mountainous terrain; Oran to Tlemcen is half that distance. Boabdil was still in Andarax at the time of the expulsion of the Jews later in 1492, when many Jewish exiles made their way to Tlemcen, and were welcomed and supported financially by its enlightened Jewish viceroy, Abraham. Under its tolerant Muslim king, the city became a well-known refuge for both Jewish and Muslim exiles from Spain, so by the time Boabdil made his crossing in the autumn of 1493, it would have been an obvious place to aim for; one where he would have been assured of a warm greeting, as is stated on the marble slab of his alleged tombstone. That epitaph also describes how death surprised him there, as if he died suddenly and unexpectedly in 1494. The harrowing time he had been through, followed by the rigours of the journey, would have weakened his constitution, and the local famine and the presence of the plague in that area all combine to suggest that an untimely death is a strong possibility. The person whose grave was covered by the marble slab must have been highly respected, given that some wealthy individual, maybe even the viceroy Abraham himself, had been willing to pay for it and to take the trouble of composing such an eloquent and poignant epitaph. No such memorial exists in Fez. For the present, the location of Boabdil's tomb, far from the mausoleum of his ancestors in Mondújar, remains a matter for speculation until such time as conclusive evidence can be found that he is buried in either Fez or Tlemcen.

What of the people who remained in Granada after Boabdil had gone into internal, then external, exile? For a period of eight years, Granada was a predominantly Mudejar city, remaining almost totally Islamic, with most of the leaders of Boabdil's administration and local government still in place, although the city was ruled by a small group of upper-class Christians, soldiers, lawyers and clergymen. We are lucky to have the detailed travelogue of a German physician, Hieronymus Münzer, who studied at the University of Pavia and went to Nuremberg to practise as a doctor. Münzer, who was also a good geographer and astronomer, made a long journey through Spain, France and Germany between 1494 and 1495, and spent five months in the Iberian peninsula travelling on horseback, during which time he arrived in 'the great and glorious city of Granada' on 22 October 1494, two years and eight months after Boabdil surrendered power, and one year after his exile. Münzer shows a markedly pro-Christian attitude towards the Granadan war, claiming that Ferdinand's generous mind conceived the 'elevated undertaking of throwing the Saracens out of Granada'. He dwells on what he perceives as the cruelty and corruption of the Muslims, who had apparently kept over 20,000 Christians prisoner in the city in terrible suffering, dragging chains and forced like beasts to plough the land and carry out the most sordid, denigrating tasks. He also points out that the city fell partly because of the large amounts of gold and silver used to grease the palms of the Moorish governors of many fortresses, who handed them over to the Christians and used the money to fund their escape to north Africa. Gold and silver become symbolic in an apocryphal anecdote that Münzer includes in his account, in which the king of Granada – evidently Boabdil, though he is not named directly – finally realised that Ferdinand was determined to take his city, and called together his nobles and lords, then spread a checked rug on the floor before them. He placed a silver tray laden with gold upon it, and said: 'Whoever can lift the tray without treading on the rug can have the gold it carries.' As no one was able to do this, the king began to roll up the rug little by little, so that the tray was driven off it and could be easily reached. 'The neighbouring cities,' he said, 'are the rug and Granada is the tray of gold. The king of Castile is taking over those cities, and so in the end, Granada will fall into his hands.'

Münzer's view that Ferdinand aimed to expel the Muslims from Granada clashes with his findings as he explores the city. He describes the splendid main Mosque, 66 yards wide and 113 long (60 by 103 metres), with rush mats on the floor and a patio with a central fountain for ablutions, as well as nine rows of columns, thirteen on each side, plus 130 arches. 'We saw many beautiful lamps lit and priests wearing a white tunic and white headcloth chanting their hours in their own way, which was a very sad clamour rather than singing. The temple was made with extraordinary richness.' There was also an enormous candelabrum bearing over one hundred candles, used for festivals. Münzer records over 200 smaller mosques in the city, so that at night the clamour from the minarets was so loud it was hard to imagine. He singles out the small mosque in the Albaicín, which was lovely, he asserts, with eighty-six free-standing columns, smaller but more beautiful than the main mosque, with a pretty garden planted with lemon trees. The German makes special note of the Muslim beliefs and rituals he observed, such as Friday prayer meetings, ritual washing before entering the mosque, the fact that only men were permitted to enter (against Koranic instructions) and Muslim generosity in the giving of alms. He admires the diligence of the Muslims at prayer, as the muezzin calls two hours before dawn, at midday and in the evening, as well as sometimes at two in the morning, as happened in the mosque adjacent to his inn, he notes. He remarks that they greatly venerated the Virgin Mary, Saint Catalina and Saint John, after whom many named their children. Münzer examines a kind of rosary made from date stones shown to him by an old Muslim who told him that the stones allegedly came from the palm tree whose fruit the Virgin ate on her flight into Egypt. He claimed it was beneficial for pregnant women, and brought good luck.

Hieronymus Münzer was enchanted by Granada. His doctor's eye perceived the advanced sewerage system with running water, as well as urns used as urinals, and plentiful wells of clean drinking water. He knew the Count of Tendilla, who took him to the Alhambra, where he saw its ceilings and cupolas made of gold, lapis lazuli, ivory and cypress wood. Tendilla told him that Boabdil had a helmet in the shape of a pomegranate, the symbol of Granada, bearing the motto *Only God is Conqueror*, a motif Münzer saw painted on many walls of the Alhambra in sky blue. He also saw the special door Ferdinand had made that allowed him to enter and leave the Alhambra unobserved, thus both avoiding having to mix with the Muslims in the street, and preventing their humiliation at the sight of their conqueror. The German declared that there was nothing similar to Granada in all of Europe, 'since it is all so magnificent, so majestic, so exquisitely fashioned, that the onlooker cannot be sure that he is not in a kind of paradise'.

His travel diary shows that, in spite of Christian wishes to the contrary, over two and a half years since Granada fell, Islam was still thriving in the city. The terms of Boabdil's capitulations, which had included an amendment by Ferdinand and Isabella to forbid the Muslim call to prayer, had clearly had little effect at that stage. Hernando de Zafra again came to the fore and used his wiles to encourage the Granadan military aristocracy to follow Boabdil into exile, hoping, no doubt, that with the old leaders gone there would be no incitement to rebellion. By 1495, Zafra reported, most of the Abencerrajes and other powerful leaders were selling all their property and packing up ready to leave, and by the end of that summer there would be only farm workers and craftsmen left. Just five years later, the end of Islam as a public religion in Granada arrived, as Christian hopes of a quiet conversion to their religion were foiled by armed revolt by Granadans outraged at the brutal Inquisitor General Cardinal Cisneros, whose mass burning of Arabic books in the Plaza Bib-Rambla of Granada and his obsessive zeal for conversion made nonsense of the concessions once agreed to and now so treacherously abandoned by the Catholic Monarchs.

The peerless Granada described so clearly by Münzer, where Islam had still flourished, was now once more a place of trauma for its Muslim inhabitants. Contemporary evidence confirms this. Sometime in the first half of the sixteenth century, a young man from the town of Arévalo in the province of Ávila in Castile, where Queen Isabella spent time when she was a girl, wrote a commentary on the Koran known as the *Tafsira*, or treatise. Although we don't know his name, we do know that he was a crypto-Muslim, in other words he continued to practise Islam clandestinely after conversion to Christianity was forced upon the Spanish Mudejars by the decrees of 1501 and 1502. He wrote his treatise in Aljamiado, a secret language invented by crypto-Muslims which was written in Castilian although it used the Arabic alphabet. The young man was learned and expert in the reading of Arabic, Hebrew, Greek and Latin, and his work includes the fundamentals of the faith and rites of Islam. What is particularly interesting is his record of his travels throughout the Iberian peninsula, copying down the knowledge of the old Moriscos he met. He interviewed several of the survivors of the fall of Granada, and provides us with an intensely personal interpretation of the tragedy of the Muslim community in Spain after 1492. His encounters with some of the most prestigious figures of the Morisco community reveal their pain, hopes and fears as they struggled to cope with the reality that faced them. With a modern-day journalist's eye for detail and for the circumstantial, the young Morisco describes the detailed conversations he held in the aftermath of Boabdil's surrender of the city.

One extraordinary figure interviewed by the Morisco from Arévalo was a very elderly woman known as the Mora de Úbeda, a Moorish woman who originally came from the town of Úbeda on the border between Granada and Castile. When he met her she was ninety-three years old, and lived in the Albaicin in Granada, close to the Puerta de Elvira. Her powerful physical presence had a strong impact on the young man, who recounts that her body and limbs were so large they scared him. He had never seen anyone like her before, a woman whose little finger was bigger than his middle finger. She wore rough twill clothes and esparto-grass sandals and lived alone in great simplicity, having never been married. She had been very influential in the time of Boabdil and his fifteenth-century predecessors and was a prestigious commentator on the Koran. Although she couldn't read, she could argue with great judgement and wisdom. The young Morisco tells us that although her speech was rough and coarse, no one could equal her in teasing out the most transcendental meanings of the Koran. She was greatly impressed by her interviewer, and told him that if he remained in her company he would inherit her books and possessions, which he declined, remarking tartly that he was not greedy like the Spanish. The Mora no longer fasted during Ramadan, prayed sitting down and did not leave her house because of her great age; since things had changed for the worse for Muslims, she had withdrawn from public life, he says, into the shadows of her unhappiness to weep over the fall of the Nasrid Islamic state. Before this she had an important role at the Nasrid court, which was to sign and seal the books of the kings of Granada, and she had been given certain volumes by Boabdil when he left the city. This ancient sage was directly affected by the Christian conquest of the city, during which she lost all her relatives except for a niece, Aixa. She also witnessed the terrible destruction of Arabic books in the Plaza Bib-Rambla, and was greatly moved by it as she was in effect present at the destruction by edict of the culture of her elders. The young man reports her words: 'I saw the Holy Book in the hands of a merchant who was tearing it up to use as paper for children, and I gathered up all the pieces, which broke my heart.'

The young man takes his leave of the Mora and at her suggestion visits another distinguished figure in the local community, an Islamic teacher called Yuse Banegas, whose classes on the Koran he attends, given in the strictest secrecy and at the risk of their lives. Yuse had an expert knowledge of Arabic and Hebrew, and his possession of books in those languages shows that their prohibition by the Christians was scorned by the Morisco minority. Yuse was a person of some material as well as cultural wealth, which has led to the supposition that he was a member of the prestigious Banegas or Venegas family of Granada, which was involved in the surrender capitulations. That family enjoyed certain civil liberties, including in all likelihood religious freedom. Yuse clearly saw the tragedy that had struck down the Moriscos. He describes his personal losses and the enormous pain and indignation he felt in witnessing the shaming and selling of Muslim women at public auction. In a sermon delivered out in the *vega* beside a stream, Yuse laments:

> In my opinion nobody ever wept over such a misfortune as that of the sons of Granada. Do not doubt what I say, because I am one myself, and an eyewitness, for with my own eyes I saw all the noble ladies, widows and married, subjected to mockery, and I saw more than 300 young women sold at public auction. I will tell you no more, as it is more than I can bear. I lost three sons, all of them died defending our religion, and I lost two daughters and my wife, so that one daughter was left to be my consolation, though she was only seven months old at the time.

The failure of the Christian authorities to fulfil the terms of the capitulations meant that the Muslim community lost its privileges and freedoms; it also threatened their religious and cultural identity. Yuse expresses his horror at the realisation that his own relatives created an atmosphere favourable to the handover of the city, without suspecting the consequences. Finally, the young Morisco from Arévalo visits another Granadan Muslim, Ali Sarmiyento, who had been an imam in Granada, who offers his version of the fall of the city. He owned a safe-conduct in Latin from King Ferdinand dated 1499, and he had protected status, enabling him to continue to maintain a large Muslim household. Precisely why he was granted such privileges by the Christian king is not clear, although there are plausible theories that he was an informer for the Christians, and it is likely that he played a significant role in the surrender of Granada. When the young man visited his home in a village outside Granada, the imam was over a hundred years old, but he vividly remembered seeing the Muslim battle standards exchanged for Christian flags, women insulted and the entire Muslim nobility destroyed and in decline. He also recounts how men gambled for Muslim women and sold them in public. The terms of surrender, he sighed, were all painful, bitter aloes.

The writings of the young Morisco from Arévalo give us an insight into how the conquered Granadans felt in the immediate aftermath of Boabdil's departure. The witnesses he interviewed had lived prominent lives in Islamic, Arabic-speaking Granada, and were present at the collapse of the last Islamic state in the Iberian peninsula. There are almost no other contemporary historical accounts written from a Muslim perspective, although the despair of these eyewitnesses is echoed in a handful of poems written in Arabic which convey the deeply personal reactions of the poets who lived through the Granadan war. One Andalusian poem deploring the war is thought to have been written initially by Aboûl Baqâ Câlih' ben Chérif, a native of the town of Ronda, and finished by another poet after his death. Written in yellowish Arab ink made from burnt wool and water, it is possible to make out the date of the manuscript as Sunday 10 June 1492, six months after the surrender of Granada. The poem is an elegy, one of the classic forms of Arabic poetry, in which the poet must freely express his pain and regrets with beauty and refinement, and it consists of 144 lines. King Ferdinand rounded on Ronda in May 1485 and overcame it using artillery and by cutting off the water supply. The poet expresses his disbelief and shock at the loss of a town considered to be impenetrable because of its famous natural defences. 'Has the light really gone out in the sky over Ronda?' he asks. 'Have shadows covered the refuge of power reaching the height of the flying eagle, where Islam had perished?' The crucifix, statues and images are now worshipped and bells replace the call of the muezzin from its minarets as mosques are transformed into churches. Like the Granadan testimonies, the Ronda poet speaks of young girls stripped of their veils and taken hostage by the Christians, with no thought for their dignity or modesty. Children were torn from their mothers' arms, taken to priests and forcibly baptised, old women were left dying of thirst and hunger. The Christian chronicles are noticeably silent on such subjects.

Aboûl Baqâ blames this terrible setback on the Muslims, who have forgotten their duty to Allah. He exhorts them to repent, submit, give alms and persist in the holy war, inciting them to vengeance. The keynotes of this poem are pain, darkness, burning and tears, as it depicts the violation of the Granadan land by the Christians as if it were a woman, and praises its capital as the sublime seat of royalty, shining brightly, unparalleled and incomparable. Muslim disobedience to Allah is reiterated, and the defection of Muslims to the Christian side is gravely lamented. The Ronda poet's question 'Can Ronda ever hope to return to Islam?' is repeated by the historian al-Maqqari and other writers who describe the loss of Granada and al-Andalus, who add the refrain which has echoed down the centuries: 'May Allah assure its return to Islam'.

Ibn al-Qaysi al-Basti was born in Baza in the early fifteenth century, and became imam and governor of that town in his later years. Some fragments of his poetry survive, the incompleteness of which seems to reflect the broken lives of al-Basti and his fellow Muslims, whom he records as homeless, sleepless and exiled after the siege of Baza in 1489. He tells us that the towns of Lorca and Archidona have been violated, and he blames disunity, corruption, deception and trickery on the part of his co-religionaries. His vocabulary of fall, loss, exile, enmity, abandonment, blood and tears sums up the distress and despair of the Muslims of the kingdom of Granada as well as reflecting the real conditions of life in al-Andalus at this time.

Shame, misfortune and calamity are also the dominant word choices of what was probably the last poem produced in Islamic al-Andalus, written in 1501 in Arabic by an anonymous bard. This beautiful *qasida*, an ode traditionally used to petition a patron, is addressed to the most powerful Muslim leader of the time, the Ottoman emperor Bayazid II, who reigned from 1481 to 1512. The poet hopes to enlist his support in restoring the fortunes of Spanish Islamic rule in simple, sincere and sorrowful language. He emphasises the betrayal of the Christians, who have forced his people to convert to Catholicism, which raises the question of apostasy, punishable by death in Islamic law. He stresses the intention of the Granadans to remain Muslims in secret, invoking the doctrine of *taqiyya'*, which is a legal dispensation for an individual Muslim under threat of persecution to dissimulate or commit acts which would otherwise be blasphemous. Again he describes the violation of the terms of the surrender treaty, and Cisneros's public book burning, punishments for not attending Mass and the forced consumption of pork and wine. The poet exposes the duplicity of Ferdinand and Isabella, who had informed the Egyptian and Turkish envoys at court that any conversions of Moriscos had been entirely voluntary, when in fact, he says, it was fear of death and burning that made them comply. The significance of this last creative vestige of Islamic Spain is considerable, as it reveals a major religious crisis in a community shrouded in dissimulation, and plainly contrasts the tolerant attitude of Islam to other religions in the past with the contemporary Christian intolerance and persecution, a theme that would come to the fore in later Morisco writing.

The surrender of Granada captured the imagination of Andalusian poets, whose body of writing mourned the calamitous loss of the country to which they felt a deep sense of belonging and attachment, and incited Muslims to continue the holy war. Their verse, the eyewitness accounts recorded by the young man from Arévalo and the observations of the German traveller Münzer open a window on to a country undergoing irrevocable change. The sorrow of external exile experienced by Boabdil and the many Muslims who followed suit and emigrated to north Africa after January 1492 is matched by the grief of those who remained, who felt as if they were internal exiles, strangers in their own land. There is no blame for Boabdil in any of these writings, or indeed any significant reference to him. A new chapter was beginning for Spanish Muslims, which reached its nadir with the Morisco expulsions starting in 1609. But that is another story. In the late fifteenth century, Granadans were coming to terms with a world different from the one they had known, and the last sultan of Granada was left to languish in a foreign country, along with his memory, while more pressing issues of religious and racial tension took precedence. The enigma of his death and burial, both uncertain and unrecorded like his date of birth, befits a man whose life was full of mystery and absences. But he was not forgotten by posterity, as history gave way to fiction and legend, which recreated Boabdil's persona in contradictory and conflicting ways that often recall the divergent and confusing contemporary interpretations of his life and deeds.

8

Boabdil in Fiction and Legend

Today, in almost exactly the same place in Granada where Boabdil handed the keys of the city to King Ferdinand, a pair of life-sized bronze statues stand in a flower bed in a small gravelled park surrounded by towering blocks of flats. The park is well off the beaten tourist track, close to a large modern conference centre, and bears no sign or indication of who the statues represent. Their out-of-the-way location and understated tribute and homage belie the historical importance of their subject. In this encounter amid roses and pomegranate trees, a bearded man wearing a turban sits on a throne looking down sadly at a young woman, her head lowered in humility as she offers him a rose. This poignant monument, sculpted by the Madrid artist Juan Moreno Aguado, was unveiled on 2 January 1997 as a memorial to the last Moorish sultan in Spain. The young woman represents Granada, who offers Boabdil a rose as a symbol of love and in hope of forgiveness. There is no previous public monument to acknowledge the expulsion, or even the presence, of the Moors who were so fundamental to the city's historical memory, and it wasn't until the 1990s that the more progressive sectors of the city, albeit under the jurisdiction of the right-wing mayor José Gabriel Díaz Berbel, stirred up a polemic which resulted in the installation of Aguado's commemoration of the Nasrid emir. Its message of love and reconciliation marks a special moment in the evolution of the perception of Boabdil. This perception has been shaped by the literature, art and music which has repeatedly evoked him as a legendary figure, whose story has been adapted to confront issues relating to national identity as well as political, racial and religious crises.

The ceremonial, theatrical quality of Boabdil's surrender on 2 January 1492 was reproduced in countless celebrations of the Christian victory in Europe, but nowhere more lavishly than in Rome. Processions were organised to proclaim the success of Ferdinand and Isabella, and many other religious ceremonies and public festivals are recorded in Italian towns. The Pope's master of ceremonies, Johannes Burckard, wrote in his diary that there were fireworks and bullfights in Rome, as well as tournaments in which knights in the guise of Christians and Moors fought with each other for several days. In a show of Spanish power that harked back to the triumphal marches held in ancient Rome, two Spanish bishops had a wooden castle built with a tower, a primitive symbolic imitation of the conquest of Granada, before which a procession passed by, with riders mimicking Ferdinand and Isabella waving the palms of victory, while Boabdil went humiliated in chains.

It is not surprising that the extreme drama of the fall of Granada was translated from street procession into theatre. A papal secretary from the northern Italian town of Cesena, Carlo Verardi, was bang up-to-date when he wrote his historical drama in Latin during the winter of 1492. The *Historia Baetica* (*History of Andalusia*) aimed to present the facts of the Christian conquest in a version of history which exalts and idealises the Catholic Monarchs as the instruments of Divine Providence. Verardi was the first person to present the latest news from Spain in dramatic form, in a work which became well known internationally. The play consists of twenty-three scenes, which start with Baudelis (Boabdil) discussing surrender with his advisers, one of whom praises the Spanish king's power and wealth, while another advises surrender and assures the sultan that King Ferdinand treats his prisoners like friends. Boabdil's inevitable fall is converted into a lionisation of Ferdinand and Isabella. The play, full of spectacle and pageantry, imitates the theatrical celebrations that took place earlier in the year in Rome. The Christian rulers are almost superhuman in their greatness, and Boabdil is a man bedevilled by bad luck, vacillating and alternately hopeful and despairing, but always a worthy rival of his enemies. Over a hundred years later, the giant of Spanish Golden Age theatre, Lope de Vega, renewed the theme of the conquest of Granada in his 1599 *Famosa Comedia del Nuevo Mundo* (*Famous Comedy of the New World*), but his Boabdil character, named Mahomed, is a minor personage in a cast whose protagonist is really Christopher Columbus, as the title suggests. Interestingly, Lope presents the conquest of the last Islamic state in Spain as setting the tone for Columbus's conquest of the New World, and harks back to the Muslim conquest of Spain in 711, when Mahomed/Boabdil describes Ferdinand as the man destined to restore the country lost as the tragic punishment of King Roderick. The sultan attributes the loss of Granada both to Christian envy and to their military strength, while Christian faith and material greed vie for supremacy in their conquest of the Americas in this thinly veiled criticism of the cupidity of the Spanish monarchy.

Boabdil's life story and the Granadan war were transformed into song over a period of almost 200 years, from the late 1500s to the mid-seventeenth century, in the cycles of sung poetry known as the frontier ballads. These poems tell stories from popular legend or about intense episodes of drama relating to national or local events, and were often used to send news from one town to another. The fall of Granada inspired a magnificent cycle of frontier ballads, many written by court poets to flatter the monarchs and grandees who were directly involved in the policy of reconquest. Composed by bards who were Christian and Spanish, they reflected the perspective of the victors, idealising the military aspects of the war and contributing to the aggrandisement of the new Spain. They were unique creations of the old Granadan frontier which still live on today. Yet Christian and political issues remain in the minor key and emotion and drama in the major, as Boabdil is portrayed compassionately as a man in the grasp of desolation and despair. In a ballad about the capture of Boabdil at Lucena the news of his imprisonment reaches the capital city, where the inhabitants set up a wailing and weeping for their 'good and dearly loved king'. Two fine ballads describe the approach of the Christian army before the siege of Granada, picturing

Boabdil as unable to speak with sadness and weeping in great distress at the imminent loss of his kingdom, while other poems strive to capture the sultan's state of mind, a mixture of deep melancholy, regret and nostalgia. The ballad of the Rey Chico, or Boy King, who lost Granada tells of his sadness but also of his cowardice, and the line 'yesterday I was a famous king and today I have nothing' recalls a similar line in the ballad which bemoans King Roderick's loss of his kingdom to the Muslims in 711. History has come full circle, as the Christian kingdom lost to the Moors by Roderick is lost in turn by Boabdil. The tone of the ballads of the conquest of Granada is usually neutral or often sympathetic to the Moorish king's situation, but this particular ballad gives an uncharacteristically negative picture of the sultan. It may be the earliest written version of the traditional legend we have already come across of the Moor's Last Sigh, which repeats Aixa's cruel words to her bedevilled son in the last lines of the poem. Probably a Morisco legend passed on by word of mouth, it was also repeated in a letter dated 1526 written by a priest, Fray Antonio de Guevara, which shows that the tradition of the last sigh was already well known by this time. In the Spanish ballads Boabdil's terrible destiny chimes with the overarching theme of the tragic nature of life which is so fundamental to these popular songs.

The myth of Boabdil's cowardice and weakness which emerged in the ballad of the Boy King deepened the negative perceptions stirred up by the *fatwa* of October 1483, which had strongly prejudiced the Granadans against him. An anonymous Castilian account from the mid-sixteenth century reveals that, following the verdict of the *fatwa*, 'when the Boy king returned to Granada, his followers abhorred him for making a pact with the Christians and using them as a weapon against his own father, and all the townships and many nobles of his faction deserted him'. This clearly expressed hatred of many Granadans for Boabdil that had been fomented by the censure of religious authorities was taken by the master shoemaker and admirer of Moorish culture Ginés Pérez de Hita and woven into his remarkable and influential two-volume historical novel *Guerras civiles de Granada* (*Civil Wars of Granada*), published in 1595, over a century after the actual events. The focus of Part I is the beheading of thirty-six members of the Abencerraje family by Boabdil, a deed carried out in reality by his grandfather Sa'd. While this beguiling combination of fact, fiction, prose and ballad created a new literary hero, the romanticised Moor, it was certainly not Boabdil but his retinue of Moorish knights that were sentimentalised and acclaimed. In contrast the Rey Chico is demonised as a violent and vicious tyrant, likened by his father to a cruel Nero with a thirst for beheading. Initially Boabdil is presented as a peacemaker between warring factions, but his fatal, Othello-like flaw is his poor judgement and gullibility in believing the story invented by the Zegrys about his wife Moraima, whom, they claimed, was having an adulterous affair with Albin Mahamete, the leader of the Abencerrajes. 'Deceived and ill-fated', Boabdil is driven to a dreadful revenge in severing the heads of thirty-six of the finest and most loyal noblemen of his court, followed by his wife and their two young boys. Eventually realising his ghastly mistake, and begging forgiveness for his blindness to the truth, Boabdil capitulates to Ferdinand and surrenders Granada. His tears of despair and grief are immortalised by Pérez de Hita, in his reprise of the legend of the Moor's Last Sigh: 'And when the Moorish king reached his house, which was in the Alcazaba, he began to weep for what he had lost. Upon which his mother told him that as he had been unable to defend his kingdom like a man, he did well to weep for it like a woman.' The now familiar incident of his weeping and his mother's cutting rebuke became widely known following the success of Pérez de Hita's unsentimental portrait of Boabdil as a gullible victim of deception, and came to have great resonance in future re-creations of the life of the deposed sultan.

Outside Spain, maurophilia reached the salons of France in the seventeenth century. In 1663 the novelist Mademoiselle de Scudéry published *Almahide ou l'Esclave Reine* (*Almahide or the Slave Queen*), the first Hispano-Moorish novel to appear in France. Boabdil appears in it as a young ambitious sovereign who takes a shine to the heroine, a lovely Muslim noblewoman brought up as a Christian. When the dramatic events in late fifteenth-century Granada caught the imagination of John Dryden, the first Poet Laureate and one of the most prominent English writers of the second half of the seventeenth century, he turned to *Almahide* for inspiration. His two-part play *The Conquest of Granada by the Spaniards* was first performed in London in January 1671. The ten acts of the drama contain some magnificent scenes and sets, and it was felt to be utopian by those who saw it, although the contemporary critic Langbaine accused Dryden of borrowing, stealing and copying all the action and characters from French and Spanish romances, and especially from Mademoiselle de Scudéry's novel. For the history, Dryden probably used Juan de Mariana's *Historiae de rebus Hispaniae* (*General History of Spain*), although he also drew on Pérez de Hita. From these unpromising sources, Dryden creates something quite special, whose hero is Almanzor, a Muslim born of Christians. While the battle for Granada is the main concern, the Spanish are kept generally in the background, and the action follows the two clans who were Pérez de Hita's protagonists, the Abencerrajes and the Zegrys. Almanzor, the lost son of the Duke of Arcos who fights for the Moors, falls in love with Almahide, who is engaged to Boabdil, here named Boabdelin. She loves Almanzor too, but will not betray her vows to Boabdelin, who is torn between his jealousy and his need for Almanzor. Almanzor and Almahide remain separated until the death of Boabdelin in the last act, when impediments are removed and the forbearing lovers can be united.

Dryden said he copied the moral of the play from Homer's maxim 'Union preserves a Common-wealth, and discord destroys it', and discord is the keynote in plot and action. Dryden's Boabdil rebukes his warring clans for fighting with each other:

> *every life*
> *You lavish thus, in this intestine strife,*
> *Does from our weak foundations, take one prop*
> *Which helpt to hold our sinking Country up.*

But discord is the undoing of the sultan too, as he neglects his crown because of his wedding to Almahide, and is consumed by his conflict with Almanzor. In the end, Boabdelin dies fighting, but throughout he is inferior to Almanzor, losing to him in love, and in popularity with the Granadans.

Dryden's decade of heroic writing, from 1665 to 1675, arose from the euphoria of restoration, with its apparent unity of prince and people, and the advancement of science, letters and trade. He uses the story of Boabdil and Granada to address the issues of his time, when England was coming to terms with a series of constitutional crises all concerned in some way with the obligations of princes and people. As in medieval Spain, there was a climate of religious tension in seventeenth-century England, in this case between Protestantism and Catholicism. Writers had the liberty to celebrate greatness, warn against weak kings, dissidence in subjects and vulnerability to foreign conquests, and in *The Conquest of Granada by the Spaniards*, the exotic stage life of the play raises by positive and negative example the possibility of decency and moral discipline in national affairs.

Boabdil's life story continued to enliven the stage in the eighteenth century, when he appeared as a character in several minor theatrical works in French and Spanish, in which he was portrayed variously as the man who dethroned Abu l-Hasan, as a brave but superstitious king, and as a violent and deceitful one. At the end of the century, the French poet and novelist Florian represented Boabdil as an evil son with a model father in his famous 1791 novel *Gonzalve de Cordoue* (*Gonzalo of Cordoba*). At this time, we can see that the last sultan of Granada was still a presence in the literary imagination, but a change was taking place. The combination of popular legend, lament and triumphant Christian rhetoric which had vilified Boabdil in the preceding centuries began to give way to a more ambivalent attitude towards him which we can see in his divergent interpretations. Soon, with the development of Romanticism and its rapt interest in medievalism and orientalism in the nineteenth century, the Muslim ruler was seen from a different perspective altogether. In 1826 Viscount François-René de Chateaubriand, the founder of French Romanticism, wrote his well-known *Aventures du dernier abencérage* (*Adventures of the Last Abencerraje*), which begins with the increasingly clichéd episode of Boabdil's tears and his mother's rebuke as he looks back at Granada. Although his sultan is the perpetrator of the terrible massacre of the Abencerrajes, taken straight from Pérez de Hita, the Moorish hero of the novella weeps in turn for Boabdil and feels sympathy for his unhappiness, which perhaps Chateaubriand understood only too well as a man who loved his own country and who had felt the pain of exile. The influence of

Chateaubriand, and the exotic appeal of Granada and its dramatic history, created a flurry of British Romantic literature in which the fall of the city and Boabdil's tears became central icons that inspired Lord Byron as well as the poetry of Felicia Hemans and the Scot George Moir, among others.

Yet Boabdil found his most unlikely champion in Washington Irving, the American whose *Tales of the Alhambra*, published in 1832 in the era of late Romanticism, turns the disparaging misconception of Pérez de Hita and others on its head. The master shoemaker had his reasons for his portrayal of the Rey Chico, but Irving launches a direct attack on the *Guerras civiles*, claiming that he, Irving, had examined all the authentic chronicles and letters written by Spanish authors contemporary with the Moorish king, as well as Arabian authorities in translation, and could find nothing to justify the accusations made in that work. He goes as far as to confess that 'there seems to me something almost criminal in the wilful perversion of this work'. Irving avoids referring to Boabdil as the Rey Chico, a nickname that draws attention to his plight and station as the older king's son, and describes him from the start using another epithet, El Zogoibi, the Unlucky One. He impresses on the reader the great difficulties Boabdil had to contend with: 'an inhuman father', 'a usurping uncle' and a reign 'distracted by external invasions and internal feuds'. He draws out the complexity of the young king's situation, pointing out that 'he was alternately the foe, the prisoner, the friend and always the dupe of Ferdinand, until conquered and dethroned by the mingled craft and force of that perfidious monarch'. So, Christians bad, Muslim good!

Irving was convinced that history turned unjustly against Boabdil because of Pérez de Hita's allegations of atrocity, asserting that 'never . . . was name more foully and unjustly slandered' since, throughout his turbulent and disastrous reign, Boabdil gave evidence of a mild, amiable character. On the other hand, Irving does detect what he calls a feebleness of spirit that deprived the sultan of grandeur and dignity, a personal bravery not matched by moral courage, rendering Boabdil wavering and irresolute in times of difficulty. An interesting view of Irving's portrayal of Boabdil is expressed by the twentieth-century American writer James Edward

Brunson, who interprets Irving's Islamic characters as objects of fear and a powerful challenge to white America, which evoke white racial anxiety and guilt, projected on to the black image. Yet Boabdil's loss of his kingdom became a fitting symbol of the collapse of the Old American South, and the secret society Momus-Louisiana went so far as to introduce Boabdil at the New Orleans carnival of 1873, and associated the Moors with heroic deeds, courage on the battlefield and Southern chivalry. The *New York Times* reported that the carnival actors portraying Boabdil and the Shah of Persia were seen leaving the Saint Charles Hotel in New Orleans with a bodyguard of 150 mail-clad warriors. Ironically, the hotel, one of the most exclusive in the city, was also where the enslaved had been auctioned.

Boabdil found another advocate in Louis Aragon. Aragon was born in Paris in 1897 and became a prominent literary and political figure. In 1924, along with André Breton and Philippe Soupault, he became a founding member of the Surrealist movement; he was a lifelong and active member of the Communist Party and in 1939 married a Russian radical, Elsa Triolet, who became his literary muse. Aragon was a key figure in the French Resistance during the Second World War, and after the war he became CEO of the Resistance publishers Editeurs français réunis. As a writer of novels and poetry, he was nominated four times for the Nobel Prize for Literature. In 1963 Aragon published *Le Fou d'Elsa* (*Crazy about Elsa*), a long work written in prose and verse, concerned with his familiar theme of love and intertwined with descriptions of the medieval Muslim culture of Spain. He sets the story of Boabdil as the background to an exploration of the relationships between the Muslim and Christian worlds. Aragon said he had waited forty years to be Boabdil's defender, remarking that a conquered king is always a cowardly traitor when the conquerors write the history, and pointing out that Boabdil's deformed image was born of Spanish poetry, Morisco ballad and his enemies' legends. He presents Boabdil's surrender and the fall of Granada as the beginning of the repression of the Muslim world, which continued in the French colonisation of parts of Africa, in particular Algeria and Tunisia. Writing at the start of the process of decolonisation in France, when feelings were running high, Aragon makes a political statement about the need for tolerance and for an appreciation of the cultural treasures of others.

In the last decades of the twentieth century, Boabdil took on a new stature as writers and other artists both inside and outside Spain rescued him from the opprobrium of history. Among the key figures, the Castilian playwright and poet Antonio Gala found great success with his novel *El manuscrito carmesí* (*The Crimson Manuscript*) in 1990. Winner of the prestigious Premio Planeta book prize, it uses the ploy of a secret and hidden manuscript written on the crimson paper of the Chancellery of Granada, which turns out to be the story of Boabdil's life set down by the sultan himself. Penned in his refuge in Fez in later life and written mostly in the present tense, his reflections on his family and the Granadan war are sincere and thoughtful, intimate and personal, as he defends himself against the accusations of history, which he shows to be unjust and unfounded. In a telling passage, when Boabdil describes his captivity after the Battle of Lucena, he observes that the Christians needed to eliminate his people because they constituted an example of their own moral failings and indecisiveness, and at the same time provoked their curiosity and embodied their highest secret aspiration. It is not so much that the Other is different, but that he or she is unnervingly similar or better. As Boabdil points out, the Castilians felt an overwhelming passion for Granada, which has never diminished. The history of Christians and Muslims in Spain, he says, is too long a list of betrayals, disloyalties, abuses of trust, broken promises, a monotonous string of wars scarcely interrupted by a monotonous string of peace treaties, all part of a strange game whose end it had been agreed to delay in advance. Perhaps more than any other writer, Gala sees into Boabdil's heart: in his imaginative exploration of Boabdil's relationships with his family, his court and the Christians, he gives us an eloquent evocation of the sultan's spirit and destiny.

Many people will be familiar with Salman Rushdie's 1995 magical realist novel *The Moor's Last Sigh*, his tale of an unloved son, a rejected outsider whose emotional and physical exile are mapped on to the figure of Boabdil as exiled sultan. Rushdie takes his title from Boabdil's legendary sigh, and the protagonist's mother, India's leading artist, creates a painting with that title, as does her lover,

Vasco Miranda, both depicting Boabdil's departure from Granada. The narrator, Moraes Zogoiby, known as 'Moor', whose family name is the same as Boabdil's epithet, traces the decline and disintegration of his eccentric family over several generations, leading to his own exile and imminent death in Andalusia. Boabdil is given an imaginary Indian Jewish ancestry which links him to Moraes, although most of the novel takes place in Bombay after 1939.

Why was Rushdie so interested in Boabdil? He doesn't refer to him until page eighty of the novel, when Abraham, Moraes's father, learns of the sultan's surrender of Granada 'without so much as a battle'. The potted account of the events of 2 January 1492 told to Abraham points out Boabdil's humiliation firstly by the Catholic Monarchs and then by his own mother, describing him as 'this blubbing male' and a 'mere cry-baby'. The sultan finds consolation in the arms of a Jewess, 'the dispossessed Spanish Arab and the ejected Spanish Jew', who abandons Boabdil and escapes to India, where she gives birth to his male child, Moraes's ancestor. Many years later, Moraes sits for his mother Aurora Zogoiby as she creates her 'Moor paintings', latterly images of exile and terror culminating in her masterpiece 'The Moor's Last Sigh', in which the sultan's face is a picture of horror, weakness, loss and pain, 'a condition of existential torment'. In her fantasy evocation of Boabdil in paint, he takes on an initial role in her work as a unifier of opposites, 'a standard-bearer of pluralism', which collapses into a new imagining of the hybrid as a weak and evil figure, haunted by the phantoms of his past, finally reduced to a pitiful and anonymous being buried in garbage. Aurora herself is a cruel reincarnation of his mother Aixa. Ultimately she gives Boabdil back his humanity in her art, as his portrait becomes that of her own and only son.

Bombay is equated with Granada, whose demise is attributed by Moraes to the fanaticism of Ferdinand and Isabella, and to the weakness of Boabdil, who failed to defend his great treasure. As Moraes nears death in the final pages, he gazes out towards the Alhambra on a distant hill, 'that monument to lost possibility that nevertheless has gone on standing, long after its conquerors have fallen'. What Moraes perceives, and what perhaps attracted Salman Rushdie to the unfortunate Moor's predicament, is that the Alhambra, symbol of Islamic presence in Spain, is a testament to our 'need for putting an end to frontiers, for dropping the boundaries of the self'. In the author's view, Bombay was destroyed through fanaticism and corruption, like Granada. Although his portrayal of Boabdil reveals a certain sympathy for the Nasrid ruler, it shows him as fallible and weak before the might of the Christian kings. Righteous avengers or murdering fanatics – take your choice, as Moraes puts it.

In 2004 the Zaragozan writer Magdalena Lasala published her novel *Boabdil, tragedia del último rey de Granada* (*Boabdil: The Tragedy of the Last King of Granada*), the third in a trilogy whose protagonists are major figures of Hispano-Muslim history, starting with the great tenth-century caliph Abd al-Rahman III, followed by the famous tenth-century general Almanzor and lastly Boabdil. Lasala's readable pen portrait of the last sultan of Granada is sympathetic if sentimental. Her Boabdil is innately elegant, refined and inclined to study and write poetry, and his fierce, militant father's rejection of him because of their difference is crucial to his evolution as a character. In this imaginative recreation, his uncle El Zagal has a deep bond with his nephew, regarding him as the son he never had, and describing his character as strong, loyal and brave. Deeply opposed to war, in spite of his bravery in battle, Boabdil strives to avoid the destruction of his city, and in particular of 'our marvellous Alhambra'. Lasala is insistent on the role of destiny in the life of the Muslim ruler, and casts him as a man bearing the inescapable weight of 'the inherited disaster of history on his shoulders'. Her reprise of the legendary rebuke of Aixa is given a satisfying twist as Boabdil retorts that not even his rage-filled and fanatical mother had the power to change their destinies in the end.

Contemporary Arab writers have also returned to Boabdil and the fall of Granada to address the relationship of modern Arab literature to the West, and to its own past. Spain is seen to be both part and not part of the Western Other, as the use of Andalusian motifs have become more radical and intense. Among these writers, the Damascus-born poet Nizar Qabbani sees the fall of Granada repeated in modern times, in a climate of implacable threat and disintegration. For the Egyptian historian and essayist Husayn Mu'nis, Granada continues to provide incomparable inspiration, and the

Egyptian writer Amal Dunqul situates Boabdil's loss of Granada among the great Arab tragedies, along with the loss of Jerusalem and the amputated map of Sinai. The Palestinian playwright Walid Abu-Bakr's play set in medieval Granada draws out parallels between al-Andalus, internally divided and externally threatened, and the Arab countries of the twenty-first century. This group of writers has created an imaginary historical landscape in which Granada is the supreme symbol of their own plight, and a site of profound nostalgia and longing. The theme has reached as far as Pakistan, where the popular novelist Naseem Hijazi wrote a classical historical novel, *Shaheen* (*The Eagle*) on the loss of the capital of al-Andalus.

The figure of Boabdil has also been the focus of a number of musical works, including five nineteenth-century operas and several shorter pieces. Two of the most important were the orchestral works *El adiós de Boabdil a Granada* (*Boabdil's Goodbye to Granada*) (1873) and *El tesoro de Boabdil* (*Boabdil's Treasure*) (1888), composed by Salvador Giner Vidal, director of the Valencian Conservatoire. The Granadan Francisco Alonso's *El sueño de Boabdil* (*Boabdil's Dream*) of 1909 evoked Granada as an icon of the exotic and oriental, and gave rise to a style known as Alhambrismo, which had recurring elements such as the Andalusian cadence of Flamenco and the ornamented melody associated with Arab music. *El sueño*, a symphonic poem for a band and choir, was well received by public and critics and is soft and melancholy, evoking African nights, and then resounding, sonorous, intense and martial, with trumpets evoking their use in battle, and the galloping of horses. It is majestic and proud, sentimental and sad as Boabdil gives a heartfelt cry of final farewell to his beloved Granada. Later in the twentieth century, cellist Gaspar Cassadó from Barcelona composed a short, slow, mournful piece for cello and piano, *Lamento de Boabdil* (*Boabdil's Lament*) (1931).

From the nineteenth century onwards, Spanish history painters became interested in Boabdil. Their work was affected by the political and ideological implications of its subject matter. The legitimacy of a dynasty, or of a specific person on the Spanish throne, was a recurrent theme of Spanish art throughout the century. The legal right of monarchs to reign was fundamental in presenting an argument for the continuity of Spanish nationality, and the reconquest of territory occupied by the Muslims was seen as a process of affirmation of Spanish nationhood throughout the Middle Ages, culminating with the Catholic Monarchs. So it is not surprising that a number of history paintings portrayed moments of surrender, and in particular the handing over of keys, the point of maximum humiliation of the enemy as well as a triumphal depiction of victory, and an inheritance from the artist Velázquez, whose famous painting of the surrender of Breda paved the way for these later visions. What is interesting is that as time went on, the message changed, so that the inferior loser gained more equal footing with the conqueror.

Francisco de Paula van Halen, born in Vic in Catalonia, one of the nineteenth-century's most esteemed history painters, was known mainly for his battle scenes. His painting of the surrender of Granada was commissioned by the king consort of Spain, Francisco de Asís. The scene is shrouded in a pale, wintery light, against which Ferdinand and Isabella loom large, and Boabdil, dressed in scarlet, has only a handful of retainers. His face is turned away from the viewer and not visible, and his four companions also have their backs to us, unlike the Catholic Monarchs, who are facing the viewer. In the background, Spanish troops appear to be entering the city. As Boabdil offers the keys to the Castilians, a man kneels and offers the sultan's sword, a sign of submission. This was clearly a monarchist and imperialist painting, not surprisingly since van Halen was closely connected with the royal family.

Joaquín Espalter, a Catalan artist best known for his murals, painted 'El suspiro del moro' ('The Moor's Sigh') in 1855, which was presented at the Universal Exhibition in Paris in that year. It was again commissioned by Francisco de Asís. Shortly after, Eusebio Valldeperas painted 'Rendición de Loja a Fernando el Católico' ('Surrender of Loja to Ferdinand the Catholic') in 1862, depicting Boabdil on his knees before Ferdinand. In this painting Ferdinand avoids the discourtesy of humiliating another king by making him kiss his hand.

Alfred Dehodencq, a Frenchman who moved to Spain after the French Revolution of 1848, was known for his vivid, innovative orientalist oil paintings, often of Andalusian subjects. His 1869 canvas 'L'adieu du roi Boabdil à Grenade' ('Farewell of King Boabdil to

Granada') is in the Musée d'Orsay in Paris, and shows the sultan mounted on a powerful horse riding over the mountains. He twists back in his saddle to look behind him, while his black servant holds on to his horse's bridle with an alarmed expression. Although only mountains are in view in the background, the viewer assumes he is looking back on Granada with anguish. The contorted pose of his body suggests his psychological as well as physical discomfort. It is a sympathetic portrait, which reflected the growing change from emphasis on the victor to the heroic portrayal of the individual victim.

This sympathetic attitude finds later echoes in perhaps the most well-known of the many visual images of the last Moorish king, the two magnificent oil paintings entitled respectively 'La rendición de Granada' ('The Surrender of Granada') and 'El suspiro del moro' ('The Moor's Sigh'), both created by Francisco Pradilla y Ortiz in the late 1800s. The first of these, dated 1882, is a large canvas over ten feet high by eighteen wide (330 by 550 centimetres), which was commissioned by the Spanish Senate for its Madrid palace, and described as the most magnificent and dazzling of all nineteenth-century Spanish historical paintings. It is a great theatrical image, in which gesture and scenario are vital, and it has a strong political charge as it seeks to glorify a defining moment in Spanish history. The purpose of the commission was to represent Spanish unity and illustrate the starting point for those great future deeds done by the Catholic Monarchs and their successors. The victors show their power in their glittering apparel and armour, their strength in numbers and the disproportionately large size of the Christian personages who dominate the right side of the picture. Christians and Muslims are separated by a muddy track, symbolic of the permanent divide between them, which is in fact the focal point of the painting. Boabdil looks diminished in stature and also in numbers of retainers, dwarfed before the might of the royal Christian retinue. This painting received generally effusive acclaim from critics and public, who clearly saw it as an image of Christian supremacy. Yet it is hard not to detect sympathy in the depiction of Boabdil, whose figure is poignantly silhouetted against the backdrop of the Alhambra and the city whose keys he holds in his hand and is about to relinquish. His followers have sad expressions and bowed heads, and his page boy seems overcome, perhaps by the sight of the Christian Monarchs, perhaps with a sense of the tragedy of the situation.

If the message of 'La rendición de Granada' is ambiguous, the second painting by Pradilla, 'El suspiro del moro', dated ten years later in 1892, leaves the viewer in no doubt of the sympathy of the depiction of the vanquished Moorish king stopping on his journey into exile to look his last upon his beloved city of Granada. Its composition is unusual and striking, since the centre of attention is Boabdil's horse and his retinue, while the conquered king seems to be walking out of the picture on the right, towards the lost city. His horse is facing back in the direction it came, suggesting its master's longing to turn back to Granada. All have turned their faces away from the viewer, their gaze intent upon the hazy, distant image of the paradise they have left behind, drawing our own gaze in the same direction. The drab brownish-grey tones of the image, the stormy sky, the suggestion of wind and the rocky outcrop which dominates the foreground emphasise the impoverishment of the defeated Muslims and the barren future ahead. Apart from his horse and saddle, nothing now differentiates Boabdil from his retainers.

Another Granadan painter, Manuel Gómez-Moreno González, who painted scenes of the intimate everyday life of the middle and working classes as well as historical works, went to paint in Rome, where he completed a large canvas of 'La Salida de la familia de Boabdil de la Alhambra' ('The Departure of Boabdil's family from the Alhambra') in 1880. In this work, Boabdil's mother, wife and children are about to leave the palace, his mother proud and upright, his wife distraught amid weeping friends and servants. A servant holds back a large curtain to open their way out as they leave their home for ever. It is a sympathetic, human painting. The English painter John Harris's 'The Last Council of Boabdil at the Alhambra' is a painting of interesting perspectives, Boabdil stands to the right and listens to the pleas of his councillors, who are in the centre of the image. The sultan and a councillor are dressed in Nasrid scarlet, a reminder perhaps of the blood spilt in the war against the Christians. The exquisite decor of the palace room contrasts vividly with the strong feelings aroused by their discussion.

In December 2015 the Texas-based Iraqi artist Nazar Yahya

made the story of Boabdil the centrepiece of his exhibition *Recon-quista* (*Reconquest*) at the Meem Gallery, Dubai. It consisted of paintings, installations and sculptures and reconstructs the events that led to Boabdil's famous last sigh. Yahya aimed to highlight the achievements of the Arab world in the fields of culture and science, as well as remind the viewer of the intolerance, greed for power and political manipulation that destroyed it. The artist sees a clear resemblance to the current realities of Arabs, in terms of events in Iraq and other countries, and he uses Boabdil's life as a gateway to explore themes of exile, isolation, loss of a homeland and the strug-gle to retain identity. At a time when the homes and historic sites of Arabs are being destroyed and millions forced into exile by power struggles, fanaticism and intolerance, these themes have strong con-temporary relevance. Yahya stated that his exhibition showed the perspective of the losing side, and he included two quite different portraits of the last Nasrid sultan, in which the artist aimed to depict the dualities of his personality, and what he represents in history. He described the sultan as a spiritual, sensitive person who wanted to be a poet, not a warrior or leader. In 'Jail' Boabdil is seen behind a carved latticework window, suggesting he was the prisoner of destiny, and his surrender of the keys of Granada are painted in 'Glowing' in the style of Christian iconography. *Reconquista* reflects Yahya's struggle to retain his identity as an Arab after leaving Iraq for permanent exile in the United States.

The sculptural image of Boabdil revived in Juan Moreno Agua-do's beautiful monument in Granada harks back to the late Middle Ages, to the reliefs depicting the Granadan war on the lower choir stalls of Toledo cathedral, carved during the war and soon after, and steeped in the contemporary atmosphere. The carvings, made by the shadowy figure of Rodrigo Alemán, contracted by Cardi-nal Mendoza to embellish the fifty-four lower choir stalls, are of outstanding value as a graphic history. They were begun in 1489, when the Granadan war was raging, and Münzer refers to them in his journey through Spain in 1495, by which time they must have been finished. The sculptures begin with the fall of Alhama in 1482 and end with the surrender of Granada, and they provide a precious iconographic record of the famous historical personages involved in the Granadan war. Ferdinand appears thirty-four times, always on horseback, with short and long stirrups, dressed in civilian clothes of a distinctive style, with his armour showing and wearing a great cape, as well as a helmet, hat and crown. Isabella is there too, along with the counts of Cabra and Tendilla, and others in the Christian retinue. Among the Muslims, Boabdil is represented twice, along with El Zagal, his father-in-law Ali al-Attar, Hamet el Zegrí, the defender of Malaga, and many others.

What interests us here is how and where Boabdil is depicted. In the relief of the Battle of Lucena, he is in the middle distance, imprisoned by a Christian who restrains him with ropes with his left hand and threatens him with a dagger in the other. In the final relief of the series, in the place of honour on the right of the archbishop's stall, Rodrigo Alemán devoted two-thirds of the image to a vista of the city, with its city walls, square towers and mosques set in the *vega*. In the right foreground, Boabdil kneels, wearing an elaborately worked *marlota* and Moorish cape embroidered and embellished with precious stones and a luxurious decorated helmet. He is in the act of handing Ferdinand the key to his kingdom, reaching upwards to the conquering king on horseback. To add insult to injury, the wooden panel has been defaced, quite literally in this case, so that half of Boabdil's countenance is missing. In this visual celebration of Christian might and victory, both depictions of the sultan show him in utter defeat, firstly at Lucena, where he was captured and imprisoned, and in the last hour of surrender.

Five centuries later the American sculptor Anna Hyatt Huntington revived the idea of a three-dimensional image of Boabdil. She had already created a famous statue of El Cid on horseback at the entrance to the Hispanic Society of America in New York City, copies of which were sent to Seville and Buenos Aires. In 1943 she carved a limestone bas-relief sculpture of Boabdil on the west courtyard wall of the Hispanic Society, near her statue of El Cid. Her sculpture was intended to capture the complexity of the sultan, who is depicted in exotic robes and riding boots as he rides away from Granada, his face showing a mixed expression of sorrow, rage and despair. The sculptor's husband, Archer Huntington, wrote a poem which appears beneath:

He wore a cloak of grandeur. It was bright
With stolen promises and colours thin,
But now and then the wind – the wind of night –
Raised it and showed the broken thing within.

The sculpture is said to allude to Spain's Civil War and the loss of its colonies, which Anna Hyatt likened to Boabdil's loss of his kingdom.

The medieval past was brought sharply into dialogue with contemporary visual portrayals of Boabdil in the twenty-first century through the medium of television, where gender in its social and religious dimensions, and its influence on the stereotypical appeal of male rulers on the small screen, is crucial to his depiction. The ever-increasing popularity of historical drama in Spain produced two successful Spanish TV series set during the years leading up to the conquest of Granada. Boabdil is centre stage in Vicente Escrivá's *Réquiem por Granada* (*Requiem for Granada*), broadcast in eight episodes in 1990, and he plays a key part in *Isabella*, a three-season Televisión Española series shown between 2012 and 2014 which charts the life of the Castilian queen. Their opposing portrayals of Boabdil and the fall of Granada shed fresh light on his nature. Both series depict historical events with widely differing interpretations. The issue of who Spain belongs to is at their heart. *Isabella* is overlaid with the exultant Christian rhetoric of reconquest embodied in Rodolfo Sancho's portrayal of King Ferdinand as a warrior strong in mind and body, chivalrous yet prone to extramarital affairs. As counterpoint to the victorious king, Boabdil, played by Alex Martínez, is initially presented as his equally stereotypical opposite. For a start, he is a poet, shown on various occasions writing at his desk. His naive otherworldliness is one reason why his fierce, warlike father denies him the throne. Another is that Abu l-Hasan has married the beautiful Christian renegade, Isabel de Solís, whom he sets above his first legitimate wife Aixa, insisting that their son Nasr should inherit the throne, instead of Boabdil as legitimate heir. His father tells his brother El Zagal that Boabdil would not know how to rule because his mother Aixa has converted him into her puppet. Granada needs a warrior, he says, not a poet. The historical accounts of Aixa as a strong, feisty woman who looks out for and supports her son are magnified in this series to convert her into a veritable virago who stands up to Queen Isabella and advocates fighting to the death against the Christian threat. Despite Boabdil's belief in the horoscope that predicts his grim fate, Aixa plots with the Abencerraje clan to overthrow Abu l-Hasan and succeeds in setting her son on the throne. Boabdil insists he will go into battle to prove himself, but the fighting lessons he takes beforehand reveal him to be woefully inept. At the fateful Battle of Lucena, this Boabdil's headstrong, foolish actions result in his immediate capture by the Christians, thereby providing Ferdinand and Isabella with the perfect hostage.

So far, Boabdil conforms to his male stereotype, but then something interesting happens. The young sultan steps up to the mark. Compelled to agree to the future surrender of his city and kingdom, with his tiny son Ahmed taken prisoner of war, he vows to adopt a new way of ruling, through peace and justice. Fearing quite rightly that further war with the Christians would destroy Granada, he seeks the path of negotiation, to avoid bloodshed and keep Islam alive. Ignoring his mother's insistence that he should die fighting rather than surrender, Boabdil saves his city and people from further tragedy by relinquishing his kingdom to the Catholic Monarchs, in exchange for the return of his son. The Muslim ruler has become a courageous, wise and strong sultan, though the final scene reverts to the conventional legend in which he looks back and weeps.

In *Isabella*, the fall of Granada is set in the context of Queen Isabella's life, so the Christian perspective dominates. In contrast, director and scriptwriter Vicente Escrivá describes his *Réquiem por Granada* as 'an exaltation of Arabic culture'. His Boabdil, played by Manuel Bandera, chooses knowledge over wealth from childhood, and is courteous, noble, just and lenient, generous and compassionate. Although his desire for peace between Christians and Muslims is strong, unlike his counterpart in *Isabella*, he is a bold, brave warrior, which accurately reflects the historical reality. Man of letters and man of war, he flouts the gender stereotype in which these qualities are mutually exclusive. The issue of gender is most important in this series in its social and religious dimensions, as the plot hinges on the conflict of ancestral lineage. Inheritance through the male ruling line is even more fundamental to Islamic dynasties than to Christian ones, and through this, Boabdil is the legitimate heir to the throne as firstborn son of the emir. As in *Isabella*, this legal right clashes with the wishes of his father, who favours his son by the converted Christian Zoraya, and this creates the main internal tensions in the narrative. Yet Boabdil has an even stronger claim to rule, which inverts gender conventions. His mother Aixa, here named Fatima, was a Nasrid princess, which meant that she benefited from the link of kinship through blood relationship down the female line, which had existed in the Nasrid dynasty since the fourteenth century. By virtue of this connection, women of royal blood could transmit rights to the throne, rights which she exercised as mother of the next true Nasrid sultan. Aixa/Fatima was also believed to be the descendant of the Prophet Muhammad, a claim repeated several times in the course of *Requiem*. Boabdil's father-in-law insists: 'Don't you know that this man has the blood of the Prophet in his veins?' These circumstances intensify the conflict of succession with the illegitimate heir, who is the son of an infidel.

Escrivá also underlines opposing models of patriarchy by contrasting the cruel and deluded Abu l-Hasan, who rejects his firstborn son's claim to reign, with the strongly emphasised anxiety of Boabdil for his small son. All Boabdil's actions after his son's imprisonment are mindful of the grave risk to the child's life, as he juggles peaceful diplomacy with the need to fight and defend. As he signs the surrender document, his last act for his people is to set out terms which will enable them to continue living in Granada and to follow their religion and culture. In contrast with the scene of departure in *Isabella*, Boabdil is not scorned by his mother, but remains sad and dignified.

What are the implications of these TV portrayals of the last sultan of Granada, in which gender is fundamental to lineage and inheritance, and to the construction of the male ruler's character? Despite its insistent focus on the triumphs and challenges of the queen of Castile, *Isabella* is not unrelievedly pro-Christian. The evolution of the character of Boabdil from weakness to strength, and his depiction as a poet and thinker, hint at the idea of a new, more forgiving model of patriarchal monarch, a Muslim to boot, who was nevertheless destined to succumb to the might of Castile and Aragon. Boabdil and his ancestors, of course, represent the original invaders of the peninsula, the original immigrants. Shown from 2012 to 2014, at a time when the crisis of immigration loomed large in Spain as it still does, the clear message of Spain as the victor in season two of *Isabella* may be significant, but the scene where Ferdinand and Isabella enter the Alhambra for the first time and are spellbound by a beauty unachievable in Spanish Christian culture of the time is equally so.

Réquiem por Granada is a bold undertaking that would have been hard to make after the al-Quaeda train bombings in Madrid in March 2004. Screened in 1990 amid a climate of rediscovery of Arab culture in Spain, its unabashed admiration for Boabdil as a courageous ruler who suffers loss and exile to preserve his city illustrates the nature of a man whose life continues to pose questions.

The life of Boabdil created a rich artistic legacy that has shaped the past in many forms. He has become a symbolic point of reference, a reinventable image whose meaning has changed according to different societies and epochs, which have attuned the myth of Boabdil to their desires and standards. Up to the late eighteenth century, he was viewed from the perspective of the victors, until the dynamic changed along with the cultural climate of the nineteenth century to present a far more sympathetic portrayal of the sultan as tragic victim, and, latterly, as a kind of hero. The rewriting and reinvention of the image of Boabdil has generated new meanings and contested old ones. In the centuries after the fall of Granada, the idealised portrayal of the city and of the exotic but conquered Moor could be seen as a way of containing the power of Spain's Islamic past to disrupt the present. But the old legend of Boabdil has been remoulded to provide imaginative ways of thinking about contemporary concerns, while remaining beguilingly mysterious and strange in its historical and cultural distance from us.

9

The Moor's Last Stand

Nearly half a millennium before Christ, a Greek force of about 7,000 soldiers held off the mighty Persian army by blocking the mountain pass at Thermopylae. They kept the Persians at bay for over a week before their rearguard was destroyed in one of the most famous last stands in history. In more recent times, Colonel Custer and the 7th Cavalry's doomed battle against 3,000 Native Americans led by Sitting Bull at the Little Bighorn river in 1876, when the soldiers suffered devastating losses and the colonel himself was killed, has come to be known as Custer's Last Stand. Boabdil's last stand was strikingly different, though perhaps no less heroic. He held his ground against the opposing force of the Christians over a period of ten years, although he didn't have a great army at his disposal. Unlike the Greeks at Thermopylae, or Colonel Custer, Boabdil realised that in his situation the benefits of capitulation outweighed those of fighting on, and his final resistance to an overpowering aggressor did not end in annihilation, but in surrender, because he realised that there was no glory in the sacrifice of his people in a fight to the death. But, true to the myth of the Last Stand, Boabdil emerges as a brave, intelligent man leading his diminished band against an unbeatable enemy, even though the odds were stacked overwhelmingly against him. This image flies in the face of the uncompromising judgements of conventional history. One of my aims in this book has been to rescue Boabdil's reputation. That reputation hinges on the vexed issue of how Spain's medieval legacy is perceived.

Nowhere is this dilemma more apparent than in Granada itself. On 2 January every year, the local people celebrate the moment of Boabdil's surrender in the festival commemorating the capture of their city by Ferdinand and Isabella, known as the Fiesta de la toma (Festival of the Capture). This annual remembrance was instigated because it was one of the stipulations of King Ferdinand's will, written in the town of Madrilejos and signed on 22 January 1516, just hours before he died. Each year a procession of civic dignitaries proclaims the Christian victory, hoisting the royal standard and Ferdinand's sword, to the strains of the national anthem. Since the 1990s, the fiesta has been opposed by left-wing intellectuals and artists, including Yehudi Menuhin and Amin Maalouf, on the grounds that it is xenophobic and inappropriate, and opposition groups clash verbally during the commemorations. In 2016, 2,000 Granadans gathered at the town hall to hear the ceremony and see the procession. Those taking part wear fifteenth-century Christian costumes, with the exception of just one figure dressed in Moorish style. The Archbishop of Granada, Javier Martínez, officiated at a Mass in the cathedral where the tombs of the Catholic Monarchs lie, praising the humanity of Queen Isabella and describing the end of the Granadan war as 'probably the most exquisitely humane end to any war', in which, he said, the Christian kings sat at the same table as the vanquished. This royalist rhetoric appears to reinforce the Christian status of the city, a status it had never had before 1492, when in fact it discloses a deep-seated and continuing anxiety about its religious and cultural identity, an anxiety encapsulated in that moment of surrender, whose peaceable nature was attributed by the archbishop to the offices of the Christian queen. In reality it was Boabdil who chose capitulation over further violence and worked with the Catholic Monarchs' emissaries to achieve a hard won agreement. It was Boabdil who renounced his sovereignty and his kingdom in the hope of sparing his people further bloodshed.

The memory of the clashes between the Moors and Christians of medieval Spain is vividly present in popular culture, and the

festival of the conquest of Granada is echoed in the festivals held
in many other parts of Spain, particularly in Valencia and Alicante,
which involve staged battles between participants dressed in medieval Arab and Christian costumes in an effective ritualisation of an
ancient conflict which, in modern times, the Christians always win.
The powerful legend of the patron saint of Spain, Saint James, the
slayer of Moors or 'Santiago Matamoros', whose flag was hoisted
by the Christians in the Alhambra on the day of Boabdil's departure
from the city, is represented visually in the mounted statue of a militant Saint James with bodies of Muslim soldiers at his horse's feet,
which stands in the cathedral of Santiago de Compostela in Galicia.
But Islam still hovers at the margins of the veneration of Saint James
and of Spanish identity, even now. On 25 July each year, Día de
Santiago or Saint James's Day, the stone frontage of Santiago cathedral is temporarily covered by a façade of red and white horseshoe
arches, bearing the words 'Al patrón de España' ('To the patron
saint of Spain'). At midnight, amid fireworks and celebrations, the
quema del Castillo, or castle burning, is celebrated and the Moorish
façade is burnt down so that nothing remains, revealing the Christian cathedral behind it. For the last few years this spectacle has
been transformed into a fantastic virtual light show, presenting a
visual image of Islam in Spanish culture which is trivialised and
finally, erased. The repeated re-enactment of Christian victory over
Muslim counterparts, and in particular of their triumph in Granada,
exposes a subtext of insecurity over the racial and religious issues at
the heart of Spain's cultural history. This covert dilemma has manifested itself in a strong desire to rewrite that history, diminishing
the importance of the Arab past to carve out a pure Catholic heritage
and Spanish lineage which tends to bypass Spain's Islamic legacy.
Boabdil simultaneously bears the characteristics of the invading
Other and of the conquered enemy. He is the feared yet desired
Muslim presence who epitomises the conflicted nature of Spain's
relationship with its past and encapsulates the enduring quandary
over Spain's cultural distinctiveness. Boabdil is the scapegoat who
takes the full brunt of the historical act of revenge of the Christian
Reconquest, the figure whose reputation is sacrificed to atone for
the inner corruption of the Muslim state on the one hand, and to

represent the Christian conquest of Islamic civilisation in Spain on the other.

These two dimensions are crucial if we are to see the full picture of the last Nasrid ruler of Granada, first, as an individual within his own culture, and then as a symbolic figure on a global historical scale. Considering the events of Boabdil's life from his perspective sheds light upon the paradoxes and conflicts fundamental to his position as an emir and sultan, yet a prisoner in chains, as a shrewd negotiator and as a schemer and rebel. It gives us insight into his position as a son, husband, father and brother. He was a man of culture and a man of war, a king, yet at the same time the pawn of the Catholic Monarchs, who captured his castles and fortresses with the help of their militant bishops. These enigmatic oppositions have rendered Boabdil's life and deeds liable to conflicting interpretations, and to a certain extent this ambiguity arises because we have comparatively few contemporary sources of information about him, the majority of which are written from the Christian point of view. In piecing together the fragmented stories of his existence, we have to take account of the bias of historians and the plausibility of their interpretations of events.

The enigmatic aura surrounding Boabdil is underscored by the fact that the precise dates of his birth and death remain unclear, the latter shrouded in a mystery that has lent itself to imaginative interpretations, similar to the creative reinventions of the death of the last Visigothic monarch King Roderick. No doubt the solution to the enigma of Boabdil's demise lies in north Africa, and may well come to light as research progresses, but the current absence of any definitive record of his tomb shows how exile divested him of a significant identity among a people for whom he had little meaning. He had grown up in the Islamic state of Granada in the privileged and beautiful environment of the Alhambra city, where he was given the religious and cultural education of a royal heir who had the blood of the Prophet in his veins. Yet his family history was scarred by the terrible internecine conflicts which did so much to weaken the Granadan regime. His paradise became a kind of purgatory. Boabdil's relationship with his elder family members was extreme and paradoxical, for he grew up to be in mortal conflict with his father and uncle, while his mother was his staunchest, almost fanatical, supporter. The two men who should have been his role models were anything but, his father forsaking Boabdil's mother for an infidel whose son he planned would inherit the throne by usurping his legitimate heir, and his uncle murdering Boabdil's younger brother. Both men also attempted to assassinate Boabdil. The shock of these events must have been considerable. The only person the young Boabdil could trust was his mother, who saved his life and pressed for his rightful accession to the throne of the Nasrids. Throughout his reign she acted as his adviser, raising an enormous ransom to pay for his release from imprisonment after the Battle of Lucena. Posterity has made much of Aixa's dominating personality and her control over Boabdil, to the extent that it has been suggested that their relationship was an Oedipal one, but there is little evidence to show that she was anything other than a feisty, strong-minded woman who did all in her considerable power to protect the interests of her eldest son.

Boabdil's life as a husband and father had grave consequences for his reign. It is telling that there is no reference in any historical source to Boabdil's interest in any other woman than his wife Moraima. It was customary for the Nasrid sultans to have a harem, as well as legitimate wives, but he seems to have shunned this custom. It seems likely that the licentious life of his father, who frequented the harem and whose unconventional love affair with Isabel de Solís posed such a threat to his emotional stability and his political future, determined his attitudes to sex and marriage through negative example, although he may have already been inclined to monogamy by nature. He is recorded as having three children, although we know very little of his daughter Aixa and his third child, Yusuf. Boabdil's elder son Ahmed's imprisonment as a hostage was in my view a major factor affecting the sultan's political decision-making, and the acceptance of his mother's offer of the child as a hostage in exchange for the release of her own son was one of the most decisive and cruellest manoeuvres of the Catholic Monarchs.

The exceptional personal circumstances of the young emir were inextricably bound to his position as a monarch and to his political strategies, and affected his external relationships with the enemy.

The bitter antagonism of his father became an effective weapon in the armoury of King Ferdinand, who supported and manipulated Boabdil in his struggle against Abu l-Hasan for his own devious purposes. It was the same with his terrible contest with his uncle, El Zagal, with whom he cut off all ties after the assassination of his brother Yusuf and El Zagal's attempted murder of Boabdil himself. Ferdinand appeared to befriend Boabdil and assist him in attaining power, while using his alliance as an instrument of blackmail to win territory and sovereignty. The Christian king's greatest bargaining tool was inevitably Boabdil's tiny son, whose capture he used to secure the sultan's final agreement to surrender Granada. But despite the prevalent view that Boabdil was the mere pawn of Ferdinand, the sultan was a man of diplomacy and astute negotiating skills, who could also take radical action when necessary. He walked a tightrope between untrustworthy advisers and militant religious and judicial leaders, never knowing whom to trust, except for his mother and wife. At times he needed to be brutal. He had no compunction in ordering the beheading of the Granadan religious factions who were destroying his fragile reputation. At all times he was trying to hold the might of the Christians at bay, accepting their help when he had no option and using studied diplomatic rhetoric in his correspondence with them, but always keeping them at arm's length until the dire circumstances Granada faced in late 1491 forced his hand. His late rebellion against Ferdinand tells us that he was playing a dangerous double game, stringing the Christians along while hoping against hope for help from north Africa. While he may have started out as a young, unseasoned leader, the dire experiences of his reign turned him into a shrewd, even cunning adversary of the Catholic king and queen. To pick just one example of Boabdil's negotiating powers, we need think only of the terms of the capitulations, drafted by the Christians, and modified by the Islamic ruler to ensure above all else, as he thought at the time, that his people would be free to continue living as Muslims in their own city of Granada.

Boabdil was a man of education and refinement. Existing documents show us that he wrote in good Arabic, and spoke it with the inflection that was typical of the Granadan area. He also spoke and understood Castilian, with a strong regional accent. Boabdil

has often been viewed as a poet, unfit to rule because he was too
unworldly, but there is not much evidence for this hypothesis, other
than the elegy sent to the king of Fez and signed by the sultan. This
poem was attributed to him, but it is likely that Boabdil dictated his
ideas, which were then shaped into verse by his court poet. There
is no question that he was also a man of arms: several historical
documents show that Boabdil led his men into battle, fought with
courage, and was an expert horseman. The great medieval Arabic
and European debate over the superiority of arms or letters fails to
do Boabdil justice, as he mastered both political rhetoric and military
skills, in the manner of a chivalric knight.

His personal and public life was riven by divisions and strife
which arose from patterns of behaviour that had been repeated
throughout the existence of the Nasrid dynasty. The conflicting view
of vassalage, which made Ferdinand so irate and gave the Granadans
an excuse to turn on Boabdil because of his perceived allegiance with
the Catholics, had existed since Muhammad I became Ferdinand III's
vassal in the early thirteenth century. The repeated submission of the
Nasrid rulers to Christian kings gave vassaldom a unique meaning.
The emirs did not see themselves as vassals or subject to any Catholic monarch, but felt instead that they were entering into a mutually
beneficial agreement. Hence Ferdinand of Aragon's fury at what he
saw as Boabdil's disobedience in flouting Christian authority. For
the sultan, the vassaldom agreement in which all Muslim leaders
did deals with the Christians had been an accepted part of life on the
frontier throughout the history of his family.

The conflicts relating to lineage and inheritance which were so
pressing for Boabdil had begun with the absolute power of Muhammad I, as emir, to designate his successor. The ancient dynastic
rivalries, and fleeting, shifting family alliances that Boabdil fell prey
to were all part of an early pattern which expressed itself in repeated
violence, bloodshed and betrayal. In a similar way, his conflicts with
the religious leaders of his time also had direct parallels as far back
as the reign of the founder of the Nasrid dynasty, whose initial peace
treaty with the Christians also fell foul of the *ulama* and lost him
public support. Even Boabdil's two interrupted periods of rule were
foreshadowed by the bewildering succession of multiple reigns of

his fifteenth-century predecessors. These inherited dynastic patterns were part of a clan heritage that Boabdil was powerless to revoke, and for which he was in no way responsible.

As a result, the sultan was almost constantly faced with animosity, discord and hatreds that demanded harrowing decision-making and distressing choices to be made, which were perhaps perplexing to those writers who portray him as a man whose motivation was ambiguous and condemn him either as a weak coward and traitor or as a victim. On the basis of what we know from the available records, there is little hint of similar views among early historians whose accounts are closest to the actual events of his life. One point they do emphasise is that Boabdil was a man of destiny. Most early sources refer to the horoscope said to have been requested by Abu l-Hasan when his son was born, which predicted that he would become a sultan whose reign would mark the end of the Nasrid state. Astrologers were highly respected scholars in the medieval Islamic world, and astrological practices had become a part of everyday medical practice in the fifteenth century, as well as being respected at Muslim royal courts, so it was likely that such an opinion would have been taken very seriously. Boabdil's epithet El Zogoibi, the Unlucky One, reveals the extent to which the prediction was believed, and it cast a dark shadow over him, as the earliest historical accounts reveal. The effect this had was to reinforce a feeling that the fate of Granada was sealed long before Boabdil came to power, which to an extent absolved him of blame, but also gave him the appearance of a victim of fate.

The tone of the Arabic *Nubdhat* and the history of al-Maqqari when describing Boabdil is mostly neutral, or conveys a degree of sympathy for him as a man prey to the Machiavellian cunning of the Christian rulers and the treacherous violence of his own family. The Christian accounts, which are by far the majority, do not tend to denigrate their enemy – naturally so, for there would be no glory in vanquishing a weak foe. Boabdil is often portrayed as a man of dignity and courage, a ferocious fighter and worthy opponent of Ferdinand. There is no reference to any cowardice on the sultan's part. Nearly all early Christian historians maintain that, in the allegedly close alliance between Ferdinand and Boabdil, the former is always one step ahead, which shows Ferdinand as a clever political strategist able to outwit his astute opponent. This intricate alliance led the Granadans to accuse Boabdil of treachery, as he became more and more obliged to make secret agreements with the enemy. As so often happens, the mass of the people were not privy to what was really going on behind the scenes, and failed to understand the hard choices their sultan had to make. Yet the Christian historians do not revel in the condemnation of Boabdil as a traitor, they merely record the accusation in a neutral fashion.

The legends of Boabdil's life that grew in the centuries following his death evolved in response to the many unanswered questions posed by his story. The interaction of history and fiction offered new creative scope to question the meaning of his life within the context of Spanish and, later, of world history. The historical circumstances have become overlaid with the resonances of legend and myth in a way that revitalises and manipulates the events depending on the dictates of literary or artistic media, and of contemporary responses to them. The fall of Granada was of such magnitude, like the Muslim invasion over 700 years before, that a mythical story was needed to explain, accept, or legitimate what had happened. It was a way of making sense of the immense upheavals the conquest brought about.

History and fiction merged in the first centuries after 1492 to create an image of Boabdil which demonised him. The early legend of the Moor's Last Sigh and his mother's rebuke, which has become an iconic point of reference, began to mould his portrait as a man too weak and cowardly to die for his religion, a man in thrall to his forceful mother. The enormously popular historical novel by Ginés Pérez de Hita added insult to injury by attributing to Boabdil the appalling massacre of the Abencerraje clan. Pérez de Hita based his novel on the stories of folklore as well as the historical account of the Christian chronicler Pulgar, and his purpose was to dramatise and glamorise the Moorish court of Granada to create a compelling tale. The Abencerrajes had already caught the public imagination in an anonymous novella *La historia del Abencerraje y la hermosa Jarifa* (*The Story of the Abencerraje and the Beautiful Jarifa*) which came out about 1550, thirty years before Pérez de Hita's book, and lionised the clan at the expense of Boabdil's reputation. These works became part of the sentimental portrayal of the exotic Moor which was so popular in Spanish writing after the middle of the sixteenth century. One hundred years after the Moorish enemy had been subjugated, there was sufficient distance to idealise the old foe in literature, if not in life. This idealisation is also a feature of the Spanish frontier ballads, many of which showed respect and admiration for the figure of the Moor, and emphasised his chivalric nature. The ballads did not malign Boabdil in the same way as Pérez de Hita. Instead, these folk stories set to music presented him either neutrally or in a way which drew attention to the elegiac drama of his tragic loss.

The inherent dramatic potential of two aspects of Boabdil's fictional portrayal as either the weak, cowardly, even malevolent ruler, or as the tragic victim, were harnessed by early playwrights as they played out the triumph of Christian conquest and imperialism on the public stage. In Verardi's Latin pageant and Lope de Vega's late sixteenth-century drama about the discovery of the New World, Boabdil is a minor character dwarfed by the protagonism of Ferdinand and Isabella and Christopher Columbus, respectively. A century later, Dryden's lovelorn Boabdelin dies tragically to give way to the hero Almanzor in a play which maps the conquest of Granada on to contemporary political events in England, using Boabdil's sorry plight as a warning against civil discord. From 1492 until the eighteenth century, literary recreations of the fall of Granada represent Boabdil in a mostly negative light. They were scornful judgements of a defeated civilisation, where he represented a crucial moment when national boundaries were redrawn.

The reinvention of cultural memory seems in these cases to consist of an effort to restrain and contain the past, which implicitly raises the unresolved question of the legitimacy of the war against Granada. Their subject matter, which either foregrounds Muslim civilisation in Spain, as in the case of Pérez de Hita, or exalts the Christian victory, revives those events which need to be justified, reinforced or interrogated. The implicit desire to keep Boabdil in his perceived place as the vanquished ruler who symbolised Catholic victory over the threatening religion of Islam discloses a covert anxiety about the validity of the Christian conquest. Such misgivings are all too easily understandable amid the climate of extreme religious and racial tension that gripped Spain from 1492 until 1609, during which time not only did Granada fall, but also all Jews and Moriscos were expelled from the peninsula. There were rebel voices in both cases, men who fought against the madness of the expulsions, who questioned the wisdom of divesting Spain of a demographic and material wealth the absence of which was to prove disastrous in later centuries. In the 300 years after Boabdil's surrender, fiction writers, dramatists and opera composers both major and minor returned to the scene of the crime to retell the tale of victory while implicitly querying its meaning.

The figure of Boabdil, poised between fact and fiction, evolved into a romantic character in the nineteenth century. His legend, with its drama of monarchy and treachery, heroism and invasion, Christianity and Islam, encapsulated the spirit of the age perfectly, and chimed with the vogue for all things oriental. The characteristically melancholy tone of Romantic writing is struck by Chateaubriand, whose sympathy for Boabdil's legendary tears begins to change the focus to nostalgia and the pain of exile suffered by the sultan as a tragic victim. The many interpretations of that last sigh took a hold on British Romantic writers, who reinvented Boabdil as a patriarchal oriental despot, or as an emasculated figure whose effeminacy and weakness are reflected in his sighs and weeping, who represents a shift from absolute power to powerlessness. From the Middle Ages to the eighteenth century, male tears had reflected a refined sensibility, sympathy and sense of humanity. When the great El Cid, Rodrigo Díaz, weeps in the famous epic poem of his life, it is viewed as a sign of masculine strength. Yet Boabdil's tears were interpreted as a sign of weakness, a marker of cultural and political decline and catastrophe. Then, for the first time, Boabdil found a defender in Washington Irving, who saw through the demonising legend and pointed out the injustices of the view of succeeding generations up to that time. Irving's vindication of Boabdil was so influential that the sultan became a figure of importance for black Americans, especially in popular art, symbolising black power and chivalry.

Unlike their counterparts in Europe and America, nineteenth-century Spanish writers revisited their past by turning to the foundational myths and legends surrounding the Muslim invasion of Spain and King Roderick rather than those which marked what they saw as its reconquest. Instead, it was visual artists and musicians who were inspired by the story of Boabdil, the latter tuning in to the nostalgic side of his legend, while visual art echoed the European literary preoccupation with the Moor's Last Sigh and Boabdil as the vanquished ruler. Painters of Spanish history broke the mould of depicting the humiliation of surrender by substituting heroic, often ambiguous portrayals of the Muslim ruler as an individual victim, at times even in domestic scenes which convey his humanity.

A keynote in the development of Boabdil's legend in this century is a degree of disintegration of the story in its original form, a change in sensibility, which brings us a sympathetic portrait of the last Nasrid sultan. As the past was re-examined, new questions arose regarding the nature and authenticity of history, at the same time as a deeper, more thoughtful understanding of oriental culture emerged. Boabdil's image evolved to suggest nostalgia for the past, in which exile and racial conflict both played a part, as the reinterpretation of his legend acknowledged a dissatisfaction with his previous negative depiction. The sultan's story had resonance in the political, religious and cultural life of nineteenth-century Europe and America which heralded more radical departures over the next hundred years.

From the mid-twentieth century on, Boabdil came into his own as a symbol of political resistance, starting with his advocate Louis Aragon's plea for cultural tolerance, which was followed by several important novels written in Spain and England during the last twenty-five years that refuted the accusations of history and set Boabdil in the spotlight as a man whose life has meaning for our modern world. Contemporary Arab writers and artists have also found a rich source of inspiration in Boabdil as a kindred spirit who is the embodiment of exile, set against Granada as the site of their own nostalgia and longing for their homeland. Television too has brought the life of this medieval monarch into sharp focus, not only as the young prince portrayed with affectionate sympathy in a number of Spanish cartoons, but also as a major character in two popular Spanish TV series which bring to light difficult issues relating to gender, and to the social and religious conflicts which afflicted

Boabdil and which remain of pressing contemporary relevance. Again the old issue of the political legitimacy of Spain's rulers is raised in these productions which beg the question of whether Spain was a better place after Boabdil surrendered his city.

The historical personage of the embattled Moorish sultan, living over 500 years ago in a city of matchless beauty tarnished by violent crime, betrayal and brutal fighting, fending off fearful enemies both outside and within, may seem remote from our experience, unfamiliar, even alien, and yet bewitching. He is the stuff of myth and fairy tale, yet in the very mingling of history and legend, Boabdil comes into focus as a medieval monarch who is simultaneously mysterious and enigmatic as an individual, and recognisable and significant for our lives in the modern world. To see why his life matters today, we need to set him in the wider context of the medieval world that shaped him, viewing his actions on the broad stage of medieval Spanish and European evolution.

Boabdil's reign coincided with the end of a long historical process resulting in the substitution of the social system and civilisation of Islamic Andalusia for that of medieval Europe, of which the Spanish Christian kingdoms formed a part. It was a point of social and cultural transition springing from the clash of Islam and Christianity, out of which the complex process of European expansion and empire in the last five centuries grew. Spain is the only territory acquired during the early Arab conquests from which Islam was eventually expelled, both as a religion and as a political entity, to be replaced by the previous culture. In the broader scheme of things, this seismic shift in the history of the Iberian peninsula was part of an age-old pattern. As the historian David Day tells us in his book *Conquest*, societies have to guard against two threats, the weakening of their internal strength and viability, and the territorial ambitions of their neighbours, two key factors in the downfall of Islamic Granada. Although all peoples claim to be rooted to the particular land in which they are living, there are not many landscapes that have not been home to a succession of different groups. Supplanting societies commonly justify their invasion by arguing that they are bringing a higher order of civilisation, economic organisation, or religion to lands they depict as being in some way savage, making a claim for moral proprietorship. While all three claims were true for the Muslim invasion of Spain, in the case of its perceived reconquest, religion was the alleged nub of the matter.

The Christian Reconquest was based on a conviction that the defence of the papacy rested on the valour and military might of Spanish soldiers. It was the only response Europeans could make to the capture of Constantinople by the Ottoman army in 1453. Ferdinand and Isabella's triumph invested the Spanish with a sense of divine mission that helped underpin their subsequent actions in the Americas and provided a ready-made foundation story for their burgeoning Atlantic empire and a justification for their supplanting of the Mexica. While the Muslims had invaded Spain principally to spread Islam, what taints the Christian Spanish Reconquest with hypocrisy is their use of religion for political reasons, to increase their power and territory by supplanting the Granadan Muslims, and to gain wealth in the Americas. The more civilised, sophisticated society that evolved after the Muslims had supplanted the Visigoths eventually led, by the mid-fifteenth century, to the Arabic-speaking Islamic state of Granada, which already had many features of a modern European nation in its unity of religion, language and politics. Ironically, it was a model for the modern state system that Ferdinand and Isabella espoused after their takeover. But for that supplanting of the Granadan state in 1492, the Muslims paid a high price both in human life and in the dispossession of their lands.

The history of the end of Islamic rule in Spain lived on in a fluid, evolving story, at once unsettling and engaging, which has the power to stir the emotions. Historians tend to interpret the past with moral and cultural authority, often because history is written by the victors, and the accounts of Boabdil's reign describe events which have become parables that explain and exemplify, creating a shared cultural history which expresses the developing identity of society. One emblematic motif of these tales of conquest, that of the traitor among the defenders, was superimposed on early Christian versions of Boabdil's association with King Ferdinand and the final negotiations for the surrender of Granada, which had raised the suspicion of his betrayal of the citizens of his capital city, an accusation taken up and elaborated on by later historians and fiction writers. In her book *The Muslim Conquest of Iberia* the historian Nicola Clarke has shown that in stories of conquest, there is typically an individual who brings about the victory of the enemy by concluding a secret surrender pact, the traitor often being a person of high status, because authority was needed to sign such agreements. In Boabdil's case, when so much contact with the enemy was conducted through local treaties of peace or truce, circumstances lent themselves to the portrayal of the sultan as a traitor, a variation of the motif in which a prominent pre-conquest authority becomes a coward who conspires with the enemy. The presence of the traitor in an account signalled an explanation or excuse to show how and why a conquest mattered to the identity of those who remembered it. Some Granadans had undoubtedly felt betrayed by Boabdil, partly because they didn't fully understand the dire situation they were in, but the allegation of treachery and the subsequent blackening of his name are called into question when we discover that his situation corresponded to a convenient pattern in history writing intended to vilify the enemy and provide an explanation for events that were often equivocal.

We might think that a man conquered and accused of treason could never be a hero, but Boabdil may prove an exception to the rule. There are many different kinds of heroism, a virtue first praised in ancient Greece, where the bard Homer used the word for 'hero' to describe warriors of great courage and fighting skill, although the term was also used for poets. Later, the hero took on the quality of being almost divine, half-god, half-mortal, to which Aristotle added the idea of greatness of soul. The Romans developed the concept of the hero to embrace the virtues of stoicism, fortitude and endurance, until, in the Middle Ages, the warlike Christian hero, epitomised by El Cid, was a more complete person, often both a warrior and a scholar. As we have seen, in life and legend Boabdil was not initially thought of as a hero, and more often as an anti-hero, although some contemporary and later historians saw the ten-year battle for Granada as a kind of Spanish Troy. Granada's last sultan was a skilled, brave fighter as well as a cultivated man who showed endurance and forbearance in his stand against the Christians, and though he was not semi-divine, he was said to be descended from the Prophet Muhammad. Viewed from this perspective, Boabdil had more than a touch of medieval heroism about him.

The great Muslim hero of the Middle Ages was the twelfth-century Kurdish ruler Saladin, first sultan of Egypt and Syria. There are some revealing analogies between his life and that of Boabdil. In the prolonged confrontation between the Christian West and Islam during the Crusades, Saladin cut a rare figure because he earned the respect of his enemies, as Walter Scott makes plain in his novel *The Talisman*, whose subject is the close relationship between the sultan and the English king Richard the Lionheart. Boabdil earned a similar regard from Ferdinand and Isabella, as shown by the official documents they exchanged, by Ferdinand's honouring of the Nasrid sultan with gifts, and his refusal to humiliate him in public either after his capture at Lucena or at the moment of surrender of Granada. Yet, in contrast with Saladin and Richard the Lionheart, there was always an undercurrent of mutual manipulation between Boabdil and the Catholic Monarchs. Saladin was hailed as a great victor when Boabdil was not, though both men fought for a city – Jerusalem in the case of Saladin, which he conquered at the Battle of Hattin in 1187. Both pursued policies which aimed to extend and consolidate their power and were accused of betraying the cause of Islam, and both were men of religious principle and military achievement in varying degree. The respectful words of the French knight Robert of Clari, who wrote that Saladin had all the qualities of a Christian knight without being one, resemble those of Hernando de Baeza when he stated that if Boabdil had become a Christian, he would have been one of the best that had ever lived.

This unsuspected aspect of Boabdil as a medieval hero comes to the forefront in the modern era. Granada has become a rich focus of cultural memory for Arabs and Europeans, Muslims and Christians, whose creative reinvention no longer seeks to contain the past but to contest it and generate new meanings. The city may be a brilliant and nostalgic reminder of a glorious past which still lives on in the poetry-inscribed walls of the Alhambra, but it is also vividly alive in the cultural imagination of the peoples of Islam. This story from the past which looks towards the future has special relevance to the present moment. That the question of Islam in Spain and Europe is still firmly anchored to the history of the Spanish Middle Ages is abundantly illustrated by twenty-first-century journalism. The Granada Journal in the *New York Times* of 21 October 2003 relates how Muslims are back in their ancient Moorish stronghold, stating that a generation of post-Franco intellectuals were reassessing the country's Moorish past and recasting Spanish identity to include Islamic influences rejected as heretical centuries ago. This interest in reinstating Islam and the Muslim community in Andalusia has a darker side directly linked to terrorism. In *La Vanguardia* of 4 May 2002, an essay by Amatzia Baram on the Israeli–Palestinian conflict states that 'some radical organisations in the Arab world cherish an even more ambitious – and illusory – vision: – the reconquest of Spain as a way of returning to the golden age of Islam'. On 7 November 2001, the terrorist Ayman al-Zawahiri spoke on an al-Quada tape-recording about offences against Islam including the appropriation by the Christians of the Arab lands of Spain, expressing a wish 'not to let the same thing happen to Palestine that happened in al-Andalus'. These words were echoed in a newspaper account on the atrocities of 11 March 2004 in Madrid which reported that Osama bin Laden, 'in a broadcast shortly after 11 September, referred to the former Islamic kingdom of al-Andalus, whose artistic scholarship was crushed by the crusading Catholic Christian monarchs Ferdinand and Isabella. There are "old accounts" for Islamic fundamentalists to settle with Spain.' Such reports confirm the persistence of memories of the religious and political conflict arising from the fall of Granada.

Yet there is also a desire for reconciliation, and the Iraqi artist Nazar Yahya's exhibition in Dubai illustrates his desire to learn from what happened in Granada through the figurehead of Boabdil, who, he feels, was prey to power struggles, fanaticism and intolerance similar to those that have destroyed the lives, homes and historic sites of the Arabs. Back in Spain, the image of Boabdil with a chain round his neck to represent his imprisonment which appeared on the municipal shield and seal of the town of Canillas de Aceituno in the province of Malaga was removed in 2008. The mayor explained that they had decided to abolish what constituted a symbol of slavery with racist connotations which could only worsen racial prejudice. Unfortunately, the image remains on the munici-pal shield of several other towns in the same region. In February 2014 the descendants of the Spanish Muslims who were exiled to north Africa asked for reconciliation, requesting equivalent rights to naturalisation as those granted earlier the same month to the descen-dants of the Jews expelled from Spain in 1492 in what the Spanish government described as a move to right a historical wrong. There are an estimated 600 families in Morocco who can trace their origins back to Moorish Spain, and the push for their citizenship is part of a larger campaign to raise awareness of Islamic influence in Spain and reverse the country's estrangement from its past. So far their request has not been granted, but they will continue to press for what would amount to an institutional admission of repentance.

In recent years Islam has become a stronger presence in the south of Spain. The first Islamic university of Andalusia, the Univer-sidad Internacional de Averroes de al-Andalus, was established in Cordoba; Muslim converts from all over Spain choose the Albaicin as their place of residence, and the internet has fostered numerous Andalusian websites preaching tolerance, freedom and love for their homeland. While the converted Scot Abdalqadir al-Murabit's aim to found an Islamic caliphate with an economy of gold dinars may meet with some opposition, Islamic converts living in Granada have taken significant steps, such as lobbying to prevent the annual celebrations of the Fiesta de la toma. In 2003 Spanish Muslims were called to prayer at the Great Mosque of Granada, the first new mosque build-ing to be opened in the city since Ferdinand and Isabella claimed it for the Christians, and it has been seen as the focal point of a new Islamic revival. It took twenty years to build and, significantly, the mosque stands on a hill looking out over groves of orange trees and cedars at the iconic Alhambra palace which echoes its Islamic ethos. Its construction was initially opposed by city leaders, whose objections were overcome when it was agreed that the new minaret should be slightly shorter than the tower of the Catholic church of Saint Nicholas next door. It was funded by money from the govern-ments of Morocco and the Arab Emirates, and no luxury was spared in its construction. Its gardens abound with roses and jasmine, and its fountains are embellished with exquisite cobalt-blue and teal-green tiles, while the inner areas display silk carpets and teak doors. The president of the mosque foundation, Malik Ruiz, who calls himself the emir of Spain, has said that Granada will return to Islam after its 500-year interruption. But the terms of the surrender of Granada revised and agreed by Boabdil are still in urgent need of resolution today. The Granadan Muslim Abdalhasib Castiñeira contended in 2008 that the city's Muslim community are direct heirs to the promises made in the 1492 capitulations, and that the restoration of the rights, guarantees and statute of protection ensured by Boabdil's terms is a historical debt whose repayment, along with the righting of the wrong, is imminent.

If we leave behind the perfumed courtyards of the new mosque and the promise of a new era of *convivencia* which Granada's municipal leaders have promoted in their tourist information, we find the city is still haunted by Moorish ghosts. The fear of the marauding and invading Moor runs deep in the Spanish psyche, and the deaths of fifty Moroccan soldiers hired to serve in Franco's nationalist army near Granada in 1937, which deeply divided the city over the serious political implications of what to do with the cadavers, led to a view of the soldiers as reincarnations of the original invader. In contemporary Granada, there is difficulty in welcoming the growing number of immigrants from north Africa for similar reasons, for these young, penniless Muslims remind the Spaniards of their own oriental selves, as well as embodying the frequently voiced fear that they have returned to claim what was theirs.

Boabdil was a key figure at a crossroads in world history and several current tensions between Islam and the West have their roots in his reign and the kingdom he lost, a calamity which has been seen as the prelude to the repression of the Muslim world. Deprecated in the past as a cowardly traitor or tragic victim, he has become a potent symbol of the forces of rebellion, and an unconventional yet modern hero in his own right. Europe is becoming increasingly concerned with discovering a model for its society and with finding a way of addressing issues of racial equality, religious freedom and racial and religious intolerance. Some of these problems were tackled successfully in the Spanish Muslim society of which Boabdil was the final heir, and the cultural annihilation and physical expulsion of that society has left a scar on the Muslim psyche, and the sense of injustice, loss and cruelty of that defeat is still acute. Boabdil's last stand was a personal battle to defend his right to rule his kingdom as its legitimate sultan. It was also a last stand against religious intolerance, fanatical power and cultural ignorance, in which issues of violence, tension and prejudice between Muslims and Christians were as pressing then as they are now. A major cultural shift is taking place in the European perception of the medieval Muslim presence in Spain, in which the traditional vision of the Arab victory of 711 as an apocalyptic disaster of the greatest magnitude is changing. There is a growing recognition of the fertile cross-cultural creativity and renewal that was born out of that conquest. If Boabdil had managed to hold out, we could believe that Philip Guedalla's brave new world of Granadan enlightenment and liberal humanist Islam might have come to pass. The history of the last sultan of Granada inspires us to consider a new world of possibility and reconciliation, and better ways of understanding cultural and religious divisions. The life and legend of Boabdil exposes how what was gained by the Christian conquest of Granada, which heralded the new nation-state and the rise of Spanish imperialism, may well have been outweighed by the loss of Muslim civilisation in Spain, with all its consequences for the future of relations between the Islamic states and the West.

Principal Dramatis Personae

Abu l-Hasan Ali	Twenty-second Nasrid sultan of Granada and father of Boabdil
Aixa la Horra	Wife of Abu l-Hasan and mother of his sons Boabdil and Yusuf, and daughter Aixa
Abu Abdallah Muhammad b. Ali, Muhammad XI, known as Boabdil	Twenty-third and last Nasrid sultan of Granada
Abu Abdallah Muhammad, Muhammad XII, El Zagal	Twenty-fourth Nasrid sultan of Granada, brother of Abu l-Hasan and uncle of Boabdil
Isabel de Solís (Zoraya)	Converted Christian lover of Abu l-Hasan and mother of his two sons, Sa'd and Nasr
Moraima	Wife of Boabdil and daughter of Ali al-Attar, governor of Loja
King Ferdinand II of Aragon and V of Castile	Son of King Juan II of Aragon and wife of Isabella of Castile

Queen Isabella I of Castile	Daughter of King Juan II of Castile and wife of Ferdinand II of Aragon
Gonzalo de Córdoba, the Great Captain	Famous soldier in the Granadan war on the side of Ferdinand and Isabella
al-Mulih	Boabdil's vizier
Aben Comixa	Boabdil's vizier

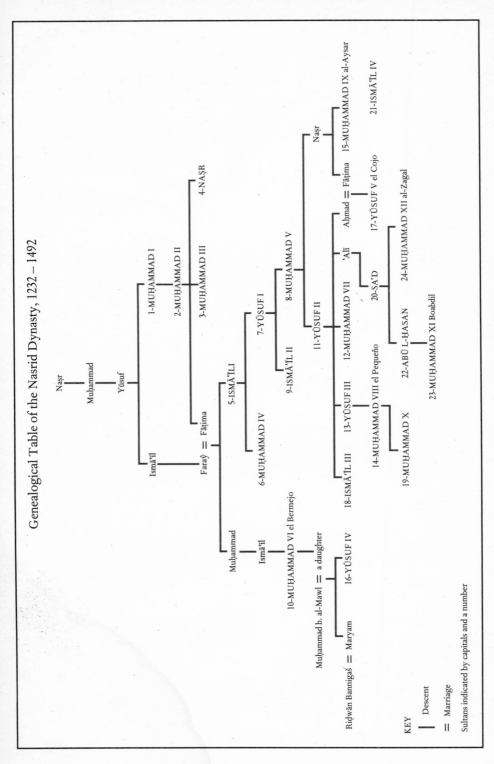

Genealogical Table of the Nasrid Dynasty, 1232 – 1492

Lineage of the Nasrid Dynasty

Glossary

al-Andalus The Arabic name for the Iberian peninsula, which came to be used in English and other European languages to refer to Islamic, rather than Christian, Spain.

emir A military commander or prince and also an independent Muslim ruler or local chief.

fatwa A ruling or opinion on a point of law, usually given by a mufti.

imam A leader in prayer, and by extension the political head of the Muslim community.

jihad Meaning 'struggle', which might be against inner weakness or as holy war against infidels. A fighter of a holy war is a mujahid.

khalifa (caliph) A successor of the Prophet Muhammed and spiritual head of the Muslim community.

madrasa A college whose main purpose is to transmit Islamic knowledge.

Morisco A Muslim convert to Christianity in Spain after 1500.

Mozarab A Christian living under Arab rule in Spain.

Mudejar   A Muslim living under Christian rule in Spain.

mufti   A Muslim legal expert empowered to give rulings on religious matters.

qadi   A judge administering the law of Islam.

sultan   Meaning 'power' or 'authority'; the title of a Muslim sovereign.

ulama   Scholars of Muslim religious learning and law.

wazir
(vizier)   Chief administrative official, generally the head of the bureaucracy, and usually the emir's chief advisor.

Reading Suggestions

Historical and cultural background

Richard Fletcher's *Moorish Spain* (London: Weidenfeld and Nicolson, 1992; repr. Phoenix Giant, 1998) is an excellent starting point for those interested in a general picture of the politics and culture of Muslim Spain. His account of the relations between Islam and Christianity from the time of Muhammed to the Reformation in *The Cross and the Crescent* (London: Allen Lane, 2003) is also a useful introduction to the medieval conflict between the two religions, as is Andrew Wheatcroft's *Infidels* (London: Penguin, 2003). *A History of Islamic Spain* by W. Montgomery Watt and Pierre Cachia (Edinburgh: Edinburgh University Press, 1996 and 2007) is something of a classic on the history, life and culture of Spain between 711 and 1492, while María Rosa Menocal's *The Ornament of the World: How Muslims, Jews and Christians Created a Culture of Tolerance in Medieval Spain* (New York: Little, Brown, 2002) is an eloquent and readable account of the cultural enlightenment of Spain in that era. Jason Webster's enjoyable *Andalus: Unlocking the Secrets of Moorish Spain* (London: Doubleday, 2004) is part travelogue, part memoir, in which Webster delves into the Moorish past of his adopted home.

The Cambridge Illustrated History of the Islamic World edited by

Francis Robinson (Cambridge: Cambridge University Press, 2009) is a useful reference work for all things Islamic. Ibn Khaldun's great work on the nature and principles of history is available in English translation by Franz Rosenthal as *The Muqaddimah: An Introduction to History* (Princeton: Princeton University Press, 2015).

Historical sources

The majority of the *historical* sources that refer to Boabdil are written in Spanish. The most important contemporary Christian histories of the late fifteenth century are the Archbishop of Seville's chaplain Andrés Bernáldez's *Memorias del reinado de los Reyes Católicos que escribía el bachiller Andrés Bernáldez, cura de Los Palacios*, edición y estudio por Manuel Gómez-Moreno y Juan de M. Carriazo (Madrid: Real Academia de la Historia, 1962), and the Catholic Monarchs' royal chronicler Fernando del Pulgar's *Crónica de los Reyes Católicos*, Vol. II, edición y estudio por Juan de Mata Carriazo (Madrid: Espasa Calpe, 1943). The sixteenth-century chronicler Jerónimo Zurita's *Anales de la Corona de Aragón* (Zaragoza: Institución Fernando el Católico, 1967–77) and the later seventeenth-century historian Francisco Henríquez de Jorquera's *Anales de Granada*, 2 vols., ed. Antonio Marín Ocete (Granada: Universidad de Granada, 1934) are also useful, though they draw regularly on material by Fernando del Pulgar and Andrés Bernáldez.

The Morisco chronicler Hernando de Baeza's *Relaciones de algunos sucesos de los últimos tiempos del reino de Granada*, ed. Emilio Lafuente y Alcántara (Madrid: Sociedad de bibliófilos españoles, 1865) is particularly interesting because Baeza knew Boabdil in person and worked at his court, which enabled him to record personal details and conversations otherwise unavailable to us.

There are only two existing Arabic sources. The first is the anonymously written *Nubdhat*, edited by A. Bustani and translated into Spanish by Carlos Quirós as *Fragmento de la época (Nubdhat) sobre noticias de los reyes nazaritas o capitulación de Granada* (Larache: Artes Gráficas Bosca, 1940) and more recently published in the original Arabic as *Kitāb Nubdhat al-'aṣr fī akhbār mūlūk Banī Naṣr: taslīm*

Gharnāṭah wa-nuzūḥ al-Andalusiyīn ilá al-Maghrib (Cairo: Makta-
bat al-Thaqāfah al-Dīnīyah, 2002). This work is the only surviving
Arabic history written around the time of the fall of Granada, and
its terse, economical style gives an alternative view to set against
those of the Christian versions. The second source, the north African
al-Maqqari's *The History of the Mohammedan Dynasties in Spain*, vol. 1
(London and New York: Routledge Curzon, repr. of 1840–43 edition,
2002) is in English translation, but has a degree of unreliability since
it was written later, in the seventeenth century, and it is not clear
which sources al-Maqqari used or whether he adapted material from
the earlier Christian histories.

The key modern history in English is L. P. Harvey's *Islamic Spain,
1250–1500* (Chicago and London: University of Chicago Press, 1990),
which gives an engaging and thorough account of the history of the
Nasrid dynasty. Miguel Ángel Ladero Quesada's work on Granada
in Spanish is also fundamental, in particular, his *Granada. Historia de
un país islámico (1232–1571)* (Madrid: Editorial Gredos, 1969).

The afterlife of Boabdil

The earlier plays, poems and novels that recreate the legend of
Boabdil are not published in English, but Washington Irving's *Tales
of the Alhambra* (Granada: Ediciones Miguel Sánchez, 1994), first published in 1832, can be bought online, and in all the bookshops on
the Alhambra site. His *Chronicle of the Conquest of Granada* (Tedding-
ton: Echo Library, 2007), originally published in 1829, is also readily
available. An English translation of Chateaubriand's *Les aventures
du dernier Abencérage* is available at www.poetryintranslation.com/
PITBR/Chateaubriand/ChateaubriandAbencerraje.htm

Salman Rushdie's *The Moor's Last Sigh* was published by
Vintage in 1996, but Antonio Gala's *El manuscrito carmesí* (Barcelona:
Editorial Planeta, repr. 2007) and Magdalena Lasala's *Boabdil. Tragedia del último rey de Granada* (Barcelona: Temas de Hoy, 2004) are not
available yet in English. Both Spanish television series *Isabella* and
Requiem por Granada can be bought online; *Isabella* has English sub-
titles, but *Requiem por Granada* does not.

A short news clip on the Fiesta de la toma can be viewed online at: http://politica.elpais.com/politica/2016/01/02/actualidad/1451730320_363776.html, and it is also possible to see the truly spectacular annual Saint James day celebrations at the cathedral of Santiago at: https://www.youtube.com/watch?v=uWi44jKQUjc.

Index